The Postwar World

General Editors: A.J. Nicholls and Martin S. Alexander

As distance puts events into perspective, and as evidence accumulates, it begins to be possible to form an objective historical view of our recent past. *The Postwar World* is an ambitious new series providing a scholarly but readable account of the way our world has been shaped in the crowded years since the Second World War. Some volumes will deal with regions, or even single nations, others with important themes; all will be written by expert historians drawing on the latest scholarship as well as their own research and judgements. The series should be particularly welcome to students, but it is designed also for the general reader with an interest in contemporary history.

Decolonization in Africa
J.D. Hargreaves
The Community of Europe: A History of
European Integration Since 1945
Derek W. Urwin
Northern Ireland since 1945
Sabine Wichert
A History of Social Democracy in Postwar Europe
Stephen Padgett and William E. Paterson

Decolonization in Africa

John D. Hargreaves

Longman
London and New York

Longman Group UK Limited
Longman House, Burnt Mill, Harlow,
Essex CM20 2JE, England
and Associated Companies throughout the world.

*Published in the United States of America
by Longman Inc., New York*

First published 1988
Fifth impression 1991

British Library Cataloguing in Publication Data

Hargreaves, John D.
   Decolonization in Africa.——(The Postwar
   world).
   1. Africa——Politics and government——1960–
   I. Title II. Series
   960'.32   DT30.5

ISBN 0-582-49150-9
ISBN 0-582-49151-7 Pbk

Library of Congress Cataloging-in-Publication Data
Hargreaves, John D.
   Decolonization in Africa / J. D. Hargreaves.
      p. 000 cm.——(The Postwar world)
   Bibliography: p.
   Includes index.
   ISBN 0-582-49150-9. ISBN 0-582-49151-7 (pbk.)
   1. Africa–History–20th century.
   2. Decolonization–Africa.
   I. Title.   II. Series.
   DT29.H37 1988
   960'.32-dc19   87-22461
                                                CIP

Set in 10/12pt Baskerville Comp/Edit 6400.

Produced by Longman Singapore Publishers (Pte) Ltd.
Printed in Singapore.

Contents

List of Tables and Maps

Abbreviations

ABBREVIATIONS USED IN REFERENCES

AAEF	Archives of Afrique Equatoriale française, Aix-en-Provence.
AF.AFF	*African Affairs*
ANSOM	Archives Nationales, Section d'Outre-mer, now at Aix-en-Provence.
CAB	Records of the Cabinet, Public Record Office, Kew.
CEA	*Cahiers d'Etudes Africaines*
CHA	*Cambridge History of Africa*
CO	Records of the Colonial Office, PRO, Kew.
Damas	Assemblée nationale: Session de 1950 No. 11348. Rapport fait au nom de la Commission chargée d'enquêter sur les incidents survenus en Côte d'Ivoire par M. Damas. (Reprinted, Abidjan, 1975)
DBFP	*Documents on British Foreign Policy*, ed E. L. Woodward
FCB	Papers of the Fabian Colonial Bureau, Rhodes House, Oxford.
FO	Records of the Foreign Office, PRO, Kew.
FRUS	*Foreign Relations of the United States*
G & L	*The Transfer of Power in Africa: Decolonization, 1940–1960*. Ed. P. Gifford & W. R. Louis (New Haven, 1982)
HEA	*History of East Africa* Vol. I, ed R. Oliver & G. Mathew; Vol. II, ed V. Harlow & E. M. Chilver; Vol. III, ed D. A. Low & Alison Smith.
HJ	*The Historical Journal*
IJAHS	*International Journal of African Historical Studies*
JAH	*The Journal of African History*

JICH	*The Journal of Imperial & Commonwealth History*
JMAS	*Journal of Modern African Studies*
K & R	D. Killingray & R. Rathbone (eds) *Africa and the Second World War* (1986)
K-G	A. H. M. Kirk-Greene (ed) *Africa in the Colonial Period. III The Transfer of Power. The Colonial Administrator in the Age of Decolonization (University of Oxford, 1979)*
Les Chemins	*Les Chemins de la Décolonisation de l'empire français 1936-1956.* Colloque organisé par le IHTP le 4 et 5 octobre 1984 sous la direction de Charles-Robert Ageron. (CNRS, Paris, 1986)
Morgan	*The Official History of Colonial Development* ed D. J. Morgan. Five volumes, 1980
M-J & F	*Decolonisation and After: The British and French Experience* ed W. H. Morris-Jones & G. Fischer (1980)
P.P.	Parliamentary Papers
PREM.	Records of the Prime Minister's Office, PRO; Kew
RFHOM	*Revue française d'Histoire d'Outre-mer*

OTHER ABBREVIATIONS

ABAKO	Alliance des Bakongo
AEF	Afrique Equatoriale française
ANC	African National Congress (according to context)
AOF	Afrique Occidentale française
ARPS	Aborigines Rights Protection Society (Gold Coast)
BDS	Bloc Démocratique Sénégalais
CDW	Colonial Development and Welfare
CIA	Central Intelligence Agency (USA)
CPP	Convention Peoples' Party (Ghana)
CRO	Commonwealth Relations Office
EEC	European Economic Community
FIDES	Fonds d'investissement pour le Développement Economique et Social des Territoires d'Outre-mer
FLN	Front de Libération Nationale (Algeria)
FNLA	Frente Nacional de Libertação de Angola
FRELIMO	Frente de Libertação de Moçambique
ICFTU	International Confederation of Free Trade Unions
ICU	Industrial and Commercial Workers Union

Abbreviations

ILO	International Labour Office
JEUCAFRA	Jeunesse Camerounaise française
KANU	Kenya African National Union
KAU	Kenya African Union
KCA	Kikuyu Central Association
MDRM	Mouvement Démocratique de la Rénovation Malgache
MNC	Mouvement National Congolais
MPLA	Movimento Popular de Libertaçāo de Angola
MRP	Mouvement Républicain Populaire (France)
MTLD	Mouvement pour le Triomphe des Libertés Démocratiques (Algeria)
NCBWA	National Congress of British West Africa
NCNC	National Council of Nigeria and the Cameroons
NDP	National Democratic Party (Southern Rhodesia)
NPC	Northern Peoples' Congress (Nigeria)
OAU	Organisation of African Unity
PAIGC	Partido Africano da Indepéndencia da Guiné e Capo Verde
PDCI	Parti Démocratique de la Côte d'Ivoire
PDG	Parti Démocratique de Guinée
PPA	Parti du Peuple Algérien
PSA	Parti Solidaire Africain (Congo)
PUS	Permanent Under-Secretary
RDA	Rassemblement Démocratique Africain
TANU	Tanganyika African National Union
UDI	Unilateral Declaration of Independence (Rhodesia)
UGCC	United Gold Coast Convention
UGTAN	Union Générale des Travailleurs d'Afrique Noire
UN[O]	United Nations [Organization]
UNIP	United National Independence Party (Zambia)
UNITA	Uniāo Nacional de Indepéndencia Total de Angola
UPC	(i) Union des Populations du Cameroun
	(ii) Uganda People's Congress
WFTU	World Federation of Trade Unions
ZANC	Zambian African National Congress
ZANU	Zimbabwe African National Union
ZAPU	Zimbabwe African People's Union
ZNP	Zanzibar National Party

Editorial Foreword

The aim of this series is to describe and analyse the history of the World since 1945. History, like time, does not stand still. What seemed to many of us only recently to be "current affairs" or the stuff of political speculation, has now become material for historians. The editors feel that it is time for a series of books which will offer the public judicious and scholarly, but at the same time readable, accounts of the way in which our present-day world was shaped by the years after the end of the Second World War. The period since 1945 has seen political events and socio-economic developments of enormous significance for the human race, as important as anything which happened before Hitler's death or the bombing of Hiroshima. Ideologies have waxed and waned, the industrialised economies have boomed and bust, empires have collapsed, new nations have emerged and sometimes themselves fallen into decline. Whilst we can be thankful that no major armed conflict has occurred between the so-called superpowers, there have been many other wars, and terrorism has become an international plague. Although the position of ethnic minorities has dramatically improved in some countries, it has worsened in others. Nearly everywhere the status of women has become an issue which politicans have been unable to avoid. These are only some of the developments we hope will be illuminated by this series as it unfolds.

The books in the series will not follow any set pattern; they will vary in length according to the needs of the subject. Some will deal with regions, or even single nations, and others with themes. Not all of them will begin in 1945, and the terminal date may similarly vary; once again, the time-span chosen will be appropriate to the question under discussion. All the books, however, will be written by expert

Editorial Foreword

historians drawing on the latest fruits of scholarship, as well as their own expertise and judgement. The series should be particularly welcome to students, but it is designed also for the general reader with an interest in contemporary history. We hope that the books will stimulate scholarly discussion and encourage specialists to look beyond their own particular interests to engage in wider controversies. History, and particularly the history of the recent past, is neither "bunk" nor an intellectual form of stamp–collecting, but an indispensable part of an educated person's approach to life. If it is not written by historians it will be written by others of a less discriminating and more polemical disposition. The editors are confident that this series will help to ensure the victory of the historical approach, with consequential benefits for its readers.

A. J. Nicholls
Martin S. Alexander

Preface

Every author has many debts to acknowledge. Archivists must find the importunities of contemporary historians trying; special thanks to the staff of the Public Record Office, of the *Archives Nationales: Section d'Outre-Mer* and Marie-Antoinette Ménier, and of the *Archives d'Outre-Mer* at Aix and Jean-François Maurel. Michael Smethurst's staff in the University of Aberdeen, and Donald Simpson's in the Royal Commonwealth Society, were as helpful as ever. Conversation with colleagues in Britain and in Europe is invaluable to those working in a rapidly developing field; I am grateful to the Social Science Research Council for enabling me to visit Aix and Paris in 1984 under their Franco-British exchange programme, and to the *Institut d'Histoire du Temps Présent* and the *Centre des Hautes Etudes sur l'Afrique et l'Asie Modernes* for invitations to contribute to their respective colloquia. I also acknowledge helpful comments from participants in seminars of the Institute of Commonwealth Studies, London, and of Aberdeen University.

Among many friends and colleagues whose help has been invaluable I somewhat invidiously mention Roy Bridges and Jean Houbert in Aberdeen, Anthony Clayton, Andrew Roberts, Robert Smith and Michael Twaddle, Marc Michel in France and Roger Louis, at Bellagio in 1977 and later. Kenneth Robinson's wise counsels have been invaluable. I was much stimulated, before retirement, by reactions from students in my Honours class at Aberdeen; and while supervising research. I have derived stimulating insights into many matters from Fewzi Borsali, Edho Ekoko, Badra Lahouel, Alastair Milne, Alan Short and Atintola Wyse. I owe a very special debt to John Kent, not least for incisive comments on draft chapters.

My greatest debt of all is once again to Sheila – though she may in turn feel grateful to the book for keeping me quiet in retirement.

Banchory, May 1987

Some Definitions

'Imperialism', wrote Sir Keith Hancock, 'is no word for scholars'; other terms commonly used in discussing modern Africa are no less liable to ambiguity because of the emotional charges they may carry. Historians are thus driven back on Humpty-Dumpty's practice of using words to mean what the author wishes them to mean. I have tried, with only moderate success, to limit my use of words ending in -ism; the following notes of intended meaning may help to reduce confusion due to my failures.

Imperialism: the use of state power in order to advance national interests and to exercise control over weaker peoples: but compare

Economic imperialism: the influence exercised by capitalist enterprises (whether or not through the agency of a state) in less economically developed parts of the world.

Imperialist: a person who openly advocates the systematic use of state power to control weaker peoples, especially through the agency of colonial governments: a politician who makes such views a major part of his platform.

Decolonization: measures intended eventually to terminate formal political control over colonial territories and to replace it by some new relationship.

Nationalist: one who, in order to promote the welfare and progress of a specific community of people for whom he claims to speak, demands that political sovereignty shall be exercised by representatives of that group.

In this book, the most common focus of African nationalists is upon an individual colonial territory: but compare:

Primary nation: a community of people, within or across colonial borders, who on account of common language, culture or historical experience claim special respect for their common identity.

Some Definitions

Populist nationalism: This somewhat imprecise term is used to denote political movements which seek to minimize divisions of class or ethnic origin by emphasizing the importance of concerted action by the mass of common people against foreign rulers or domestic oligarchies. It does not necessarily imply a rural base, as in more precise definitions of **Populism**.

Introduction

Since January 1951, when Kwame Nkrumah became Leader of Government Business in the Gold Coast, many commentators have written of an African revolution; and if political maps encapsulated historical truth nobody could doubt that revolutionary change has occurred. When the Second World War ended only three African states were not under white rule, and two of those were doubtful models of indigenous authenticity. In Egypt, the dynasty founded by a Macedonian mercenary, Mehemet Ali, continued to tolerate a British military presence; Liberia was ruled by an oligarchy of largely American descent; only in Ethiopia was there an ancient African monarchy, recently restored after Italian occupation. In the one other independent state on the continent a powerfully entrenched racial oligarchy dominated the African majority. In 1980, although this oligarchy continued to rule South Africa and its own dependency of Namibia, only two small Spanish enclaves in Morocco remained as relics of colonial government on the continent. This book aims to give an historical account of these changes.

Such simple aims are rarely met by simple narratives. The very choice of a title begs large historical questions, which an earlier volume tried to evade by the formula *The End of Colonial Rule*.[1] The word *decolonization* has not yet acquired an agreed definition. Apparently coined by an expatriate German scholar in 1932, it first featured in a book-title twenty years later, when a liberal French administrator interpreted decolonization as a natural climax of colonial rule, whose advent was however being imprudently expedited by contemporary pressures.[2] Subsequent French usage generally maintained this sense of a broad historical movement, not usually identified with anything so transient as the intentions of particular governments.

Decolonization in Africa

Leopold Senghor, with his gift for expressing African aspirations in language congenial to European consciences, defined it as 'the abolition of all prejudice, of all superiority complex, in the mind of the colonizer, and also of all inferiority complex in the mind of the colonized'.[3] The session of the 1965 International Historical Congress entitled *Decolonisation* was similarly comprehensive in scope.[4]

Certainly the end of the colonial empires can only be understood within the total context of contemporary history. Reductionists might explain it as a simple consequence of the declining power of the colonial rulers in an international system dominated, during the critical period, by two anti-imperialist super-powers. But to understand the nature of the change, and its varying effects on different countries, it is necessary to ask, not only Why?, but such questions as How? When? By whom? – in short, to study history. President de Gaulle, speaking of Algeria in 1961, declared *la décolonisation est notre intérêt, et par conséquence notre politique;*[5] this book attempts to show how the historical conjuncture of the mid-twentieth century eventually led colonial rulers to perceive that their interest lay in such policies. In this more restricted usage, 'decolonization' implies intent: the intention to terminate formal political control over specific colonial territories, and to replace it by some new relationship. This did not necessarily mean independence; neither France nor Britain, at the end of the Second World War, envisaged a general lowering of flags. But both, it will be argued, (though not, until later, Belgium, Spain or Portugal) did set out to change political relationships – to substitute collaboration for force or, in the words of Sidney Caine, counsel for control.[6] The first two chapters of this book aim to show how, when the assumed stability of colonial rule became more questionable during the 1930s, a certain number of persons in both countries conceived programmes of reform and renewal which would eventually lead towards the independence of their African colonies.

Eventually, if not intentionally. The irony of political history lies in the processes through which the results of human statesmanship come to diverge from the intended purpose. The original reform plans were formulated by disillusioned practitioners concerned to discharge their imperial trusteeship more effectively. 'Development' and 'Welfare' were the initial keynotes of the British Colonial Office, with 'self-government' added as a means towards these ends. French reformers gave even greater priority to economic and social improvement, and their political horizons remained obscure. Chapters 3 and 4 show how, while the world crisis developed from depression into war, reform plans were progressively amended, accelerated, and ultimately transformed, as pressures from their more powerful allies, and from within Africa, obliged Britain and France to formulate their political objectives more clearly.

After the war contradictions developed between the forces working for decolonization and the need experienced by both Britain and France to mobilize colonial resources to support the restoration of their international power. Chapters 5 and 6 show how these were resolved, in theory and in practice. British Ministers redesignated their development policies as 'nation-building': designs for self-governing democracies within the Commonwealth, some based on institutionalized racial partnership, within an ever-shortening future. The French, still less precisely, envisaged decolonization within the framework of the new French Union, through the full assimilation of some communities and the autonomy of others. Some of the objectives proclaimed in this period now seem to resemble mythological beasts, incapable of existence in twentieth-century Africa; what realistic plans for political evolution were made were aborted by the rapid acceleration of time-scale demanded by economic and political realities. By about 1960 those controlling policy in Britain, France and Belgium had come to regard the possession of colonies (with a few strategic exceptions) as a positive hindrance to their new national objectives. As Chapters 7 and 8 will show, they now hastened to liquidate the remains of their formal empires with the greatest speed compatible with an appearance of responsible trusteeship, sometimes without much concern about future relationships.

It may be thought that this interpretation devalues the importance of those African initiatives which at one time occupied the centre stage of contemporary historiography. Yet the most effective critics of racial injustice were always Africans who drew from their reading of European history a Mazzinian faith in the capacity of the independent nation-state to promote material progress and cultural renewal; in the euphoric 1950s the political parties they founded seemed the natural heirs to colonial authority. In the 1980s some of their hopes appear incredibly naive. Those who followed Nkrumah's advice to seek first the political kingdom did not find all else added to them. That 'Third World' which idealists once hailed as a new source of creative energy has become a heavy burden on western consciences; while in many African nations continuing immiseration and poverty is made all the more conspicuous by the prosperity of a favoured few.

Although this volume does not aspire to analyse the problems of

3

contemporary Africa, it may clarify their political context. Some will judge this a subject of secondary importance by comparison with the environmental crises, or with the constraints imposed on development by the capitalist world system. Those who, following Fanon, regard the conditions under which power was transferred to African hands as a 'false decolonization' are more likely to share the author's interest in political history; and the book may help less theoretically-minded persons to distinguish the varying responses to challenge in different successor states. Although a broad survey like this cannot enquire very deeply into the nature of the social formations and interest groups which clustered under the nationalist banner in each colonial territory it may suggest lines of comparison between the different states in which power was transferred, and also with those – less closely studied here – where it had to be fought for by military and political mobilization.

The focus of the study (as of the author's experience) is thus on the peaceful transfer of power in Black Africa. A full study of decolonization in northern Africa would involve deeper analysis of Middle Eastern politics, economics and culture than can be attempted here; the Union of South Africa, where a first decolonization took place in 1910 but the second is still incomplete, has its own distinct and complex historiography. But if there are different regions within Africa, the existence of the OAU proclaims that there is a single continent; Cairo and Pretoria are not extraneous capitals, like Delhi or Havana. So there is much about both regions, even if important questions about their recent history receive only tentative answers; Black Africa is seen in a context of continental, as well as world, history.

NOTES AND REFERENCES

1. John D. Hargreaves, *The End of Colonial Rule in West Africa: Essays in Contemporary History* (1979)
2. M. J. Bonn in *Encyclopaedia of the Social Sciences*, VII (1932) p. 613, s.v. 'Imperialism'; Henri Labouret, *Colonisation, Colonialisme, Décolonisation* (Paris 1952)
3. Leopold Sédar-Senghor, 'La décolonisation: condition de la communauté franco-africaine', *Le Monde*, 4 Sept. 1957
4. Congrès International des Sciences Historiques, xiie congrès international, Vienne, 29 Aug–5 Sept. 1965. Vol.II, pp. 133–76, Vol. V, pp. 281–309

5. Charles de Gaulle, Press conference, 11 April 1961; *Marchés Tropicaux et Mediterranéens* No 805, 15 April 1961.
6. C.O. 847/36/47238, Memo by Sidney Caine: 'General Political Development of Colonial Territories', 1947

CHAPTER ONE
Conditions of Tranquillity in Black Africa

During the 1920s those citizens of western Europe who were aware that their governments controlled substantial territories and populations in tropical Africa usually assumed this to be a fact of nature, or at least of history. Over much of the continent small numbers of white men appeared to be governing their African subjects with relative ease and economy; where signs of resistance did appear they were commonly shrugged off as the dying kicks of moribund cultures. Some regarded colonial empire as the white man's burden, some as his nest-egg for the future; but very few could have imagined that it would be substantially liquidated within half a century. The terms in which the architects of the Paris peace settlement described the inhabitants of the former German and Turkish empires – peoples not yet able to stand by themselves under the strenuous conditions of the modern world – were widely accepted as applicable to most of the African continent.

But not quite to all. Different conditions applied in both north and south of the land-mass. Around the Mediterranean coasts well-structured Islamic societies existed; in western Asia the peace-makers acknowledged that these had reached 'a stage of development where their existence as independent nations can be provisionally recognized', though subject to external advice and assistance. Egypt, never brought formally within this Mandate system, achieved nominal independence in 1922. But British troops remained, to reinforce the advice and assistance which continued to be offered by a powerful High Commissioner; and the international sovereignty of the Egyptian monarchy was still limited by treaty. And neither France in the Maghreb nor Italy in Libya believed their Muslim subjects to have reached the stage of even conditional independence.

European control was tightest in Algeria, where settlers from the European shores of the Mediterranean, numbering between an eighth and a tenth of the population, controlled half of the land north of the Sahara desert, including all the most fertile areas. French myths of assimilation contrasted with the realities of economic exploitation and racial ascendency; although ultimate control of what were technically three *départements* of metropolitan France was centralized in Paris, locally power was in the hands of *colons* who resisted even modest concessions to the Muslim majority. Morocco and Tunisia, where foreign settlement and exploitation of mineral resources were increasing on a somewhat lesser scale, were Protectorates, where international treaties obliged France to acknowledge the identity of formerly independent nations; (while in the north and south of Morocco Spain ruled on similar terms). The French administration had to some degree succeeded in appropriating the secular if not the religious authority of their clients, respectively the Sultan and the Bey; but locally they also had to strike bargains with wealthy Muslim potentates like the Glaoui family of Marrakesh, whose power rested on formidable combinations of religious charisma, commercial wealth, and private armies. The breakdown of such alliances presented the most immediate threats to colonial control; between 1921 and 1926 'Abd al-Krim led a formidable armed revolt in the Rif mountains, initially directed against Spain and later against France also. In Libya Italy faced similar threats, notably from Muhammad Idris, leader of a Sufi desert brotherhood, the Sanusiyya, and of a major rebellion during the war. In 1919 they came to terms with him, conceding substantial measures of local self-government and civil liberty throughout the colony; but with the advent of Mussolini these concessions were withdrawn. Large-scale Italian settlement resumed, and so did Sanusi resistance.

In the longer run a greater threat to alien rule than that from the essentially conservative hierarchies of Sufi Islam was presented by *salafi* doctrines of reform and modernization. The religious call to return to the foundations of the faith, as heard by younger Muslims in the growing towns, was often married with secular doctrines of revolutionary nationalism inspired from Europe. In 1919 the Emir Khaled (an officer in the wartime French army, and grandson of the nineteenth-century resistance hero 'Abd al-Kader) petitioned President Woodrow Wilson to support the claim of Algerian Muslims for full French citizenship. When it became clear that the French intended to reject such appeals to their own professed principle of assimilation, other ex-servicemen and migrant workers began to assert the rights of a separate Algerian nation. Their Paris-based organization, the *Étoile Nord-Africaine* led by Messali Hadj, received some encouragement from French Communists and other sympathizers. But the French authorities in North Africa maintained strong police surveillance (far more effectively than in more distant colonies), and locally-based political parties like the Tunisian Destour of 1920 and the Moroccan League of 1927, had to be circumspect in their demands for civil rights. And in the mosques the French encouraged more old-fashioned Muslim clerics to temper the influence of *salafi* doctrine.

Modernizing influences enjoyed more freedom in Egypt. After 1922 the British could still use their influence to persuade the monarch to appoint moderate ministers, prepared to tolerate continued military occupation in practice. But the nationalist demands of the largely middle-class *Wafd* party were stimulated by threats of violent action from radical students, Muslim fundamentalists of various schools, trade unionists and army officers. One continuing cause of anti-British protest was the government of the Sudan, which a diplomatic compromise of 1899 had constituted as an Anglo-Egyptian condominium, but where Egyptians were in practice allowed little influence over government. So long as educated Sudanese tended to sympathize with Egypt, British administrators sought alliances with the more conservative Muslim orders, treating them as more authentic spokesmen of the Sudanese people; they eventually allied themselves with the powerful brotherhood led by 'Abd al-Rahman al-Mahdi, posthumous son of the prophet who had resisted both the Egyptians and the British in the 1880s.

Muslim North Africa was thus not a tranquil region, even in the 1920s. But the European military presence was relatively strong, and it was widely assumed that the physical and cultural barrier of the Sahara desert would prevent its rebellious spirits from infecting Black Africa.

The south of the continent seemed somewhat more tranquil, being under the control of settled populations of European origin who were fully confident of survival in the strenuous modern world. The United Kingdom had completed its formal decolonization of the Union of South Africa in 1910, the war of 1899–1902 having shown that its important economic and strategic interests would have to be protected by collaboration with representatives of that population rather than by military force. The First World War proved the value of that strategy when the less intransigent Afrikaner nationalists had joined with London-oriented capitalists in supporting the allied cause; but J. C. Smuts, the key figure in that coalition, had displayed, notably by the terms on which he assumed the Mandate for former German South-West Africa, the clear intention of white South Africans to pursue their own imperial mission at the expense of earlier inhabitants of the region. This new empire would be based on some form of compromise among the agrarian, mining and industrial interests of the white population; even if in the longer run there might be limited opportunities for an African *petite bourgeoisie,* the primary role of the Africans would be to provide reserves of unskilled labour in their constricted and impoverished homelands.

This programme for post-colonial development, would, it was already clear, be challenged by different groups within the Union. Afrikaner extremists aimed to establish an exclusive racial hierarchy based on *apartheid* – a term implying separation from the Anglo-Saxon enemy as well as from the non-white majority. In 1922 Smuts had to use force to suppress Afrikaner Republican commandos who supported white miners, on strike to preserve their differential privileges. Threats to the Smuts consensus from non-whites were less immediate. The Coloured population, which under the 1910 settlement still enjoyed substantial civil and political rights in Cape Province, seemed easily reconcilable; the immigrant Indian community of Natal, where Gandhi had served a political apprenticeship, was more articulate, but no great threat in isolation. The protests and petitions of the relatively small elite of educated African Christians, as voiced through the South African Native National Congress founded in 1912, still tended to be deferential in tone, expressing hopes that the British monarch would intervene paternally to protect his South African subjects against those to whom he had entrusted their government. Potentially the greatest threat lay in the growing African labour force. The Industrial and Commercial Workers Union (ICU) of Clements Kadalie, an immigrant worker from Nyasaland, led strikes of Cape Town dockers in 1919, and of miners on the Rand in 1920. Later in the decade the ICU claimed 100,000 members, some in the impoverished rural areas from which the migrant miners came. But there was no united labour movement; most white trade unionists regarded Black workers as threats to their own high living standards, rather than as allies against capitalism. Even the attempts of the South African Communist Party to recruit African members were marred by doctrinaire tactical errors, as well as by the inherent difficulties of

9

mobilizing temporary migrants. So the many manifestations of African resistance, whether constitutional or militant, failed to challenge white control. Instead of political rebellion African victims of social and racial injustice looked for consolation to independent churches, 'Ethiopian' or Zionist, which claimed a million members by 1936. Though many whites feared that these might foster dangerous racial doctrines, they presented no immediate threat.

FOUNDATIONS OF COLONIAL CONTROL IN BLACK AFRICA

Although, with the partial exception of Egypt, internal challenges to European control in north and south Africa were in their early stages, they were stronger than among the Black peoples who inhabited the vast central regions of the continent. That they existed at all caused some concern to foreign rulers in those regions who appreciated their historic links of commerce and religion with the Muslim North, or the sense of racial solidarity which might be aroused during temporary labour-service in the Union. A perceptive officer of the Kenya government had noted during the war the danger of a conjunction between Islamic propaganda and 'Ethiopian' ideas of 'Africa for the Africans'.[1] But in the 1920s the peoples of Black Africa seemed centuries short of any capacity to stand by themselves under the strenuous conditions of the modern world. With no immediate threats evident from anti-imperialist parties in the metropolis, from foreign states, or from their African subjects, colonial governments appeared stably balanced on a sort of tripod of acquiescence. What has been called 'the tranquil assumption of the long-term character of colonial rule'[2] was rarely questioned.

This confident tranquillity was not based on the presence of overwhelming military force. A Commission of 1935 declared somewhat smugly that:

> To set down two or three British officials at an outstation to rule
> 100,000 natives, with a handful of police to keep order, is a customary
> British risk which many years of colonial development has proved to be
> successful.[3]

But it was not only in British colonies that small numbers of white men, unsupported by any considerable investment of metropolitan resources, were able to impose laws, collect taxes and exact labour from African subjects. During periods of conquest small but well-disciplined armies had used modern firearms to overcome courageous resistance from larger African forces, and later the deadly new weapon of air-power was used effectively and economically against rebels in Somaliland and the Sudan. But continuing foreign rule depended more on collaboration than on force. Colonial armies were organized for external defence as much as internal security – or, in the French case, as reinforcements of imperial power. Even so, they were of modest size. Belgium's African empire, which maintained a *Force Publique* of sixteen thousand for a population of around thirteen million, was heavily militarized by comparison with the four British West African colonies, whose Frontier Force numbered eight thousand in a population twice as large. Settler colonies did have the reserve resource of white militias, but men with farms and businesses to run could be mobilized only in real emergency.

In normal times public order in British Africa was the responsibility of civilian police forces, separated from the military at early stages of colonial rule. These were rarely powerful repressive agencies, as regards either their capacity to gather political intelligence or their numerical strength. When the forces of Northern and Southern Nigeria were amalgamated in 1930 there was an establishment of eighty-five officers (plus some African Chief Inspectors) for a population estimated at twenty millions. The total strength of the Nyasaland Police was usually around 500 men.[4] In rural areas police duties were executed by Native Administration forces (who often adapted crude pre-colonial methods of law enforcement) or by small units of uniformed Court Messengers. There were indeed frequent complaints about the ways in which such forces collected taxes, recruited labour, or enforced colonial law, but these usually alleged unsupervised acts of extortion, partisanship or vindictiveness rather than centrally-directed tyranny.

The confidence with which most District Commissioners and *commandants de cercle* exercised their extensive powers was thus not founded wholly, or even primarily, on the coercive force at their direct disposal, but on their belief that their technical, moral and racial superiority was acknowledged by their subjects. Power, good imperialists believed, did not flow only from the barrel of a gun, but from scientific and technological knowledge; having expedited conquest, this would now ensure the material and moral progress of the conquered. Their faith in colonial expertise now seems to have been complacently exaggerated; the fallibility of western science and the relevance of much indigenous technical knowledge have become familiar themes in recent literature. But the early colonizers could perform enough spectacular conjuring tricks to convince many Africans that they did possess superior magical powers: that it was wiser to collaborate with their rule, when once established, than to try to reject it.

During the 1920s, then, the 'thin white line' of administrative officers could maintain control through the more or less gentle supervision of African hierarchies, invented or reconstituted. Britons inspired by Lord Lugard extolled the virtues of Indirect Rule; Frenchmen philosophized about their new *politique d'association*; Belgians developed their own rhetoric of centralized paternalism. In all these systems the essential practical task was to identify Africans of standing who could be induced to collaborate actively with colonial officers in administering justice, collecting revenue, and directing reluctant populations into approved forms of labour. Europeans who found themselves controlling a varied group of African peoples (of different 'primary nations', to adopt the language of a historian who was formerly an administrator, and always a Breton patriot) needed intermediaries who understood their national languages and cultures. Africans willing to assist them could find opportunities to protect the interests of their own peoples, within the severe constraints of the new order.

The extent of such opportunities depended on the political preferences and local aims of their new masters. Some administrators (chiefly but not exclusively British) gave priority to convincing the successors of pre-colonial elites that they, and their people, would benefit by actively collaborating with the new order. Others (chiefly but not exclusively French), judging that essentially new forms of *commandement indigène* were necessary in order to establish viable colonial economies, elevated formerly subject peoples in the new colonial hierarchy. But whether or not the persons recognized as agents of colonial authority also enjoyed legitimacy as traditional 'chiefs', by the 1920s most colonial governments had identified Africans to collaborate in maintaining order and solvency in their large dominions. This did not imply close control over African life; agents of native administration, whether historic potentates like Nigerian Emirs or petty functionaries like France's 'canton chiefs', became skilled in using the powers and patronage devolved upon them to promote the interests of their clients and kinsmen. Those who had secured such areas of autonomy thereby reinforced their interest in collaborating with rulers they could not in any case hope to evict.[5]

Africa in the 1920s was predominantly rural; but the growing number of administrative capitals, ports and communication centres, and mining towns had to be administered by other methods. Here colonial governments, missionary churches and foreign businessmen needed the services – as clerks, constables, school-teachers, storemen, dispensers – of a *petite bourgeoisie* whose education had emancipated them, at least partially, from the authority of their traditional rulers. In East Africa immigrants from the Indian sub-continent were often employed, but on the west coast a numerous population of educated Africans was already available. Moreover they possessed relatively sophisticated spokesmen in African lawyers, editors, physicians or businessmen, whose importance had been more or less reluctantly recognized by appointment to some form of representative council. West African politicians, as will be seen, were already criticizing their rulers quite sharply and acutely; but their opposition was essentially loyal opposition, recognized as legitimate even by those who resented it. These critics were asking for more colonial government rather than less – more schools, more roads, the establishment of a District Headquarters in their own territory rather than that of traditional rivals. So long as there was no serious threat to empire from outside there was thus reason for confidence in its stability, even though this might represent temporary equilibrium rather than inherent structural strength.

The argument here must be distinguished from the complacent assumption of some contemporaries that, barring a handful of trouble-makers, Africans were passively accepting their dependent status. Every study of the period which seeks an African rather than an imperial perspective supplies evidence that they were not. But historians of the 1950s who discern nationalist movements everywhere preparing to challenge the colonial order can be almost equally misleading. Manifestations of resolve to protest against injustice, to defend the traditional values and future opportunities of local communities, even to seek common action with fellow-subjects, do not add up to effective political movements with broad popular support. During the 1920s links between such village Hampdens and more sophisticated leaders in the capitals were rarely strong, and colonial governments were watchful that they should not become so.

EARLY AFRICAN RESPONSES

During the early stages of colonial occupation many local communities offered 'primary resistance' in the form of armed revolt.

Its forcible suppression did not necessarily mean that nothing had been achieved. Separate risings by the Temne and the Mende in 1898 did not secure withdrawal of the hut-tax, nor reverse the Governor's plans to develop the Sierra Leone Protectorate; but they slowed down the application of these by his successors and inhibited enthusiasm for direct taxation throughout the African empire. In Sierra Leone hut-tax remained at the low level of 5 shillings until 1937 – technically indeed until 1955, when it was African Ministers who were imprudent enough to impose new burdens on the farmers.[6] For many peoples in French West Africa the moment for revolt arrived with the imposition of conscription during the First World War. 'No more taxation, no more work on the roads, no more soldiering', cried the Somba of northern Dahomey as they attacked the representatives of French authority in May 1917.[7] Others resisted by simply migrating into the bush, or across colonial boundaries. In the short term this resistance obliged the French to improve conditions of service for future conscripts; more generally, it underlined the crucial importance of ensuring that colonial agents retained sufficient respect locally to control the rural populations.

But as the development of colonial economies imposed new demands and opened new opportunities, maintaining the structures of collaboration became more complicated. For most Africans the colonial occupation was not their first experience of having to pay taxes and provide labour to alien rulers. But the spread of cash-crop production, under more or less direct government pressure, and the movement of men into forced or waged labour in ports, mines, or administrative centres, extended the horizons of many Africans and gradually altered their social perceptions. Farmers who were directing more of their productive energies towards export or urban markets, and so becoming dependent on monetary incomes to pay labourers or meet debts, began to form new associations to help meet their new needs. Gold Coast cocoa farmers, an early and outstanding example of entrepreneurial response to market opportunities, were forming local Growers' Associations before the First World War, and in 1919 John K. Ayew, an Akwapim farmer, founded a United Gold Coast Farmers' Association to try to by-pass the European oligopoly which controlled cocoa exports.[8] Such bodies did not aim to challenge colonial authority (many farmers were, as chiefs, involved in upholding it); but they served notice that rural Africans were not ignorant 'bushmen', but were becoming peasants with a steadily expanding social consciousness.

In urban areas, where change was more obvious, the range of new associations through which migrants sought to protect their interests and redefine their identity was wider. People from particular villages, meeting together for mutual assistance, self-help, and recreation, became aware of affinities with others who spoke different versions of their language; the notion of a single Igbo people was formed among the local 'Descendants' Unions' of Lagos. Cultural and sporting associations – dance societies, football clubs, brass bands – to varying degrees brought together people of different ethnic origins. Consciousness of a wider common identity as members of a working class, though retarded by stronger loyalties to the village communities to which most African workers intended eventually to return, made some precocious appearances. Although trade unions nowhere enjoyed full legal recognition, labourers and government employees had taken effective industrial action in some West African towns since the nineteenth century; there were well-organized railways strikes in Sierra Leone in 1919 and 1926, in Nigeria in 1921, in Senegal in 1926.

For many Africans, however, religion still offered the most meaningful way of coming to terms with new experiences and new troubles. In rural areas traditional cults with some local focus often retained their authority, directing primary resistance to colonial aggression as well as responses to natural disasters like famine. But authority was increasingly claimed by clergy of a new type, who combined understanding of traditional cosmologies with appreciation of the spiritual power of the missionary religions, and of discrepancies between Christian teachings and colonial practice. In many colonies, as well as in the Union, the emergence of independent churches, millenarian movements, and new syncretic cults provided the strongest manifestations of discontent with the new order.

Many European contemporaries tended to reduce these varied attempts to find meaning in a rapidly changing universe to political subversion, mentally updating a famous dictum of James VI to read 'No missionary, no Governor'. The sub-conscious fears of white South Africans which John Buchan articulated in his novel *Prester John* (1910) seemed briefly realized in January 1915, when followers of the Reverend John Chilembwe attacked Europeans in southern Nyasaland. The terms in which some charismatic prophets denounced the sins of their generation seemed to contain latent challenges to the authority of colonial Caesars. Although William Wade Harris, during his remarkable mission to the Ivory Coast in 1913–15, preached orthodox Protestant morality, hard work, and respect for authority, French officials feared that, with a hundred

15

thousand disciples, Harris was becoming a rival authority himself, and obliged him to transfer his ministry to Liberia. Simon Kimbangu, who between his messianic vision on 18 March 1921 and his incarceration by the Belgians six months later powerfully interpreted the Gospel of evangelical Christianity through the religious traditions of the Bakongo, was similarly suspect because of his appeal to Congolese who felt oppressed by white administrators or white missionaries. Though innocent of political intent, Kimbangu spent the remaining thirty years of his life in gaol; this however enhanced, rather than reduced, his extraordinary spiritual authority among the Bakongo.

New Christian movements like these, which developed widely in colonial Africa, must be understood as primarily religious phenomena. The mission of their leaders was to preach the Gospel more directly to the hearts and minds of their countrymen; they offered spiritual rather than political emancipation. Chilembwe's insurrection, however alarming to whites, was exceptional; Kimbanguism became involved with Congolese nationalism only after the prophet's death. Yet in the longer run, some colonial apprehension was justified: visions of communities founded on human equality and liberty in Christ *were* essentially subversive of racially-structured colonial governments.

There were comparable contradictions in colonial attitudes to Islam: recognized as a religion capable of satisfying the social and political needs of African populations, it was feared as a possible cause of irresistible *jihad*. The French in particular transferred to Black Africa some of the ambivalence towards Muslim authorities which marked their search for stable forms of government in Algeria, Tunisia, and Morocco. During the period 1895–1912 they twice sent Ahmed Bamba, saintly kinsman of the Wolof resistance leader Lat-Dior, into exile. But gradually they came to see that the Muridiyya, the Sufite order he had founded which inspired some 400,000 Wolof, was actually rendering great service to the Senegalese colony, not only by maintaining social and political discipline but by mobilizing its disciples to cultivate the groundnuts on which the colonial economy had come to depend. In Anglo-Egyptian Sudan the Mahdiyya provided another example of how a Sufite order once associated with resistance could help Africans adjust to life under colonial rule. Elsewhere urban immigrants, severed from the local context of ancestral religions, often found a mosque or an Ahmadiyya school new centres for communal life, which became growing points for the spectacular expansion of the Muslim religion in colonial Africa.

Secular prophets could also, without formulating explicit challenges to the colonial order, express the desire of changing communities to achieve a new identity. André Matswa, or Grenard, born near Brazzaville in 1899, has been variously described as a protonationalist, a martyred revolutionary, a spokeman of Bakongo personality, and an assimilationist who wanted the Congolese to become fully French.[9] Although he did not think in narrowly 'tribal' terms, Matswa was closely identified with the Balali (or Lari), a section of the Bakongo people which provided much of the indigenous enterprise in French Equatorial Africa. Besides supplying much labour to the colonial capital and the railway, Balali farmers used mutual aid societies (*temo*) to mobilize labour and capital and supply cassava to new urban markets; their sons enthusiastically accepted the schooling offered by Roman Catholic missionaries, and so came to provide most of the *moyens cadres* required by government and foreign trading houses.[10] Matswa, having worked as Catholic catechist and customs clerk, made his way to Europe in 1921, served as an NCO in the French colonial army during its Moroccan campaign, and became a book-keeper in Paris. Although, like many other colonial immigrants, he associated with French Communists he did not militantly denounce imperialism; in 1926 he founded, and legally registered, a Friendly Society, the *Association amicale des originaires de l'Afrique Equatoriale française*. In 1928 Matswa sent two emissaries to establish branches in the Congo; their speedy success in collecting 110,000 francs from 13,000 supporters alarmed Governor-General Antonetti, who withdrew his initial patronage. Fearing that the claim of these *amicalistes* for the rights of French citizens would draw attention to the existing disabilities of French subjects, Antonetti confiscated their funds, charging Matswa and his associates with embezzlement. But Balali chiefs refused to redistribute the subscriptions collected, and Balali workers came out on strike; it became clear that Matswa's initiatives commanded widespread support. Some French officials attempted to enlist the *amicalistes* as collaborators, seeking 'to enter openly into the new orientation of the Balali movement in order to follow, direct, and canalize it in the direction of work, order and discipline.' But others thought it dangerous to permit such African initiatives outside official control; on the eve of war French relations with the movement remained ambivalent.[11]

Harris, Kimbangu, Ahmed Bamba and Matswa were each, in different ways, assisting Africans to adjust their lives to cope with a rapidly enlarging scale of social and economic relationships. As

Decolonization in Africa

pre-colonial states were incorporated into larger unities, people also
began to change their political identities. Within southern Nigeria,
young men from Ilesha and Ijebu who attended school in Ibadan or
Oyo were taught to write a standard form of the Yoruba language and
to identify themselves as Yorubas (a term previously reserved for
subjects of the Oyo empire). A few even came to think of themselves as
Nigerians.[12] People were simultaneously becoming conscious both of
their identity within 'primary nations' united by language and
culture and of their membership of colonial states which, however
arbitrarily constituted, had the potential to command a secondary
national allegiance.

Individuals' horizons might extend even beyond that. 'Some
people when they became Christians, including myself, were no
longer interested in Kikuyu things', Harry Thuku recalled in old age.
In 1918, as a young telephone operator in Nairobi, he made friends
among Kenyans of varied origins, becoming a spokesman for the
grievances of returning servicemen. By 1921 he had founded an East
Africa Association, with assistance and advice from the Asian
community, and was corresponding fraternally with the 'Young
Baganda', with the charismatic Jamaican Marcus Garvey in New
York, and with sympathetic Members of the British Parliament. All
the same, it seems to have been Thuku's influence among his fellow
Kikuyu as much as these cosmopolitan contacts which led the
colonial government in 1922 to arrest and deport him to enforced
residence near the coast.[13] But Kikuyu hostility to official policies
concerning land, agriculture, the *kipande* or African pass, continued
to grow, was reinforced by conflict with missionaries over the
established Kikuyu custom of initiating nubile women by an
extremely painful excision of the clitoris, and was expressed through
a Kikuyu Central Association. Its secretary Johnstone (later Jomo)
Kenyatta had even wider horizons than Thuku; in 1929 he travelled to
London with petitions against Colonial Office policies and when
rebuffed visited Moscow. Yet his Pan-Africanism was still rooted in
the Kikuyu primary nation; if Kenyatta's prestige soon eclipsed
Thuku's it was because he did remain keenly 'interested in Kikuyu
things', of which he became a leading academic student.

There is a semantic problem, of some substantive importance, in
deciding at what point in the expanding horizons of groups or
individuals it is appropriate to hail the advent of nationalism. Some
distinguished students of modern African history use that term
eclectically, to embrace:

any organisation or group that explicitly asserts the rights, claims, and aspirations of a given African society (from the level of the language group to that of 'Pan-Africa'), in opposition to European authority.[14]

Others emphasize the political focus provided by highly articulate groups and individuals in West African towns who had long used the language of European nationalism with much skill. Some of these had even believed that the British might be persuaded to begin to transfer their power on the coast before they had consolidated it on the mainland. But colonial governments knew that such men lacked any real mass following; if they continued to tolerate the political activities of these early nationalists after the partition, it was precisely because they doubted their capacity to make effective contact with larger formations of African society. Even the autocratic Lugard (who found most educated Africans personally antipathetic) conceded their right to 'a sphere of civic usefulness' in colonial capitals; but this was now all they could effectively hope to achieve.[15]

Senegalese patriots seemed to have achieved a little more in 1914, when the former customs officer Blaise Diagne was elected to the French Parliament by the organized votes of urban Africans, who thus captured a bridgehead bequeathed by the assimilationist principles of the French Revolution. During the 1870s the Third Republic had conceded the franchise and other citizen rights to natives of four coastal towns, but the territorial expansion which followed seemed to preclude any general extension of such enlightened practices. Racialists urged abolishing the 'black vote' completely; liberals would do no more than defend it in the four *communes*, while envisaging slow extensions of citizenship among the conquered populations in an indeterminate future. Diagne, adopted by the colonial establishment as a valuable collaborator, confined his energies to consolidating the rights of fellow-*citoyens*, while helping to recruit 134,000 *sujets* to fight for France in Europe. Subsequent elections turned less on mass participation than on negotiations with the religious heads of the Muridiyya and Tijaniyya orders, who marshalled the growing number of urban Muslim voters but discouraged any mobilization of political energies in the countryside. Their legal immunities as citizens permitted some Senegalese to establish newspapers, trade unions, and other organizations, even in other colonies; but on the rare occasions (such as 1923 in Porto Novo)[16] when political activists threatened to win broader support, colonial authoritarianism quickly reasserted itself.

Spokesmen for the four British West African colonies, who in 1920 formed the National Congress of British West Africa (NCBWA) and delivered to London a deferential petition for fuller civic rights, had similarly limited success. The intellectual basis of their claim to speak for a West African nation, or for the whole populations of their respective colonies, was vigorously refuted in a famous speech by Governor Clifford of Nigeria; but in 1922 Clifford himself partially implemented one of their main demands, reconstituting the Nigerian Legislative Council to include four members elected by the more prosperous residents of Lagos and Calabar. Similar constitutions followed in Sierra Leone and the Gold Coast. Although Clifford based his initiative on the 'sphere of civic usefulness' principle, the elected members could now claim a certain 'national' legitimacy; Herbert Macaulay, able manager of the Lagos electorate, entitled his machine the Nigerian National Democratic Party. But there seemed little immediate prospect of such bodies effectively penetrating the rural population of the Yoruba hinterland, still less the dozens of primary nations which had been agglomerated into British Nigeria.

African political consciousness had advanced a little further in the Gold Coast. During the 1890s the Aborigines Rights Protection Society (ARPS), organized by African lawyers, merchants and clergy, had voiced the fears of chiefs and others about British attempts to control the disposal of African lands, and succeeded in persuading the Colonial Office (warned by the recent risings in Sierra Leone of the deep passions which apparent threats to African property rights could arouse) to withdraw its Bill. Drawing creatively on their understanding of Akan law and custom, J. E. Casely Hayford and J. Mensah Sarbah expounded constitutional theories which substantially limited the sovereignty of their colonial rulers. British authority in the southern Gold Coast, they argued, derived from the free consent of chiefs who retained certain inherent rights; these they continued to exercise as trustees for their people, and subject to indigenous democratic practice. They themselves, as the chiefs' educated kinsmen, were their proper counsellors in the difficult process of adjusting customary law to the needs of modern ('civilization'; the colonial government had no right to interfere in this process, nor to impose direct taxation.

Administrators, however, were equally quick to perceive the importance of working with 'natural rulers', and by the 1920s they had established working collaboration with leading state chiefs (*amanhene*) like Ofori Atta I of Akim Abuakwa who recognized that the colonial government's support was now essential for the preservation of their influence, prestige and perquisites. In founding the NCBWA Casely Hayford was recognizing that the nationalists too would have to seek influence through the central government, even at the price of accepting new taxes. The result was a split among the nationalists, based partly on ideology, partly on personal faction, partly on the professional self-interest of lawyers like W. E. G. Sekyi and Kojo Thompson. When these new leaders of the ARPS resorted to court filibustering and litigious intervention in local disputes Governor Guggisberg was enabled to consolidate his alliance with the chiefs. Here as elsewhere colonial rulers, by conceding a small share of public patronage to licensed critics, seemed able to contain any threat from nascent nationalism.

METROPOLITAN BASES

Tranquillity in Africa required the acquiescence or consent not only of the subject Africans but of the outside world. But so long as colonial control was inexpensive in money and European lives few citizens of the ruling power actively opposed it, some were strongly committed to maintaining it, and the majority, so far as their views can be ascertained, felt a general proprietorial satisfaction. The crucial contribution made by African soldiers to national security gave particular point to French colonial propaganda. The *parti colonial*, a coalition of interest-groups and ideologues, publicized the material and moral benefits supposed to flow to colonizers and colonized alike, organized support within most political parties, and spread pride in colonial empire widely, though shallowly, through many sections of society. After the First World War French leaders were keenly conscious of falling birth-rates; troops from both northern and tropical Africa not only played a role comparable to that of Britain's Indian Army in upholding imperial interests throughout the world but provided some reinsurance against the dangers of a revival of German power in Europe. Officers of the Colonial Army – an autonomous branch of the service, with intense pride in its historic achievements – were to prove the most determined defenders of colonial empire.

In other countries the 'hegemony' of the Imperial idea was promoted through a variety of official and unofficial channels. World maps proudly identified colonies in the appropriate national colour; school-children were instructed about the exotic marvels of 'their' African dependencies, and participated in such rituals as Britain's Empire Day; they returned home to read ripping colonial yarns in youth magazines, or to affix postage-stamps to the 'Empire' albums of Messrs Stanley Gibbons. Sir Stephen Tallents, secretary of the Empire Marketing Board established by Leopold Amery in 1926, commanded sufficient public funds to enlist creative artists in new enterprises of public relations, notably in documentary film. The British Empire Exhibition of 1924–5 attracted twenty-seven million visitors to Wembley; the Colonial Exhibition of 1931 drew more than thirty-three million to Vincennes. In Belgium lavish permanent displays had been financed from the profits of Leopold II's Congolese enterprise. In Portugal and Spain pride in the residue of past imperial glory was cultivated as assiduously as were hopes of a greater imperial future in Mussolini's Italy.

How deeply such emotions had penetrated European society is another matter. Beneath the diffuse enthusiasm evoked by publicists lay great depths of ignorance and indifference; imperial euphoria never rose to what the great Lord Salisbury called income-tax point. But active hostility was weaker still. Although there were penetrating critics of imperialism, both socialist and liberal, in every European country, during the inter-war years they mostly confined themselves to monitoring excesses of colonial rule. Although imperialism was being challenged in postwar Ireland and Egypt, India and Indo-China, only small groups of the far Left could imagine independent states in Black Africa within a foreseeable future.

Nineteenth-century humanitarians in many countries had displayed paternal concern for African welfare through the anti-slavery movement; in the 1890s new manifestations of this international conscience secured reforms in the brutal regime of Leopold II's Congo Free State, and its eventual transfer to the Belgian government. But such interventions were always selective; European watch-dogs normally had access to information about Africa only when missionaries, traders, or public servants called attention to specific scandals – which they usually attributed to other denominations, rival firms or foreign governments rather than to the colonial system itself. During the 1920s Josiah Wedgwood was enabled to enforce some Parliamentary scrutiny of the Kenyan settler lobby through the vigilance of two former officials, Norman Leys and MacGregor Ross, and of missionaries like J. W. Arthur. André Gide, invited to Equatorial Africa by the progressive governor de Coppet, used his literary prestige to denounce the concessionary companies on which the French administration there still had to depend. The burden of African misery was sometimes lightened through the efforts of such estimable men. Yet the most effective critics of colonial misrule shared the underlying assumption of imperial ideology: that

Africans were 'backward', inarticulate, people, who could only acquire the capacity to 'stand by themselves' through gradual exposure to colonial capitalism, under the watchful eyes of colonial 'trustees'. Gide warned his readers:

> against confusing these Congolese concessions with the ordinary concessions which may be made to colonists or great financial companies for bringing land into cultivation or exploiting mineral wealth. These do contribute to the enrichment, not only of the colonist or company, but of the country or its inhabitants. If an anti-capitalist political party disapproves, that doesn't concern me; I don't have to identify with that party to attack the abuses of AEF.[17]

E. D. Morel, hero of the Congo Reform campaign, convinced the British Labour Party of its duty to defend African land rights; but he remained allied to Liverpool merchant interests, and in 1911 published a eulogistic account of British rule in Nigeria. Following this tradition, C. R. Buxton was to argue 'that British imperialism in West Africa ... should serve as a model to the Labour Empire builders in the next Labour government.'[18] The existence of such critics helped to guarantee the good faith of the Imperial 'trustees', and so to reinforce, rather than to challenge, their imperial ideologies.

Stronger critiques of imperialism were developed within the Labour movement, which inherited the old radical thesis that colonial expansion usually resulted from hidden conspiracies by sectional interests. After 1902 J. A. Hobson's *Imperialism*, inspired by recent observation of mining capitalists in South Africa, provided socialists with new insights. In 1907 the Stuttgart conference of the Second International condemned 'the barbarous methods of capitalist colonialism', implicitly rejecting not only 'social imperialism' but also the cautious reformism of Ramsay MacDonald, who believed that British socialists should aim to secure 'the establishment of Imperial standards and the safeguarding of Imperial traditions.'[19] Marxists however were usually more concerned about the effects of colonial empire on class relationships in Europe than with the immediate problems of 'backward' Africans. One conclusion drawn from Lenin's famous pamphlet of 1916 was that African colonies were an epiphenomenon of international finance capitalism, which could be effectively combated only by the class-conscious working class of the industrialized world. Colonial freedom, however desirable, would have to await the overthrow of capitalism in Europe.

Was this analysis correct? Were African colonies indeed providing the capitalist economies of the metropolitan states with essential sources of profit? It is easy to exaggerate both the extent of capitalist stakes in Africa and the degree to which they were dependent on the exercise of influence through a particular national government. Certainly Africa's contribution to world trade increased under colonial rule; in 1913 the continent supplied 3.7 per cent of world exports and took 3.6 per cent of world imports, but by 1937 these figures were respectively 5.3 per cent and 6.2 per cent. And usually the metropolis was the main beneficiary, even if it did not impose direct fiscal discrimination; by the 1930s Africa was the only continent with which Britain still had a favourable balance of trade. At first sight investment too appeared to follow the flag. Leaving the Union of South Africa aside, only in the Portuguese empire, where the concessionary companies which controlled vast territorial fiefs in Angola and Mozambique were largely financed by foreigners, do official figures suggest substantial movements of capital across national boundaries.[20] But the total sums invested seem relatively modest, and often represent loans raised by colonial governments to construct the transport infrastructures required to facilitate exports. Only clearly identified mineral resources attracted private capital on any scale. By 1936 the Belgian Congo accounted for 12 per cent of all foreign investment between Sahara and the Cape (compared to 43 per cent in the Union); three-quarters of this came from private sources, principally the powerful *Société Générale* of Brussels.[21]

Official figures however do not always indicate the cosmopolitan character of capitalist enterprise. The economic partition of Africa – launched, as A. G. Hopkins notes 'from three initially competing power bases: Europe, South Africa and India' – had never closely followed national flags. By the 1920s the age of independent entrepreneurs looking to their consuls to get them out of trouble was giving way to the modern era of multinational companies. In mining areas the heavy initial investment required international participation; until British companies were stirred into action by their government's strategic worries, the Northern Rhodesian copper-belt was developed by American and South African capital.[22] Trading giants like the United Africa Company, *Compagnie française de l'Afrique Occidentale, Société Commerciale de l'Ouest africain*, continued to operate across West African boundaries; W. H. Lever, denied plantation concessions in British West Africa, secured them through his *Huileries du Congo Belge*. The banking groups which regulated international exchanges and controlled internal credit tended to operate regionally, if largely within the empires where they were founded;[23] shipping lines received postal subsidies and gave priority to their nation's colonies, but fixed their charges through transnational conference systems.

Relationships between capitalists and colonial governments can therefore not be easily generalized. Foreign businessmen had found ways of operating in Africa before colonial rule, and most of them would prove capable of adjusting their methods in order to continue to do so after independence. The judgement of a scholar who has studied one major multinational company in depth is that British entrepreneurs in general were neither fervently committed to prolonging their country's rule in Africa, nor anxious to see it liquidated.[24] While it lasted, they naturally did their best to protect their interests. British Ministers and officials claimed to treat their requests on merit, arbitrating impartially between their own interpretation of African interests and of the advantages of proposed development, but seeing no necessary incompatibility between them. Practitioners of what has recently been called 'gentlemanly capitalism', they were naturally predisposed to assist those whom they regarded as 'reasonable, efficient and patriotic businessmen,'[25] but did not regard the maximization of production or profit as the highest end of government.

How these relationships worked out in practice can best be studied through particular encounters in differing contexts. British examples seem to suggest that, if gentlemanly capitalists were often sympathetically treated in Whitehall, their specific demands might be received with more reserve by colonial administrators, better placed to see how they could prejudice the interests of African farmers or other groups with essential roles in the colony's economy.[26] The pressure groups with the strongest political leverage were often not multinational corporations but resident settlers. Families trying to create – even to earn – standards of material prosperity in Algeria, Kenya or Rhodesia to which they could not aspire at home could often marshal formidable political support among their kith and kin, or their creditors. In the last resort however it seems that imperial rulers *believed* that they were free to decide how to exercise their trusteeship in Africa, beholden neither to self-interested pressure from their capitalist constituents nor to imperfectly informed complaints from their doctrinaire critics.

THE INTERNATIONAL CONTEXT

Before the First World War, the only external threats perceived by colonial rulers (apart from a possible Islamic peril) came from rival practitioners of their own trade. Although Frenchmen and Britons long suspected each other of plotting to re-open the colonial partition, after the Fashoda crisis of 1898 Africa was never a likely cause of European war. Colonialism was in many ways a *fait européen*;[27] a few fanatical chauvinists apart, common interest in preserving white rule was stronger than any pressure to enlarge the national share. Those Germans who sought a great consolidated *Mittelafrika* did so in the hope of preserving European peace, not as a call for war; indeed some imperialists favoured proclaiming the neutrality of the African continent. This of course did not happen; after fierce battles in the German colonies these were re-allocated among the Allies and the result ratified by the Paris peace settlement. But although few Germans recognized the legitimacy of this repartition the Weimar Republic, disarmed and isolated, could give no priority to reversing it. Any new external threat to the African empires could only come from the intervention of non-colonial powers.

In the Soviet Union it was indeed being claimed that the 1917 October Revolution had opened a new historical era for Africa, as for the world. The founding manifesto of the Communist International declared that 'the colonial question in its fullest extent [had] been placed on the agenda in the colonies themselves'. But it still remained some way down the revolutionary agenda. Since in the circumstances of March 1919 the survival of Soviet Russia and of the revolution itself depended on the outcome of struggles in Europe, 'emancipation of the colonies [would be] possible only in conjunction with the emancipation of the metropolitan working class.'[28] To African patriots this cheque on an indeterminate future offered more emotional appeal than immediate opportunities.

Pro-Soviet emotion was nevertheless strengthened when the promises of the Comintern were backed by successful acts of decolonization by the Soviet state, terminating Russian sovereignty over the former Tsarist empire in conditions which largely preserved its unity. It was the Georgian Stalin who, after 1917, faced the problem of reconciling Lenin's clear recognition of 'the right of the oppressed peoples in dependent countries and colonies to complete secession' with the political and military necessity of preventing the Asian dependencies of Tsarist Russia from passing, like its western territories, under counter-revolutionary control. Stalin's solution was to acknowledge the credentials only of 'those national movements which tend to weaken imperialism and bring about the overthrow of imperialism, and not to strengthen and preserve it', and could thus be deemed to be waging an objectively revolutionary struggle.[29] Under this formula local Communist parties (however weak, however strongly influenced by 'progressive' immigrants from Europe) became the only legitimate heirs of Tsarism; and by 1924 the territories secured under such control could be re-united in the Union of Soviet Socialist republics. This is not the place to evaluate the freedoms thus secured for Armenians or Kazakhs; as a means of implementing a formal change of political status, Stalin's achievement appealed to many with exemplary power.

During the internal war years this example, no less than the doctrines of the Russian revolution, commanded the admiration of many Asians. In Africa however the Comintern's declaration of war against colonialism remained largely formal and ineffective, rather like the Anglo-French offensive against Germany in 1939. It was difficult for revolutionaries to penetrate the controls of colonial police and customs men and secure access to influential Africans. The small Communist Party founded in Egypt in 1922 was soon driven underground; those in Algeria and South Africa survived, but under leaders of European origin who tended to impose on their African disciples policies influenced either by their own sectional interests or by ill-informed directives from Moscow. There seemed better prospects for influencing African students and workers overseas, whose political consciousness had often been sharpened by wartime experiences. But this African diaspora had political traditions of its own, emphasizing conflicts of race rather than of class; its members were not easily recruited for campaigns whose strategy was made in Moscow.

During the nineteenth century a sense of racial solidarity had developed among people of African origin on both sides of the Atlantic. By 1918 alternative versions of Pan-Africanism were being preached by the Afro-American intellectual W. E. B. DuBois and by the charismatic Jamaican Marcus Aurelius Garvey; though their movements differed profoundly in both ideology and social base, both seemed possible recruiting grounds for the Comintern. But neither proved easy to penetrate. Garvey, whose eloquent evocation of the pride of 'a mighty race' secured genuine mass support among workers in northern American cities, already enjoyed prestige in many parts of Africa, where his reputation spread by word of mouth, as well as through his multi-lingual newspaper *The Negro World*. Many colonial rulers were seriously worried by Garvey's influence, which a few mistakenly equated with Communism, or indeed any other subversive movement they had heard of.[30] But such panics were unjustified: Garvey's demagogic advocacy of Black capitalism proved a prophylactic against Communism, among American workers as well as aspiring young Africans.

DuBois's influence was more diffuse. His contribution to Pan-Africanism during the 1920s was to organize occasional conferences in European capitals, which allowed African students and others to discuss common grievances across colonial boundaries within an eclectic ideological framework. In the USA his was one voice within an Afro-American intellectual community whose bases were among creative artists in Harlem and teachers in segregated Negro Colleges. Communists did make occasional converts among the few African students, notably Bankole Awoonor-Renner from the Gold Coast. One of their leading agents was the Trinidadian George Padmore; he tried to recruit Nnamdi Azikiwe for a political organization modelled on the Kuomintang in order 'to foster racial consciousness and a spirit of nationalism aiming at the protection of the sovereignty of Liberia.'[31] But although Azikiwe did become an active champion of Liberian independence he continued to pursue his own road 'in quest of the Golden Fleece'; analogies with the Kuomintang of 1927 were in any case hardly propitious for Communism.

Soon afterwards the Comintern transferred Padmore to Europe, to try to organize Negro students and workers there. In Britain the party had only occasional success with individuals. Members of the West African Students Union founded in London in 1925, after occasional contacts with anti-imperialist radicals, usually returned home to reasonably secure positions within colonial society, from which reformist rather than revolutionary activity seemed the most reasonable course. In France there was a stronger Communist Party, which ran clubs for African seamen and sponsored political discussion among people from all the French dependencies (including Matswa). In 1924 a well-to-do Dahomean, Tovalou Quenum (or Houénou) founded a *Ligue Universelle de la Défense de la Race Noire,* but this proved more Garveyite than Communist in outlook. In 1926 it was succeeded by a more radical *Comité de Défense de la Race Nègre,* led by a Senegalese postman, Lamine Senghor – a Communist, but concerned to defend the autonomy of African aims against 'deeply chauvinistic' attitudes in the French party.[32] Shortly before his death in 1927 Senghor assisted at the foundation in Brussels of the League Against Imperialism, a broadly-based front promoted by the Comintern. The revolutionary cause was then taken up by Tiémoko Garan Kouyaté, who tried to establish his *Ligue de la Défense de la Race Nègre* in Dakar. But he found it difficult to escape colonial supervision; patriotically-minded African students in the city never got to hear of him. And as racial solidarity began to conflict with Party loyalty, both Kouyaté and Padmore fell out of Communist favour. The blow which the Russian Revolution claimed to have dealt to imperialism thus had less immediate effect than the growing, if still diffuse, sense of Pan-African solidarity.

If alliance with Soviet Communism proved counter-productive, some Pan-Africans hoped for support from the USA, whose growing power was reflected in the eminent role played by President Woodrow Wilson at the Paris peace conference. The anti-colonial rhetoric of 'the first new nation' heartened many Africans from Algiers to the Cape; but it soon became clear that American policy was more responsive to the needs of white business than to those of Black voters. Wilson was anxious to eliminate the preferential commercial advantages which some Europeans enjoyed (through legal restrictions, tariff discrimination, or simply established usage) in their colonies; his main achievement was the mandatory regime which Article 22 of the League Covenant imposed on the heirs of Germany's empire. This placed few effective restraints upon the new rulers (though they might have proved more serious had not Wilson's electoral defeat removed American membership from the League); but some colonial administrators did resent this token of foreign interference with their self-appointed mission.

But American anti-colonialism was less dangerous than the Soviet variety; indeed, international supervision was not anathema to all imperialists. Before the 1880s few Europeans had regarded colonial partition as the most effective way to open Africa to commerce and civilization; some did not do so now. In 1918 the British Board of Trade suggested establishing an international customs administration across all equatorial Africa, with power to enforce the hitherto nominal provisions of the 1885 Berlin Act concerning African welfare. Besides gratifying American, and Labour, internationalism, the author assured Lloyd George, 'the degree of Federal Control suggested ... would be to the advantage of our trade interests, to say nothing of the interests of the natives.'[33] Nothing came of this immediately; colonial empire was still too closely identified with nationalism, and American pressure tended to strengthen their alliance. But was government by forty separate bureaucracies indeed the best way to develop African resources? If colonial rule came to seem less securely inexpensive than at present, it did seem possible to devise satisfactory alternative arrangements.

NOTES AND REFERENCES

1. Minute of October 1917, quoted John Lonsdale, 'Some Origins of Nationalism in East Africa', JAH, 9, 1968, pp. 132–3.
2. K. E. Robinson, *The Dilemmas of Trusteeship* (1965) p. 7
3. P. P., 1934–5, VII, Cmd 5005, 'Disturbances on the Copper Belt ...' p. 61
4. T. N. Tamuno, *The Police in Modern Nigeria* (Ibadan, 1970) p. 66; John McCracken, 'Coercion and Control in Nyasaland: Aspects of the History of a Colonial Police Force', JAH, 27, 1986, pp. 130–1; cf. D. Killingray, 'The Maintenance of Law and Order in British Colonial Africa', AF.AFF, 85, 1986, pp. 211–37
5. The seminal essay on collaboration is R. Robinson, 'Non-European Foundations of European Imperialism: Sketch for a Theory of Collaboration', in R. Owen & B. Sutcliffe (eds) *Studies in the Theory of Imperialism* (1972); cf. D. A. Low, *Lion Rampant* (1973) Ch. I
6. Sierra Leone: Report of Commission of Inquiry into Disturbances in the Provinces. (Freetown, 1956) p. 98
7. M. Michel, *L'appel à l'Afrique: Contributions et Réactions à l'Effort de guerre en AOF (1914–1919)* (Paris, 1982) p. 120
8. See K. Arhin (ed) *The Minutes of the Ashanti Farmers Association, 1934–36* (Accra, cyclostyled, 1978)
9. Respectively by A. Hastings, *A History of African Christianity 1950–1975* (Cambridge, 1979) p. 84; Woungly-Massaga, *La Révolution de Congo* (Paris, 1974) pp. 90–99; M. Sinda, *Le messianisme congolais et ses incidences politiques* (Paris, 1972) p. 16; J. M. Wagret, *Histoire et Sociologie politiques de la République du Congo* (Brazzaville, 1963) p. 45
10. G. Balandier, *The Sociology of Black Africa* (1970) Part III
11. AAEF, 3B 2375, Solomiac to Mandel, 10, 13 Jan. 1939; Reste to Mandel, 12, 30 April; 3B 2376, Solomiac to Cortinchi, 6 Jan. 1939 illustrate contrasting attitudes
12. J. D. Y. Peel, *Ijeshas and Nigerians: The Incorporation of a Yoruba Kingdom* (Cambridge, 1983) p. 162
13. *Harry Thuku: an Autobiography*. With assistance from Kenneth King (Nairobi, 1970)
14. T. L. Hodgkin, *Nationalism in Colonial Africa* (1956) p. 23
15. F. D. Lugard, *The Dual Mandate* (Edinburgh, 1922)
16. J. A. Ballard, 'The Porto Novo Incidents of 1923: Politics in the Colonial Era', *Odu* II,i, 1965
17. André Gide, 'La détresse de notre Afrique Equatoriale', *Revue de Paris*, 15 Oct. 1927, in *Journal d'André Gide, 1939–1949*; Souvenirs (Paris, 1966) pp. 1029–34
18. Article in *The Manchester Guardian*, Jan. 1935, quoted S. Rohdie, 'The Gold Coast Aborigines Abroad', JAH VI, 1965, p. 407
19. J. Braunthal, *History of the International, 1864–1914* (1966), Ch. 20; J. Ramsay MacDonald, *Labour and the Empire* (1907) p. 50
20. Figures from A. J. Latham, *The Depression and the Developing World* (1981), pp. 87–9, 71
21. B. Jewsiewicki, 'Belgian Africa', CHA, VI (1986) pp. 492–3

22. A. G. Hopkins, 'Imperial Business in Africa', JAH, XVIII, 1976, p. 275; A. D. Roberts, 'Notes towards a Financial History of Copper Mining in Northern Rhodesia', *Canadian Journal of African Studies* 16, 1982
23. R. Fry, *Bankers in West Africa* (1976) pp. 62, 90, 220, for market-sharing arrangements between the *Banque de l'Afrique Occidentale* and the Bank of British West Africa (which did establish itself in Morocco)
24. D. K. Fieldhouse, *Black Africa, 1945–1980* (1986) pp. 9–12
25. C.O.267/667/32040, Minute by G. Clauson, 27 Jan. 1939; cf. P. J. Cain & A. G. Hopkins, 'Gentlemanly Capitalism and British Imperialism', *Economic History Review* XXXIX, 1986, pp. 501–25 & XL, 1987
26. e.g. John Miles, 'Cocoa Marketing on the Gold Coast and the African Producers, 1919–1939', Ph.D. thesis, University of London, 1978; J. Lonsdale & B. Berman, 'Coping with the Contradictions: the Development of the Colonial State in Kenya, 1895–1914', JAH 20, 1979, pp. 487–505; D. Meredith, 'Government and the Decline of the Nigerian Oil-palm Export Industry, 1919–1939', JAH 25 1984, pp. 311–29
27. Paul Reynaud, 1931: *cit.* R. Girardet, *L'idée coloniale en France, 1871–1962*, (Paris, 1972) pp. 131–2
28. Manifesto of the Communist International, 6 March 1919, in J. Degras, *The Communist International*, I (1956) p. 43
29. Josef Stalin, 'The National Question' (1924) in *Marxism and the National and Colonial Question* (1936) pp. 191–5
30. cf. G. Gautherot, *Le Bolchévisme aux Colonies* (Paris, 1930) p. 270. 'In 1919 Dr Du Bois joined up with the negro Marcus Garvey; the latter then held in Madison Square, London, a first Pan-African Congress, in which the leader of the British Labour Party, Mr Ramsay MacDonald, participated along with American negroes.' It would not be easy to include more misconceptions in a single sentence
31. N. Azikiwe, *My Odyssey* (1970) pp. 138–9
32. Front Culturel Sénégalais: *Lamine Senghor: Vie et oeuvre* (Dakar, 1979) pp. 22–5. See also P. Dewitte, *Les Mouvements nègres en France 1919–1939* (Paris, 1985)
33. Scottish Record Office, Edinburgh, GD 40.17/49, Llewellyn Smith to Lloyd George, Conf. 8 Jan. 1918

CHAPTER TWO

Forces of Change in the 1930s

AFRICA AND THE WORLD DEPRESSION

The first great shocks to colonial tranquillity originated in the economic depression which began to affect the international economy from about 1929. The financial crisis, which led to cuts in investment, large-scale unemployment and impoverishment in industrial countries, drastically reduced demand for the minerals and agricultural produce on which the export trade of every colony depended. If African farmers tried to maintain their incomes by increasing production, this only accelerated the fall in the prices they received; and although the cost of manufactured imports also fell it rarely did so proportionately. There were of course variations in the effects of world price movements on different colonies and in different years, and detailed econometric research is still proceeding, notably on the French empire; but for the 1930s the general picture is one of deterioration in Africa's net barter terms of trade (the quantity of imports obtainable for a given quantity of exports).[1] There was one major exception. Falling commodity prices meant rising prices for gold; after an initial crisis the national income of South Africa rose by nearly 80 per cent between 1932 and 1939, and new investment stimulated industrial growth. The continent's first modern iron and steel plant opened in Pretoria in 1933.[2] In Southern Rhodesia too, to a lesser degree, gold provided some protection against the worst effects of the Depression; and the settler economy in Algeria also seems to have benefited from changing prices.[3] But elsewhere the growth of the 1920s, such as it had been, seemed decisively checked.

Apart from such differential effects of global tendencies on individual colonial economies, important distinctions must be made within territorial boundaries. *Countries* do not get richer or poorer; people do. Not all sections of African society suffered equally, and some whose needs were still largely met from within the regional economy may hardly have suffered at all. White settlers in Kenya whose standard of living involved heavy fixed costs found it harder to adjust than African farmers growing food for local markets. Yet the crisis extended beyond those groups of farmers and workers wholly engaged in production for export; when cocoa farmers were short of cash, entrepreneurs in the expanding domestic economy – yam farmers, fish and cattle traders, weavers of *kente* cloth – were also affected. The Depression revealed how widely the welfare of African communities had become dependent on developments beyond local control.

One effect was to increase movements of African males in search of paid employment. Labour migration had in many areas begun long before the colonial occupation; nineteenth-century groundnut production in Senegambia was expanded largely by *navétanes* or strange farmers, travelling long distances over established routes to spend a season working for Wolof or Mandinka landlords. Those who needed cash to meet the demands of creditors and tax-collectors, or to pay increased prices in the market-place, might see wage-labour as a preferable alternative to growing more cash-crops at lower prices. Many inhabitants of densely populated regions in Upper Volta and the northern Gold Coast willingly travelled south to work for African cocoa farmers, though constraint might be needed to make them work on European mines, plantations or timber concessions. Colonial constraint, through high taxation or direct administrative pressure, was still more important to mining companies in southern Africa who needed to recruit unskilled labourers on short contracts; the new growth of gold production in the Union was made possible by expanding the frontier of such recruitment more deeply into Nyasaland and Mozambique.

Increased labour migration greatly sharpened official perceptions of attendant social problems in capital cities, ports and mining centres. Although relatively few Africans were engaged in wage-labour – a 50 per cent increase between 1933 and 1936 raised the proportion of the population of French West Africa only to 1.63 per cent – they were particularly vulnerable to the Depression; in 1932 2291 Senegalese were classified as 'unemployed', a concept hitherto used only in more 'advanced' societies.[4] But those who lost their jobs represented a lesser social problem than the growing number of single men who had moved to town in search of a better life, but were in fact living in squalid poverty in over-crowded quarters like the Dakar *medina*. Many Europeans began to regard these dangerous classes with alarm, as 'de-tribalized' persons beyond existing forms of social control. This was a misleading term; most immigrants maintained networks of kinship which not only provided links to rural communities on whose resources they could fall back in emergency but also helped to structure life in the new urban environment and sometimes provide a basis for new economic initiatives within its 'informal economy'. But continuing links with the countryside in the long run made the new proletariat more, rather than less, dangerous to governments whose powers of control were also weakened by the Depression.

For colonial governments were in their own way as badly hit as any of their subjects. The political representatives of metropolitan tax-payers almost invariably insisted that the costs of administration and development in the colonies (and to some extent those of their defence) should be met out of local revenues, derived in varying proportions from the taxes or unpaid labour services of their subjects, and from indirect duties on trade. In order to finance the construction of ports, railways and other forms of social overhead capital necessary for commercial growth, colonial governments had borrowed substantial sums, at rates which, even if relatively favourable at the date of the loan, constituted fixed prior charges on colonial budgets. Colonial governments also had heavy commitments, difficult to reduce, for the salaries and pensions of their own officials, the highest of course being payable to expatriates. When falling prices slashed the value of customs revenue (the Sierra Leone Government's income, for example, fell by almost a third between 1928 and 1934), governors had little choice but to penalize African subjects: by reducing expenditure on schools, roads, and medical services, by cutting the public pay-roll at the expense chiefly of junior African staff, or by increasing direct taxation. None of these courses was adopted willingly, for each was liable to undermine such legitimacy as the colonial state had been able to achieve in the eyes of its subjects; and some provoked ominous new forms of African resistance.

SOME AFRICAN INITIATIVES

Connections between hardship and rebellion are not usually direct, and the Depression years were not a period of generally increased disorder; many populations may have felt too wretched to see the purpose of revolt. In towns of the Ivory Coast, for example, Africans are said to have reacted by withdrawing into pre-colonial methods of production and exchange rather than by strikes or demonstrations.[5] And locally-focused studies are revealing many strategies by which rural populations reacted to the new hazards of a commercial economy as well as to the familiar challenges of their environment. Tax-collectors and labour-recruiters could be evaded by deception, or if necessary by emigration: falling prices for cash-crops countered by cultivating extra land or shifting to grow food for regional markets. More overt reactions ranged from syndicalism to millenarian religion (or even combined both). By way of illustration, two of the more conspicuous threats to colonial tranquillity produced by the Depression will be briefly described.

During the 1920s a spectacular growth in copper production had turned Northern Rhodesia into a classic single-product economy. Multinational mining companies practised a rigorous industrial paternalism; while skilled jobs were reserved for whites by a South African-style colour-bar, African workers, recruited on contract from throughout the Protectorate and beyond, were fed and housed in austere compounds, and subjected to strict, sometimes brutal, labour discipline. In 1931 the world copper price crashed from twenty-four to around six cents a pound. One of the three mines temporarily closed; but disastrous effects were felt throughout the territory. Unemployed workers, white as well as black, emigrated or became destitute; tax revenues, predominantly dependent on copper, collapsed; the government was forced to make fierce economies, especially in health, education and agricultural services. The fall in the African labour force from 30,000 to 7000 seemed the least of the government's worries, for they assumed that migrant workers could survive by returning to their villages. But rural areas were hit by the depression too; and in 1933 drought and locusts ruined the harvests which should have fed the returning labourers.

By this time the copper market was beginning to revive; but the competitiveness of Northern Rhodesian mines depended on their low wages and tight labour discipline. Life in the towns and mining compounds remained hard for the workers, still harder for those who had come to rely on paid work and could not find it. Some took to crime, others to religion; witch-finding societies flourished in the countryside and the millenarian Watch Tower movement (whose lurid propaganda had long alarmed sensitive whites) in the towns. While some migrants found a new community focus in *mbeni* dance

35

societies, others joined local improvement associations, where African clerks emerged as more authentic spokesmen for their people than the accredited 'tribal elders'. The depleted administration had little information about such developments, and less control. In May 1935, in a well-meaning attempt to promote equity between urban and rural tax-payers, it raised the tax payable by Africans on the Copper Belt; this, on top of grievances over pay, rations, work discipline, and racial injustice, triggered violent protests. Local leaders called brief but effective strikes at one mine after another; stones were thrown at blacklegs and officials; eventually a disorganized police detachment at Luanshya opened fire and killed six strikers. A Commission of Enquiry recommended reforms; but neither these nor the gradual recovery of the copper industry removed the injustices inherent in this colour-bar economy.[6]

In the Gold Coast, though there were fewer white residents, African leadership was more sophisticated, and the government's response to the Depression strained the alliance which Guggisberg had established with the *amanhene* against the urban nationalists. Even before the financial crisis became acute Governor Slater had been planning to establish Stool Treasuries which would levy taxes in each chiefdom and share the proceeds with central government; but, hoping 'to divide the opposition to direct tax' by showing that townsmen would also be affected, he first introduced a Bill imposing tax on annual incomes of £40 or more. But this could affect chiefs, traders and cocoa farmers as well as clerks and lawyers; instead of dividing the opposition it threatened to unite town and country in opposition to direct taxation. Cocoa farmers, already frustrated by the failure of their latest attempt to hold up deliveries until the foreign export houses offered higher prices, joined other commoners in denouncing chiefs who accepted Slater's new fiscal programme. In Western and Central Provinces some chiefs turned against the government; those who did not faced protests from the *asafo*, military companies which claimed a historic right to depose chiefs who violated custom. When Ofori Atta I, the governor's leading ally, withdrew his support from the Native Revenue Bill, both aspects of Slater's financial package had to be abandoned.[7]

The financial plight of the Gold Coast was less serious than that of other colonies; gold-mining provided some hedge against deflation, and after the boycott the farmers compensated for falling prices by increasing production. By 1934 some of the budgetary cuts could be restored; but the government decided to transfer the costs of improved water supplies in three coastal towns by charging water-rate. This new form of taxation, and also new penalties for possession of 'seditious literature', were approved by the Legislative Council against united African opposition; two deputations, led respectively by Ofori Atta and by Sekyi of the ARPS, went to London to protest and demand constitutional reform. There they were greeted by George Padmore, and advised that their grievances formed part of a wider African crisis.

Padmore, increasingly disillusioned with the Comintern since it had adopted a strategy of Popular Front with the French and British governments against Hitlerite Germany, had begun to build a group of radical Pan-Africans, which included Jomo Kenyatta and the Trinidadian Marxist C. L. R. James. In September 1935 a new focus for racial solidarity appeared when Mussolini invaded Ethiopia. This reversion to the morality of earlier European generations aroused spontaneous anger among Black people throughout the world; the young Nkrumah, in passage to the USA, felt 'as if the whole of London had suddenly declared war on me personally.'[8] This anger, originally concentrated against Italy, spread more widely after the abortive exercise in appeasement of Hoare and Laval; the western democracies, the Soviet Union, the Catholic church, the League of Nations, all seemed to have become accomplices in the martyrdom of Africa's last independent kingdom. Like the submerged nations of nineteenth-century Europe the London Pan-Africans resolved to create an overseas base from which national liberation movements might develop. While still prepared to work with sympathetic Europeans (like the League of Nations Union, appalled by the Hoare–Laval pact for somewhat different reasons) Padmore and his friends preached that Black people had ultimately to depend on themselves alone.

An opportunity to introduce this new cosmopolitanism to the Gold Coast arose when a wealthy African merchant, J. A. Ocansey, decided to publish a new newspaper, *The African Morning Post*. As editor he engaged Nnamdi Azikiwe, returning to Africa after nine years' study in the USA; and Isaac Wallace-Johnson, a sharp-witted Sierra Leonean who had visited Moscow, became a contributor. This talented pair introduced more polemical styles of journalism, supported the election of the *frondeur* Kojo Thompson to the Legislative Council, and founded an organization called the Youth League which secured support in many urban centres.

While this new political style was winning applause at the coast, the Farmers' Associations, in Asante as well as the Colony, were displaying increased effectiveness in organizing another hold-up of

37

the 1937–38 cocoa crop. This time brokers, drivers and market-women recognized a common interest in supporting the ban on sales; and it was underwritten by the authority of many chiefs. This was not a political protest; although lawyers like Sekyi eagerly offered advice and support the farmers insisted that their grievance was against the foreign merchant houses and their price-fixing 'pool', not against the colonial government. (Local officials indeed showed much sympathy for the farmers, who provided most of their revenue, although the merchants found more sympathy in the Colonial Office.) The impressive unity of the farmers and their allies secured the appointment of a Commission which made far-reaching proposals for public control of cocoa marketing; but they were not yet ready to accept the leadership of urban nationalists.[9] But although the colonial government felt able to proceed with attempts to establish closer supervision over local government in the countryside, it had been reminded of the limits of the control which, even with the collaboration of the *amanhene*, it could exercise over rural society.

Nor was the Gold Coast the only colony where nationalist rhetoric was winning popular applause. In 1938 Wallace-Johnson moved from Accra to his native Sierra Leone, where he not only attracted lively audiences in Freetown but formed Youth League branches in several provincial towns. Though most of his supporters were fellow-Krio, trade unions which he formed in Freetown and at the new iron-mine of Marampa began to recruit more widely; the visiting academic W. M. Macmillan thought that 'the ventilation of constitutional or labour grievances had begun to bridge the deep cleavage between the Creoles and the peoples of the Protectorate.'[10] In 1939 the government was provoked by strikes to introduce laws which severely restricted civil liberties; but it also initiated more constructive labour legislation. If the impact of the Depression had not undermined the authority of colonial rulers, it did remind them forcefully of the need to justify that authority by serious measures of improvement.

IMPERIAL SOLUTIONS TO EUROPEAN CRISES?

Meanwhile in Europe the Depression was increasing interest in empire among those who hoped that economic weaknesses might be relieved by creating protected trading areas abroad. The degree to which metropolitan industries had already benefited from protected

African markets is difficult to measure; in many colonies differential tariffs were excluded by international treaty, but even there substantial advantages could be gained through administrative favour, subsidized transport and communications, familiarity with language and legal systems. A fine study of French experience shows how colonial empire helped declining industries to survive in France. By 1928 the empire (primarily Indo-China and the Maghreb) had become France's largest customer, taking 17.3 per cent of her exports; already these were largely supplied by old industries like cotton which elsewhere were handicapped by foreign competition. It was these least progressive sections of French business which after 1929 began to call for greater protection within an autarkic imperial economy. They were opposed, not only by free-traders, but by financiers who favoured industrial development in the colonies, in order to transfer some of the more labour-intensive processes overseas and encourage investment in more modern technology at home. But in France, as to a lesser extent in the Britain of the Ottawa agreements, protectionism reinforced by imperial sentiment tended to prevail. Algeria's share of French foreign trade grew to one-eighth, that of Black Africa to a twentieth. By 1936, when the empire took a third of all French exports, certain industries (cotton textiles, cement, sugar, groundnut oil) found over 80 per cent of their markets there.[11]

Opportunities to solve domestic difficulties in Africa were also perceived in Germany, but here political pressure for reversal of the Paris peace settlement counted for more than economic calculation. The rise of Hitler alarmed those European governments which held former German colonies as mandates, but had done little to develop them (preferring to invest available resources in colonies to which their title was more secure); mandates suddenly became weak points of colonial empire. The local threat was twofold. Germans who had returned after 1919 to reclaim their property resumed their dominant position in many colonies and supported reunion with the Reich. In British Cameroons most of the 300 German residents, who heavily out-numbered the British, were ardent Nazis. As late as October 1939 the local Nazi leader who acted as their spokesman could proudly report that 'pictures of the Fuehrer hang everywhere and everybody greets the other with "Heil Hitler".'[12] But pro-German sympathies also appeared among Africans. Administrators in French Cameroun became somewhat paranoid when Duala chiefs petitioned the League of Nations in the German language, when musical ensembles wore caps in German national colours, when social clubs adopted such names as *Bund der Freunde*. Judging it expedient to temper repression with concessions still denied to subjects in their other colonies, in 1938 they tentatively authorized a political association of the French-speaking elite, the *Jeunesse Camerounaise Française*, or JEUCAFRA.[13]

But although the lost colonies featured in Hitler's list of grievances against the Treaty of Versailles, the recreation of an African empire came low on his agenda. While he maintained a sort of shadow Colonial Office within the Nazi party under an old Wilhelmine imperialist, Ritter von Epp, Hitler's priority remained the creation of a new European order through expansion in eastern Europe; colonial grievances were only brought forward when this seemed tactically expedient. His talented economic adviser Hjalmar Schacht tried to persuade him that a successful colonial policy could make other risks unnecessary; he wrote in retrospective self-justification;

> If Germany had been able to concentrate her energies on developing her colonies, instead of trying to concentrate them on her export trade, she would have been able to obtain the bread and fats she needed from colonial production instead of being compelled to upset the industrial markets of the world by excessive competition.[14]

But this argument reflected Schacht's political caution rather than his economic expertise, and there is no sign that Hitler ever considered it seriously. The detailed plans prepared in von Epp's office were to be implemented only after Germany had consolidated her control of continental Europe.

Nevertheless, within two months of Hitler's accession to power British Ministers were contemplating appeasing Fascist land-hunger by restoring some or all of the mandated territories. They saw powerful objections to abandoning Tanganyika, and the Union of South Africa clearly had no intention of relaxing control of Namibia; but the Colonial Secretary, Cunliffe-Lister, noted that both Togoland and Cameroons 'seem liabilities rather than assets', and objections from his staff centred on the probable damage to British prestige in the empire and the international community rather than more direct costs.[15] Only when Hitler's re-occupation of the Rhineland on 7 March 1936 made France and Britain eager to seek some comprehensive agreement to prevent further aggression did the Committee of Imperial Defence establish a military and civilian sub-committee under the Earl of Plymouth 'to consider in all its aspects the question of the possible transfer of a Colonial Mandate or Mandates to Germany.'[16]

Their report did not encourage the view that sacrificing colonies might preserve European peace. As the Foreign Secretary announced on 27 July, there were 'grave difficulties, moral, political and legal' in any restoration of mandates. Togoland and Cameroons, the only possible candidates, were unlikely to satisfy either Hitler's political appetite or his economic needs. But Plymouth's committee, like the Board of Trade in 1918, did see possibilities of reducing political grievances through some form of economic internationalism: an International Commission to guarantee equal opportunities in tropical Africa, in colonies as well as mandates, might prove 'a useful piece of window-dressing'. In conversations with the French Premier Leon Blum, Schacht showed sufficient interest in this sort of imperial restructuring to encourage Neville Chamberlain's hopes of appeasing German 'moderates'; after Lord Halifax's visit to Hitler in November 1937 Chamberlain presented somewhat vague proposals on these lines to the Cabinet's Foreign Affairs Committee. Those better informed rightly doubted whether his scheme, drafted without consulting France, Belgium or Portugal, was relevant to the containment of German expansion; and indeed Hitler's planned annexation of Austria was in no way affected by the offer of participation in 'a new regime of colonial administration' built on the frail international structure introduced to the Congo basin in 1885.[17]

But Chamberlain's blundering initiative did have positive effects on British African policy; it obliged opponents of colonial appeasement on Left and Right to reconsider the moral basis of colonial authority. By late 1938 rumours of the proposal reached Africa; governors reported alarm, on the part not only of settlers in Tanganyika but of African bodies like the Nigerian Youth Movement, more conscious of the racial menace of fascism since Ethiopia. Conservatives who cared more about the empire than about eastern Europe began to have doubts about appeasement. The Labour Party, echoing this concern, initiated a Parliamentary debate on colonial policy – a rare event indeed; and the Colonial Secretary, Malcolm MacDonald, gave an assurance (watered down by a grudging Chamberlain) that any transfer of territory was 'not now an issue in practical politics'.[18]

But something more positive was needed to ensure African loyalty in face of Hitler's challenge. MacDonald went on to repeat a statement, informally aired at an administrators' Summer School a few months earlier, that the ultimate, if distant, aim of British colonial policy was evolution towards self-government. In the meantime, the primary purpose of colonial policy would be 'the welfare and progress of all the inhabitants'. Presented as a recapitulation of established principles, this statement in fact reflected extensive reconsiderations within the Colonial Office. The German threat had reinforced a lesson of the Depression: that those who publicly justified their rule by the benefits it brought to Africans needed to take more active measures to produce positive results.

TOWARDS COLONIAL DEVELOPMENT

The experiences of the early 1930s undermined the tranquil confidence which colonial administrators had shown in the beneficial effects of economic liberalism lightly supervised by paternal governments. Such modest improvements in services to African populations as commercial expansion had permitted were halted, and some of those populations were beginning to manifest discontent in hitherto unfamiliar forms. Although the external challenge of Nazi Germany was unlikely to attract African patriots, that which Japan was mounting in Asia had more sympathetic racial implications; and if either resulted in war African loyalties would be severely tested.

One response of the colonial powers, in Africa as at home, was to experiment with new techniques for state intervention and planning of economic development. The emphasis was usually on building an imperial economy to serve the needs of the metropolis. The British Colonial Development Act of 1929, prepared by Joseph Chamberlain's disciple L. S. Amery but enacted by the Labour Minister J. H. Thomas, authorized grants or loans of up to £1,000,000 annually 'for purposes of aiding and developing agriculture and industry [in the Colonies] and thereby promoting commerce with or industry in the UK.' Opinions differ as to how far this measure, justified to Parliament by its advantages to Britain, was really expected to assist the development of Africa. Like the Imperial Preferences agreed at Ottawa in 1932 (which in colonial Africa treaty commitments allowed to be significantly used only in Sierra Leone and the Gambia), the intention seems to have been to foster an imperial economy to insure established interests against the Depression. In any case a total expenditure of $6,523,193 over ten years could have only local effects (e.g. around the open-cast iron mines which Baird's of Glasgow were assisted to develop in Sierra Leone).

In France, wartime experience of corporate planning, though not always successful, had encouraged enthusiasts for an imperial economy. In 1921 Albert Sarraut had presented to Parliament an abortive programme of loans and subsidies intended to improve the transport facilities, productive capacity and social overhead capital of the colonies; as the Depression set in his plan was revived and refined by André Maginot, with priority now given to a grand, ill-prepared, technocratic scheme for irrigated cotton cultivation in the middle valley of the Niger. At the same time preferential arrangements for colonial trade were helping to palliate the effects of depression. Between 1927 and 1936, while the value of French exports to foreign countries fell by 65.8 per cent, exports to the empire declined by only 1.7 per cent, and indeed rose to dominate the market for such industries as cotton textiles. The total effect was that Africans were confirmed as principal suppliers of cotton and oil-seeds to French industry and principal consumers of many products. It was still widely and naively assumed that the benefits of such colonial development would automatically be shared by the Africans whose taxes and unpaid labour made it possible.

Similar assumptions underlay the neo-mercantilism of the corporate state which Antonio Salazar had been establishing in Portgual since 1928; government and capitalists were to collaborate in developing colonial production so as to improve Portugal's balance of payments and permit the regeneration of the empire. The colonial development fund set up in 1937 to improve transport and irrigation facilities was financed chiefly from budgetary surpluses achieved by rigid financial controls in the colonies: in other words, by the Africans themselves.

But as technocratic economic planners became influential in metropolitan capitals officials closer to African realities emphasized different priorities. When the Governor of Nyasaland declared in 1930 that 'without more money, the country will not develop', the official head of the Colonial Office pointed out that social development was a necessary pre-condition for economic growth:

> The natives are underfed and underpaid; they have little and, in many cases, no opportunity to trade; their education has been almost entirely neglected by Government; they are leaving the Protectorate in large numbers; at the same time such important social services as medical and sanitary work, agricultural and technical training and research, development of native institutions and law, have been so restricted as to fall far below the standard normally attained by backward British Dependencies.[19]

By this time Europeans were becoming more conscious of the extent of their ignorance about Africa, and of the difficulties of applying their own scientific and technical knowledge to the problems of its peoples and environment. Missionaries and retired administrators, the two most experienced groups, formed the International Institute of African Languages and Cultures in 1926, and the Paris-based *Société des Africanistes* four years later; meanwhile a few imperial enthusiasts were beginning to extend interest in the academic study of African problems from South Africa to British universities, and to interest the great American foundations in sponsoring studies of contemporary problems. With their support the massive *African Survey* of Lord Hailey was published in 1938 – a magisterial prospectus of 1837 pages, summarizing the perceptions of a distinguished Indian pro-consul about what was currently believed, and what most urgently needed to be discovered, about environmental, social, economic and political problems of sub-Saharan Africa.[20]

Meanwhile the British Colonial Office had been improving its capacity to incorporate specialized expertise in the formation of policy. Officials in the 'geographical' departments, who by tradition handled every aspect of policy in a cognate group of colonies, were increasingly reinforced both by specialist advisory committees, drawing on the experience and knowledge of academics, missionaries and others, and by full-time specialist Advisers. The first of these were in medicine (1926) and agriculture (1929); by 1945 a former PUS somewhat incredulously counted thirteen such appointments, plus six assistants.[21] At the same time separate departments for economics (1934) and social services (1938) became increasingly active in initiating policy.

Measures introduced for sound scientific or technical reasons could profoundly alter colonial relationships. Agriculturalists who noted how many African farmers maintained incomes by increasing acreage became alarmed by reports from America and the Union of South Africa about environmental catastrophes caused by soil erosion. Although some fears were influenced as much by socially conscious journalism as by comparative ecological study, fallow periods *were* being shortened, and there *were* dangers of over-grazing by cattle evicted from former pastures. Reports from the field, interpreted by the Agricultural Adviser, fostered an 'ideology of conservation'[22], which decreed that African farmers must plant in strips separated by grass barriers, plough along contour-lines, control the size and condition of their cattle herds, and generally employ their land and labour in ways not self-evidently remunerative. Such interventions by well-intentioned bureaucrats in the lives of African farmers were liable to evoke political reactions, unless quickly justified by visible improvement.

Political implications of research on urban problems could be even more far-reaching. In the growing towns, where conditions of labour, diet and housing were in varying degrees deplorable, the new labouring classes were liable to become 'dangerous classes' even more rapidly than in nineteenth-century Europe. The International Labour Office, prompted by scientists like John Boyd-Orr, placed special emphasis on nutritional problems, and in 1936 a Colonial Office survey agreed that malnutrition was almost everywhere a major obstacle to improvement. Initially they nevertheless continued to hope that paternal oversight by experienced administrators could keep the problems of the new proletariat under control; Major G. St. J. Orde-Browne, who became the first Labour Adviser in 1938, won his credentials by supervising migrants in Tanganyika. But wider travels soon showed him that a good deal of research and investment in measures of welfare would be needed to maintain social control, as well as a constructive approach to the new associations of African workers. Old-school Governors had regarded trade unions as subversive, where they were not actually illegal; the 1926 strike on the Sierra Leone railway had been interpreted as a 'serious trial of strength between authority and the spirit of indiscipline.'[23] But the influence of the British Labour movement and of the ILO led to appreciation that it would be wiser to tame than to suppress such organizations; a Labour Minister wrote in 1930, 'I would like to think that we were in good time to guide and keep our Colonial Labour movements on sound and constitutional lines.'[24] Since economic development would radically change African society, welfare policy should aim to channel change in directions which in Great Britain had led to social stability.

Between 1938 and 1940 these various impulses towards reform were drawn together in the British Colonial Office under the political guidance of Malcolm MacDonald, son of the former Prime Minister. Particular urgency was provided by a series of disorders in West Indian colonies between 1935 and 1938; faced with falling demands for sugar and their other crops, these plantation societies had no 'traditional' agriculture to cushion the impact of depression. A wide-ranging Commission of Inquiry under Lord Moyne produced in December 1939 a report so bleak that it was not published until 1945; the Cabinet perceived how easily Nazi propaganda could have used it to discredit British colonial rule. But it arrived at the right time to reinforce MacDonald's principal proposals. In February 1940 the

Cabinet approved a Colonial Development and Welfare Bill, which was enacted three months later during the greatest emergency of the war. The sum of £5,000,000 was to be allocated annually for ten years to support plans, which each colonial government was required to prepare, 'to bring their services [for education and social welfare as well as economic infrastructure] up to a reasonable standard'; these might now include Exchequer grants for recurrent as well as capital expenditure. An annual sum of £500,000 was ear-marked for research. Even had wartime priorities allowed the disbursement of these sums – which they did not – they could not have proved adequate for the unquantified need; but the availability of British funds for development planning signalled a more active role for the colonial state, which could not fail to have political consequences.[25]

The reactions to crisis of the other colonial powers have been less closely studied (at least by this author), though the Belgian Government's provision of capital for a major medical centre in the Congo as early as 1930 seems to indicate a similar concern.[26] In France the reforming impulse became most visible under the Popular Front governments of 1936–38, although apart from limited improvements in labour legislation and some relaxations of administrative autocracy results were meagre. Following a Governors' Conference in November 1936 Marius Moutet, the Socialist Colonial Minister, appointed an impressive committee, including the ethnologist Lévy-Bruhl and the writer André Gide, to study 'the application to overseas countries of the great principles of the Rights of Man', but this proved a substitute for rather than a prelude to effective reform; Gide quickly recognized the sterility of summary 'inspections' of Senegalese schools, carried out *par acquit de conscience*.[27] Vested interests and inherited prejudices were too strongly entrenched in Parliament to permit fundamental reform or improved funding for development. Perhaps the most important result in the long run was to advance in the colonial service a new generation of officials, inspired by new ideals of 'colonial humanism'.

Moreover, these discussions of reform in the metropolitan states had drawn in persons and groups who raised questions of political value, concerning the wisdom of anticipating grievances or the justice of maintaining authoritarian control. The Popular Front's evocation of the Rights of Man led some, like the young Socialist governor Hubert Deschamps, to take seriously the assimilationist ideal once cherished by good Republicans. Blum's government even tried to take a modest step in this direction by an abortive Bill to add some 24,000 Muslim notables to the existing, largely white, Algerian electorate of 200,000, so extending the principle already established in Senegal that a Muslim could become a full French citizen without renouncing personal status under Islamic law. Similarly, MacDonald's statement of December 1938 that Britain's ultimate aim was to bring the colonies to self-government articulated an intention which, though many vaguely believed it to be latent in the historical evolution of the Commonwealth, had never previously been formally applied to the African colonies. Assimilation and self-government were still no more than remote principles; nobody in France or Britain was actually planning their early implementation. But the Second World War was about to increase the pressures to do so, from both inside and outside Africa.

NOTES AND REFERENCES

1. Cf. A. G. Hopkins, *An Economic History of West Africa* (1973) pp. 182-5; *Afrique et la Crise de 1930*, special issue of RFHOM, LXIII, 1976
2. D. Hobart Houghton & J. Dagut, *Source Material on the South African Economy* (Cape Town, 1973) III, pp. 108-15
3. J. Marseille, *Empire colonial et capitalisme français: Histoire d'une divorce* (Paris, 1984) pp. 68-75
4. Hélène Almeida-Topor, 'Recherches sur l'évolution du travail salarié en AOF pendant la crise économique, 1930-1936', CEA, XVI, 1976, p. 105; Monique Lakhroum, *Le travail inégal* (Paris, 1982) p. 126
5. P. Kipré, 'La crise économique dans les centres urbains en Côte d'Ivoire, 1930-35', CEA, XVI, 1976, pp. 139-41
6. P.P. 1934-35, VII, Cmd. 5009, Report of the Commission appointed to enquire into the Disturbances on the Copperbelt, Northern Rhodesia; R. I. Rotberg, *The Rise of Nationalism in Central Africa* (Cambridge, Mass, 1966) pp. 161-68
7. Jarle Simmensen, 'Commoners, Chiefs and Colonial Government: British Policy and Local Politics in Akim Abuakwa, Ghana, under Colonial Rule' (Ph.D. thesis, University of Trondheim, 1975, Chap XI; B. M. Edsman, *Lawyers in Gold Coast Politics, 1900-45* (Upsala, 1979) pp. 151-59
8. *The Autobiography of Kwame Nkrumah* (Edinburgh, 1957) p. 27; S. K. B. Asante, *Pan-African Protest: Africa and the Italo-Ethiopian Crisis 1934-41* (1977)
9. John Miles, 'Cocoa Marketing ...'; R. Crook, 'Decolonization, the Colonial State and Chieftaincy in the Gold Coast', AF.AFF, 85, 1986
10. C. K. Meek, W. M. Macmillan & E. R. J. Hussey, *Europe and West Africa* (1940) pp. 76-77
11. Marseille, *Empire colonial ...* pp. 44, 54; cf. CHA,VII, p. 62
12. A. Ndi, 'The Second World War in Southern Cameroon and its Impact on Mission-State Relations, 1939-50', K & R, pp. 206-09

13. R. A. Joseph, 'The German Question in French Cameroun, 1919–1939', *Comparative Studies in Society and History*, 17, 1975, pp. 65–90
14. H. Schacht, *Account Settled* (1949) p. 93
15. C.O.967/108, Memoranda on Mandates and Arguments against Surrendering Mandates. The file also considers, and rejects, a possible transfer of Palestine to Italy.
16. Report of Plymouth Committee is in DBFP, 2nd series XVI, App.III
17. DBFP, 2nd series XIX, No. 465; Cabinet committee on Foreign Policy 24 January 1938; cf. W. R. Louis, 'Colonial Appeasement, 1936–1938', *Revue Belge de Philologie et d'Histoire*, 1971
18. Hansard, Commons, 7 Dec. 1938, 1247. For Chamberlain's amendments, see PREM I/247
19. Samuel Wilson to Treasury, 11 April 1930, quoted Morgan, Vol. I, pp. 53–5
20. K. E. Robinson 'Experts, Colonialists and Africanists', in J. C. Stone (ed) *Experts in Africa* (Aberdeen, 1980)
21. Cosmo Parkinson, *The Colonial Office from Within* (1947) pp. 55–60
22. David Anderson, 'Depression, Dust Bowl, Demography and Drought: the Colonial State and Soil Conservation in East Africa during the 1930s, AF AFF,83,1984, p. 339; cf. W. Beinart, 'Soil Erosion, Conservationism, and Ideas about Development: a Southern African Exploration', *Journal of Southern African Studies* XI,1984. For other examples of misapplied agronomic expertise, R. H. Green & S. H. Hymer, 'Cocoa in the Gold Coast: A Study in the Relations between African Farmers and Agricultural Experts', *Journal of Economic History* 25 1966; Alastair Milne, 'Experts and Farmers: British Agricultural Policy in the Gold Coast', *Bulletin, Aberdeen University African Studies Group* 19, 1983, pp. 11–13
23. Slater to Amery, 20 Jan. 1926, quoted Akintola Wyse, 'The 1926 Railway Strike and Anglo-Krio Relations: an Interpretation', IJAHS 14,1981, pp. 93–4
24. Minute by Drummond Shiels 11 April 1930, quoted P. S. Gupta, *Imperialism and the British Labour Movement* (1975) p. 144
25. P.P. 1945, VI Cmd. 6607, West India Royal Commission Report, 21 Dec. 1939; CAB 65/5 War Cabinet 42 (40) 15 Feb. 1940
26. R. Anstey, *King Leopold's Legacy* (1966) p. 85
27. *Journal d'André Gide* (Paris, 1949) p. 1297; cf. W. B. Cohen, 'The Colonial Policy of the Popular Front', *French Historical Studies VII, 1972*. For 'colonial humanism', R. Girardet, *L'idée coloniale en France, 1871–1962* (Paris, 1972) Ch. IX

CHAPTER THREE

War and the African Empires, 1939–1945

THE GROWTH OF AFRICAN INVOLVEMENT, 1939–41

The immediate effects in Africa of the declaration of war by Britain and France against Germany on 3 September 1939 were limited and localized. Between Cairo and Cape Town operational activities were at first confined to a few ports and airfields. Freetown, an important staging-post and assembly-point for naval convoys, was quickly affected. Six weeks after the outbreak of war its European population, normally 400, was varying between 5000 and 18,000; from thirty-five to fifty merchant ships were normally in harbour, and Admirals were 'three a penny'.[1] Mombasa, Lagos, Dakar and other towns also experienced concentrated military activity, and its attendant social problems.

The most intensive military recruitment took place in the French empire, which to an even greater extent than in 1914 was expected to redress the demographic weakness of the metropole; by June 1940 Africans provided almost 9 per cent of the French army in France, and some 100,000 troops had been mobilized in AOF alone.[2] In their impoverished colonies of Equatorial Africa however the French failed to reach their recruitment targets, as regards either the infantry which they sought chiefly in Chad or the labour contingents which were to be the main contribution of the southern territories.[3] This was an early warning of the strains which might be imposed by requiring African contributions to the war.

After the double shock of Italian entry and French defeat in June 1940 the war began to affect Africa more directly. At first it seemed possible that France would continue to fight from her imperial base in North Africa; by July this was unlikely, and a pre-emptive British attack on their fleet at Mers-el-Kebir confirmed the belief of military and civilian leaders in the Maghreb that they would best serve France's long-term interest by remaining loyal to the Vichy regime and its policy of neutrality. But the Guyanese Governor of Chad, Felix Eboué (a socialist and freemason) and his Chief Secretary Henri Laurentie (a Catholic humanist) had already made contact with the British in Nigeria; when de Gaulle issued his famous call for continued resistance they responded ardently, as did many officers of the Colonial Army. During 'three glorious days' in late August patriotic Frenchmen in Fort Lamy, Brazzaville and Duala executed *coups d'état* which resulted in the consolidation of a Gaullist dominion covering all of Cameroun and AEF (though only after fighting in Gabon), with Eboué as Governor-General. In AOF many Frenchmen remained uncertain about their patriotic duty, or their interest; but Governor-General Pierre Boisson, a stern nationalist equally distrustful of Britain as of Germany, declared for Vichy and successfully resisted a maladroit attempt by de Gaulle and the British to take over Dakar in September 1940. Vichyite authorities hoped, by asserting their strict neutrality, to avert the danger of direct German intervention in Africa; but the price was acutely hostile relations with their British neighbours for more than two years.

Africans played only minor roles in these dramatic events. Many Senegalese, including Al Haj Seydou Nourou Tall, head of the Tijaniyya Muslims in Dakar, were openly pro-Allied; but their opinions counted for little with French officials, whether Gaullist or Vichyite. The Free French regime in Brazzaville allowed even less freedom to the *amicalistes* than its predecessors; Matswa died in prison in 1942. Eboué's much-acclaimed new 'native policy' proved to be essentially authoritarian paternalism, envisaging an increasing role for chiefs on the North Nigerian model.[4] In Dakar Boisson and his colleagues welcomed the opportunity to suppress such constitutional liberties as African citizens had enjoyed under the Third Republic; critics accused them of complicity with Nazi racialism.[5] Wartime conditions thus initially strengthened the authoritarian tendencies latent in all colonial administrations in both sections of *Afrique noire*.

Political doctrines apart, all France's African subjects suffered new hardships in consequence of the interruption of peace-time patterns of production and trade, and of increased demands by their rulers. Although Allied measures of blockade against AOF were intermittent and incompletely enforced, imports and exports decreased on the instructions of the German conquerors. To compensate by increased food production, administrators made more intense demands for forced labour and compulsory cultivation; this command economy was also required to support an army raised to 100,000 to defend the frontiers against the British. There were serious shortages, inflation, and other hardships, leading to much overland migration. The economy of the Gaullist territories was under-written by a British agreement to buy up export crops even when no shipping was available; but since de Gaulle and Eboué were determined to mobilize a major contribution to the Allied war effort in production and manpower, here too Africans experienced increased demands for taxes, unpaid labour, and compulsory deliveries of crops. It was a similar story across the Congo, where the exiled Belgian government made its main contribution in production rather than in troops: Africans experienced increasing governmental pressure, especially in the widening areas where the mines of Katanga, whose copper, uranium and cobalt were so vital, recruited their labourers.

Meanwhile Italy's declaration of war on 10 June 1940 brought military operations to the soil of both north and east Africa. As the Middle East became the British empire's principal theatre of land-based operations, major battles were engaged astride the Egyptian-Libyan border; and imperial resources were mobilized to eliminate the 290,000 Italian troops in Ethiopia and Somalia. The Sudan Defence Force was doubled in size; in Kenya the two Brigade Groups of King's African Rifles were reinforced by two West African brigades and a South African division. The government of General Smuts, which on 4 September 1939 had carried South Africa into the war by a majority of only 80–67, expanded its white fighting units and began to enlist labourers and other non-combatants in its Non-European Army Services. Meanwhile a Command headquarters, established at Achimota to defend the suddenly vulnerable frontiers with AOF, extended military recruitment into regions without previous military traditions; the total strength of the Royal West African Frontier Force rose quickly to twenty-three battalions, with a wider range of technical and supporting arms. By May 1941 the imperial forces in East Africa, reinforced by Indian divisions, had overcome the feeble Italian defence; Ethiopia thus became the first African state to be freed from colonial rule, and largely by African arms.

In most British colonies the political impact of war was still indirect, but it quickly began to diffuse. Colonial governments, tacitly assuming that their subjects would recognize moral obligations to assist the war against fascism, greatly expanded public information services; publications in African languages, as well as in

51

English, were sponsored, broadcasting and rediffusion services, though still accessible only to limited audiences, were expanded, mobile cinemas mixed propaganda films with Charlie Chaplin. Much of the material used now seems staggeringly inept; if in retrospect these wartime innovations seem to mark the start of a communications revolution, care is needed in assessing immediate effects. Although military enlistments, like the much-publicized contributions by Africans to Spitfire funds and other designated war works, were supposedly the fruit of spontaneous loyalism, in practice pressure from chiefs or other government agents counted for more than civic spirit.

It was wartime economic necessities which had the most drastic effects on African life. Dislocation of prewar trade patterns, shipping shortages, and maritime blockades weakened whole sectors of the commercial economy, while others were strained by increased demands – for strategic minerals, for example. Restrictions on imports – including some essential foods, as well as consumer goods – created inflationary pressures, in the colonies of neutral Portugal and Spain as well as in the belligerent empires. Governments were obliged to adopt interventionist policies which existing machinery was ill-prepared to execute. Command economies were improvised on the basis of forced (or heavily constrained) labour, compulsory cultivations, hastily-created marketing controls; under-manned colonial states began to make heavier demands on their subjects than ever before. Prices paid to producers of essential commodities were held down, and the ensuing profits temporarily appropriated by the British Treasury in the over-riding cause of imperial survival. And from 1942 the extension of the war and the loss of Allied empires in South-East Asia meant that all these pressures were greatly intensified.

A TRULY WORLD WAR, 1942–45

After Japan's occupation of South-East Asia in the early months of 1942 denied the Allies vital sources of minerals, raw materials and foodstuffs, planners in London and Washington required colonial governments to impose still heavier demands on African populations which seemed capable of supplying these needs. While Africans were sent abroad in thousands as soldiers and labourers for North African and Asian theatres, those who remained came under increasing duress to work harder, whether on their own farms, on those of foreigners, in mines, or in direct employment of the colonial state. Areas whose resources seemed relevant to special strategic needs received particularly intensive pressure. From 1942 the Tanganyika government enforced labour conscription for European plantations, hoping to increase production of sisal and revive that of rubber, while almost 100,000 workers were being conscripted in largely vain attempts to extract more tin from northern Nigeria. Wherever there seemed opportunities to assist the white man's war, colonial states assumed unprecedented powers to ensure that they were taken.

For some Africans these demands entailed sufferings comparable to those of the battle-fronts. Conscious cruelties by labour contractors were often less serious than the totally inadequate arrangements made for the health and diet of men displaced from their home environment, or the devastating effects on many areas of drought and famine in 1942-43. Sanitary conditions in Nigerian tin-mines were particularly scandalous, and many hundreds of workers died. But even where minimal standards were maintained and wages regularly paid, shortages of imported goods and local food supplies inflated prices, depressing living standards for the prewar labour force as well as for the new recruits.

This is not to say that all effects were negative. The extension of exchange economies based on cash laid foundations for postwar growth. Shortages of imported consumer goods stimulated some light industrial development around many ports and capitals. Enterprising West Africans accumulated some modest fortunes as farmers supplying new urban food markets, as commodity traders, above all as government contractors. In Kenya, if settlers were the most obvious gainers from the corporate economy of the later war years, some African peasant farmers prospered too, often by evading official marketing regulations. As always, the costs and benefits of war were most inequitably distributed; Africans were often, but not always, losers. The principal gainers however were white South Africans. The requirements of the war not only provided large markets for the mining industry and for capitalist farmers but allowed the Union to consolidate the industrial advances begun in the 1930s. During the war its manufacturing output increased in value by 116 per cent; the industrial labour force grew by 53 per cent, representing 125,000 new workers, of whom only 19,000 were white. Its economic and military contributions to the Allied cause strengthened Smuts's South Africa as a regional power, which claimed to possess not only material resources but scientific expertise and political experience relevant to the development of the African continent.

The Japanese entry made Africa strategically important in relation to Asia as well as to the Middle East. In May 1942 British troops seized the Madagascan port of Diego Suarez; later the rest of the island was occupied by forces including troops from East and South Africa, and its administration handed over to de Gaulle. Between 1942 and 1944 five East African brigades and two West African divisions were sent to Asia, for eventual service on the Burma front. But until 1943 African war efforts were still focused on the Mediterranean. Two South African divisions took part in the North African desert war; after one surrendered at Tobruk the other was re-equipped with armour for the Italian campaign. As pressure on South African manpower increased, Smuts contemplated, but rejected, the idea of arming non-whites; nevertheless Non-European Army Services supplied much military labour in Egypt, as did East African and Congolese units. The Allied armies were also reinforced by the Sudan Defence Force, and in February 1943 by a Free French column which fought its way across the desert from Chad.

The protection of African supply routes was a crucial contribution to the Middle East war. Extraordinary efforts were made to develop the African Line of Communications by which bulky supplies were moved up the Congo river, across to Juba in southern Sudan, and thence to Egypt. Air supply routes through west Africa had even higher priority. Since 1940 the British had been assembling military aircraft at Takoradi for onward flight to Khartoum and Cairo, and Roosevelt had sought ways to evade American neutrality laws so as to involve the resources of Pan-American Airways in this work. By 1941 that airline had developed landing facilities in Liberia which after America entered the war became, together with Monrovia harbour, the basis of a considerable military establishment. Elsewhere too transatlantic air traffic greatly increased; Accra, Lagos, Kano, and many smaller airfields, as well as major ports, became centres of an American military and civilian presence which could overshadow that of the British.

In November 1942 American and British forces landed in Morocco and Algeria, and six months later the African armies of the Axis surrendered in Tunisia. These events set off a complicated series of shifts in allegiance by French pro-consuls. Initially the Americans used the authority of the Vichyite leader Admiral Darlan, fortuitously present in Algiers, to secure the collaboration of the officials in post; later they tried to work through the *émigré* General Giraud; but eventually de Gaulle secured Allied recognition as head of the provisional government of the French empire. The intrigues and contradictions of Algiers, where Frenchmen who had taken conflicting positions in 1940 were obliged to work together, were mimicked in Dakar, where for several months American influence succeeded in sustaining Boisson. But eventually AOF acknowledged its allegiance to de Gaulle, who insisted that both officials and subjects should intensify their contributions to the war effort as a means towards the re-establishment of French power.

After the North African landings American influence increased throughout Africa. Roosevelt sent a personal representative, Admiral Glassford, to Dakar, which senior officers were coming to covet as an essential base for the post-war defence of the western hemisphere. Although Glassford claimed to be interested only in promoting efficient prosecution of the war, the increased American presence created ambitions on one side, apprehensions on another, about possible postwar developments. Businessmen as well as servicemen began to perceive new frontiers of opportunity. Pan-American Airways and the Socony-Vacuum oil company, while performing their patriotic duties, were clearly establishing strong bases for postwar expansion, and seemed to the Colonial Office to be aiming at 'a permanent position of economic predominance.'[6] Contacts with American troops stimulated new tastes and aspirations among African consumers, from Camel cigarettes and chewing-gum to jeeps and modern radios. The living standards of Black American troops could become a cause of envy, even if they also suffered a segregation starker than the familiar muted racialism of the British. When in May 1942 Lord Swinton, a former Colonial Secretary, was sent to represent the War Cabinet as Resident Minister in Accra, one of his main duties, beyond the co-ordination of military and economic war efforts, was to handle international problems, notably those caused by the American presence. Soon Swinton, protesting at the 'apparent subordination of British interests to American control', was reporting widespread rumours that after the war Americans would take over the West African colonial empires.[7]

If there was some paranoia in such reports, it was clear that the war was giving an overwhelming impetus to the growth of American technological, industrial and financial power. When the war ended this growth could only be sustained by a vast expansion of export markets; Africa, where (with a few exceptions, including South Africa and Morocco) America's prewar trade had been negligible, was one obvious target area. Such perceptions gave point to the call, in the

'Atlantic Charter' of August 1941, for 'access on equal terms to the trade and to the raw materials of the world', and so to the ideological anti-colonialism which Wilson had ineffectively articulated in 1918.

By 1942 the war had destroyed the old confidence of France and Britain that there would be no serious external challenge to their imperial authority in Africa. Challenges did not come only from the USA. The expansion of South Africa's economic and military strength was accompanied by signs that General Smuts would seek to pursue an active 'Pan-African policy'.[8] In the Rhodesias, in British East Africa, even in Belgian Congo and AEF, wartime contacts strengthened influences from the Union. Thoughtful officials began to fear that South Africa's invaluable wartime collaboration might be purchased with grave prejudice to Britain's reputation among Africans whose collaboration would be equally vital in future; but they feared to criticize Smuts too openly for fear of encouraging Afrikaners who opposed participation in the war and looked for a future based on apartheid.

The Soviet Union was a still more embarrassing ally, though still remote. As in Europe, the heroism of Stalin's armies could induce roseate images of his regime; in 1943 Bankole Awoonor-Renner, one of the Comintern's few remaining converts, published a volume of adulatory prose and verse, with commendations from Kobina Sekyi and J. B. Danquah.[9] Although revolutionary access to Black Africa remained difficult, and the disruption of colonial rule never became one of Stalin's priorities, the new super-power status of the Soviet Union was another threat to colonial tranquillity.

American pressure remained the most immediate. Even before Pearl Harbor it was clear that the British empire could not survive the war without American supplies, American financial assistance, eventual American military participation. A price would have to be paid, partly by directly gratifying American demands (as for Caribbean bases in 1940), but also by aligning policies with the general interests of the USA. Enthusiasts for Anglo-American alliance believed such concessions justified by long-term benefits to be derived from the 'special relationship'. Churchill accepted the 'equal access' clause of the Atlantic Charter without too much regret for the British interests which would thereby be exposed to direct American competition; but he was shaken to discover that in Roosevelt's view 'the right of all peoples to choose the form of government under which they will live' extended to Asians and Africans as well as Czechs and Poles. While assuming the public role of equal ally Churchill found himself pressed, no less hard than the exiled representatives of other European empires, to expedite the independence of British colonies, and meanwhile to accept some form of international control over their government.

In the event, American anti-imperialism failed to focus on specific programmes; its immediate effects were less serious than some feared, and others hoped. Roosevelt, who when visiting Casablanca in 1943 insisted on interviewing the Sultan of Morocco, seems to have envisaged installing multinational administrations to prepare colonies for early independence: (there were unconscious echoes here of Wilhelm II's Moroccan visit of 1905). The President's insistence that independence was the only legitimate goal of colonial policy reflected memories of America's own colonial past, rather than awareness of the more eclectic techniques currently being used to decolonize the United States' own empire. But the State Department favoured the more limited aim of strengthening and extending the League's system of national mandates; and the Joint Chiefs of Staff opposed any system of universal trusteeship which might obstruct their own growing determination to secure new Pacific bases of their own. With counsels thus divided, British cultural diplomacy succeeded in persuading influential Americans that *enlightened* colonial government might be temporarily tolerated without violating their democratic consciences.

It was still necessary to prove that British colonial policy *was* compatible with prevailing ideas of liberty. In a Parliamentary statement of 13 July 1943 Churchill's Colonial Secretary, Oliver Stanley, defined his goal as 'self-government within the framework of the British Empire'. Some critics claimed this was evasive verbiage, incapable of translation into good clear French; but there were reasons for caution about the word 'independence'. One was the desire to maintain the serviceable ambiguities of Commonwealth status, with its implication that nations might freely accept constraints on their freedom of action to secure advantages of membership in a larger entity. Although nineteenth-century African patriots like Africanus Horton had spoken of independence, until Roosevelt raised the stakes nationalist groups like the NCBWA had generally accepted 'self-government within the empire' as their aim. But in 1943 a delegation of West African journalists led by Azikiwe envisaged 'independent and sovereign political entities, aligned or associated with the British Commonwealth of Nations', and in 1945 a Pan-African Congress in Manchester would declare 'that complete and absolute independence for the Peoples of West Africa is the only solution.'

Uncertainties about the relationship between independence and Commonwealth membership apart, some officials doubted whether even 'self-government' (as opposed to 'the healthy growth of local institutions') was a viable political and economic option for all colonial territories. As Lord Moyne observed at the time of the Atlantic Charter:

> Some Colonies are so small, or strategically so important that complete self-government seems out of the question; and I cannot, for instance, imagine any conditions under which we would give Dominion status to Aden, Gibraltar, the Gambia or British Honduras.

A senior official added several names, including Mauritius, to this list.[10] Other colonies, including Nyasaland and Sierra Leone, might not fall below any magic threshold of size, but still raise doubts about their capacity to finance and man the apparatus of a modern state. For – and here lay the deepest cause for scepticism about universal independence – not only were the functions of government everywhere increasing, but many of them seemed to require action on an international scale. In the supervision of labour conditions, the control of narcotics, organization of air traffic, promotion of public health, ecological control of the natural environment, governments everywhere were becoming committed by international agreement to specific and often expensive responsibilities and membership in international agencies. This indeed seemed to reflect the growing interdependence of the capitalist world. When the war was showing even Britain the limits of her own independence it seemed unnecessary for every colony to learn that lesson from scratch.

With such matters in mind Stanley devoted much of his speech of 13 July to defining 'social and economic foundations' of self-government, and describing British attempts to lay them by economic and educational initiatives at all levels. In replying to the debate he startled his more attentive listeners by a new suggestion. Many colonial problems, Stanley emphasized

> are common problems, and can only be solved in co-operation, for problems of security, of transport, of economics, of health, etc., transcend the boundaries of political units;

the British government therefore suggested

> the possibility of establishing Commissions for certain regions ... [to] comprise not only States and Colonial Territories in the region, but also other states which have in the region a major strategic or economic interest.

Africans were to be associated with these Commissions, and would thus progressively shape the development of their countries even before self-government.[11]

Although experience in the Caribbean had already shown that there could be important work for such Commissions to do, the primary aim of this proposal was to divert pressure for more rigorous forms of international control. The detailed proposals of the Colonial Office, worked out over the next eighteen months, suggested six Regional commissions, three of them in Africa, which would complement the 'functional agencies of the World Organization' then in process of gestation. American membership was suggested in West Africa (as well as in the Caribbean, South Pacific and South-East Asian Commissions); this would involve her in the practicalities of socio-economic development, as well as in future defence arrangements. South Africa would inevitably be a prominent member of the Commission for Central, Eastern and Southern Africa, but could be excluded from the West and the North-East; and there would, conveniently, be no grounds for Soviet membership in any group.[12] Regional Commissions without executive powers, though with broad consultative roles, seemed the safest way to recognize the legitimate interests of Allied powers with the minimum prejudice to the authority of existing 'parent states'.

In retrospect this elaborate scheme seems of transient interest: a method of averting international control through a vitalized mandate system rather than a serious attempt to improve colonial government. Once the Yalta conference of 1945 had decided to involve the United Nations in supervision of colonial affairs, the British abandoned the plan in favour of less formal approaches to regional co-operation. The real importance of the international pressure had been to concentrate attention on the future of colonies at high political levels, to create a certain consensus (among French as well as British leaders) on the urgency of reform. Old Empire patriots like Amery and Lord Cranborne found themselves working with Clement Attlee (who as late as September 1942 still favoured 'an international system of responsibility and control') to give closer definition to the 'self-government' which MacDonald had promised in 1938. British leadership of a reconstructed Commonwealth was in the long run to replace direct control of the dependent empire.[13] In planning the 'social and economic foundation' to which Stanley's speech referred critics and defenders of empire began to co-operate in translating old imperial ideas into democratic language more appropriate to the mid-twentieth century.

THE RESPONSES OF LIBERAL IMPERIALISM

A perceptive historian of Europe has distinguished four modes in which modern warfare may affect society.[14] In colonial contexts, two of these (military participation and psychological trauma) are most applicable to the experience of African populations: the others – effects on productive capacity and challenges to established institutions – are best approached through colonial states. Initial wartime challenges were similar to those presented by the Depression, and the British Colonial Office's early response was to pursue its new policies to promote development and social welfare. But the increased demands of the war effort upon Africans, and the growing interest of the United States, made it more urgent to change political relationships between state and subjects, British and French leaders came to realize that they could only resist external and internal pressures for independence by initiating their own programmes of decolonization.

Continuities between reforming ideas of the Depression and those of the war years are well personified by Lord Hailey, whose commanding authority in African affairs had been established by the *African Survey*. During the first days of war Malcolm MacDonald invited Hailey to undertake a new enquiry into local structures of government in British Africa. Hailey's Indian experience seemed clearly relevant to two large questions which were preoccupying MacDonald: whether and how the more or less ramshackle structures of 'Native Administration' could be rendered capable of executing the new policies of improvement, and what practical steps might be taken towards the ultimate goal of self-government which MacDonald had re-affirmed in December 1938. As the Colonial Secretary told an informal Brains Trust at the Carlton Hotel, it was now necessary to consider how the future development of Native Administrations and of Legislative Councils (institutions for collaboration with, respectively, traditional and modern elites) might, in the conditions of different colonies, be harmonized.[15]

Hailey's Report, finally drafted in 1942, was widely distributed only in 1944, by which time it was becoming partially dated. But his insights into potential forces for change within new social formations influenced by 'African racial consciousness' must have disturbed the continuing complacency of many officials. Anticipating the increasing load which development policies and wartime needs would place on government, Hailey could not feel confident of 'that degree of acquiescence, in our rule which is a necessary condition of administrative progress'. An urgent need was therefore to create an African political class, more capable of managing a modern state than the existing Native Authorities and local Councils, whose varying levels of efficiency in each territory formed the main subject of his report. Hailey's preferred method was to encourage the emergence of able local leaders by enabling them to serve political apprenticeships in the affairs of their own communities. Reformed Native Authorities should then be encouraged to send representatives to Regional Councils, which might serve as electoral colleges for the central legislature; gradual progress towards decolonization could thus be made by expanding the range of self-government from below, rather than by sweeping constitutional changes at the centre.

Hailey returned to find the Colonial Office, like other Ministries, increasingly engaged in comprehensive planning; in April 1941 he was asked to chair an official committee on postwar reconstruction in the colonies, which eventually produced an agenda of over fifty subjects for more or less urgent action.[16] The emphasis still fell on development and welfare rather than political reform. The Colonial Office had fought the Treasury to prevent the complete sacrifice of the 1940 Act to military priorities; in June 1941 Lord Moyne enjoined all governors to balance the contributions which their subjects would be required to make to the war effort against the recompense due to the poorer inhabitants – which should if possible be visible in immediate improvements as well as post-dated promises.[17] Moyne, a proconsular imperialist, attached more value to material progress than to political rhetoric; but even he felt that Hailey's approach in *Native Administration and Political Development* was over-cautious and 'hardly democratic'.[18]

Pressures from all directions – international, African, and domestic – were now working towards political reforms. When the Labour Party entered Churchill's coalition government in May 1940 one effect was to speed up the appointment of Labour Officers to oversee conditions and encourage trade unionism in the larger colonies. George Hall, a Welsh miner who spent two years as Under-Secretary at the Colonial Office, encouraged 'experimental appointments' of British trade unionists to these posts. Many of these men, who saw a responsibility to go beyond the encouragement of peaceful collective bargaining and educate African workers in the principles of social democracy, made new and distinctive contributions to African political life. Outside the government a few socialists with African interests or experience formed the Fabian Colonial Bureau in 1940; this became an influential pressure group, less through its political weight than because of overlaps in outlook and membership with the liberal imperialists inside the Colonial Office. Fabians emphasized progressive social engineering – welfare provision, education, economic planning – as necessary preparations for self-government; but they also cautiously endorsed calls from their African friends for greater freedom and early constitutional reform. A colonial version of the coalition government's consensus on the need for postwar reform gradually emerged, influenced less by theoretical critiques of colonialism than by the experience of disillusioned practitioners. Even those who dismissed Roosevelt's anti-imperialism as ill-informed, self-interested or mischievous acknowledged that discontents fomenting in Africa would require at least homeopathic doses of political freedom.

Not all the solutions suggested pointed in the same direction. White settlers in Kenya and the Rhodesias, whose contribution to the war had earned them enhanced influence within the colonial state, claimed that *they* were best qualified to take responsibility for African development; many of them regarded Smuts as a more inspiring leader than Churchill, certainly than Attlee. New inter-territorial institutions linked Northern Rhodesia and Nyasaland a little closer to the already autonomous settler regime in Salisbury, though London continued to resist pressure to amalgamate these three territories. Settlers in Kenya, their farms flourishing as never before, took active roles in wartime administration, and expected political rewards. In 1942 Lord Cranborne, as Secretary of State, showed sympathy for an elaborate plan which would have conceded internal self-government to the White Highlands as one of five provinces in a new East African Union; but his Under-Secretary, Harold Macmillan, effectively challenged the assumptions behind this scheme, suggesting that nationalization of land in the Highlands (on lines which would broadly be followed twenty years later) would prove 'less expensive than a civil war'. Although Cranborne remained unwilling to 'rule out the idea of a white-controlled self-governing administration under a Governor-General', his officials saw the danger of creating an island of white power within an ocean registering the early swells of African consciousness; as an earnest of intent the moderate nationalist Eliud Mathu was nominated first African member of the Legislative Council.[19]

In West Africa enlightened governors could see that more substantial gestures – even concessions – towards educated African leaders were necessary. The constitutional ideas of Sir Alan Burns, a vigorous reformer appointed Governor of the Gold Coast in 1941, went far beyond Hailey's. Alongside Governor Bourdillon of Nigeria Burns successfully insisted on appointing African Members to his Executive Council; and by late 1942 he was proposing an African majority on the Legislative Council. His intention was to recover African confidence rather than to transfer power; only a few Members would be directly elected, and the Governor would retain ultimate power to over-ride the Councils. Nevertheless Hailey and others resisted Burns's proposal, arguing that such concessions to 'groups of politically-minded Africans' should wait until the welfare and political consciousness of 'the vast bulk of African cultivators living under tribal conditions' had been greatly advanced. But spokesmen for the cultivators of Asante had already been in touch with politically-minded Africans, notably with J. B. Danquah, a subtle lawyer, scholar, and kinsman of Ofori Atta. In October 1943 the Asante Confederacy Council submitted petitions which the Colonial Office could only meet by accepting Burns's proposal, and drafting a new constitution. There was to be a substantial African majority in the Legislative Council, though largely elected indirectly through regional advisory Councils formed through Native Authorities. Warmly welcomed by African leaders in 1944, the new constitution was not however implemented until 1946.[20]

Although this African initiative moved political reform higher up the Colonial Office agenda, the priority, as in Stanley's statement of July 1943, remained the laying of 'social and economic foundations'. In Whitehall (where the ardent Fabian reformer Andrew Cohen became head of the Africa Division in 1943) and also in the Resident Minister's Office in Accra, the machinery of government, already expanded and adjusted to new wartime needs, was painfully adapted to the even less familiar work of development planning. Late in 1944 the Treasury agreed that the Colonial Development and Welfare scheme should be extended, and allocated £120,000,000 for the period 1946–56. Although this would be manifestly inadequate to finance the hundreds of desirable projects already identified, additional investment was expected from British companies and from the substantial sterling balances which many colonial governments were accumulating in London. In two crucial fields funds were to be ear-marked for expenditure under central Colonial Office control: research (with an annual allocation of £1,000,000) and the development of Higher Education.[21]

By appointing two high-level Commissions in 1943 the Colonial Office recognized that the foundation of African universities would form an essential part of their long-term preparations to decolonize.

Besides acting as local centres of research and enquiry, their role would be to educate, not only cadres of administrators and professional specialists, but also political leaders. 'Somewhere in West Africa within a century, within half a century', Walter Elliot's Commission declared, 'a new African state will be born'; the time needed to train its counsellors was already running short. A few critics questioned the wisdom of concentrating so many scarce resources on the fortunate few who were to constitute the new African elites; but in any plans to transfer power in a modern state the preparation of the inheritors would clearly be crucially important. Educational initiatives were necessary at other levels too – not only in primary, secondary and technical schools but in informal sectors: hence a new interest shown by officials in subjects called Mass Education and Community Development, and in training leaders for the trade unions and co-operative societies which Labour leaders were so anxious to encourage. But the decisive test of this exercise in building African nation-states on European models would be the extent to which the values and interests of future rulers harmonized with those of their British peers. Ormsby-Gore had once written of the Englishman's 'instinctive dislike of assimilation'; but as far as educational policy was concerned, reason had now triumphed over instinct.

Among Frenchmen, although the word was temporarily out of fashion, the idea of assimilation never disappeared. De Gaulle, recognizing strong international pressures for decolonization, was determined to move in that direction in his own way, not by weakening the bonds of empire but by gradually eliminating unjust differentials in the condition of its peoples. By July 1943, having established himself as sole President of the Algiers Committee of National Liberation, de Gaulle realized that American and Soviet anti-colonialism, as well as his moral and political obligations to those colonies which had provided Free France with its territorial base, would make it imperative to 'modernize our methods and concepts of colonial rule, and not maintain these states and territories in their present condition.' Assisted by Henri Laurentie, the Colonial Commissioner René Pleven organized a conference of governors from tropical Africa to meet in Brazzaville in January 1944.[22]

Although preparations for this conference took place in improvised offices in Algiers, without the backing of bureaucratic experience and expertise which went into British colonial planning, there was considerable continuity between the ideas of Brazzaville and those of the Popular Front. After opening orations by Pleven, Felix

Gouin and de Gaulle the dominant voices were those of experienced administrators, reforming graduates of the *École Coloniale*; their most reactionary colleagues had excluded themselves by collaboration with Vichy. Their views were largely echoed by politicians in the Consultative Assembly in Algiers, whose overseas committee was chaired by P. O. Lapie, formerly Free French Governor of Chad. Though Pleven proudly proclaimed that this was the first conference to focus upon the problems of the African himself, no African was present: the organizers assumed it would be impossible to identify persons competent to speak for the many distinct peoples of French Black Africa. But a few decorous memoranda received from African *évolués* were printed in the conference report.[22]

Unsurprisingly, there was much agreement among governors about the need for new programmes of development and welfare. After some inconclusive philosophizing about France's respective obligations to the masses and to the elite, they committed themselves to work towards two reforms of huge practical significance for all France's African subjects: the progressive suppression, after the war, of the hated system of arbitrary justice, the *indigénat*, and the phasing out within five years of forced labour. Their proposals for economic modernization, building on inter-war projects by businessmen and technocrats, gave more emphasis than the British were contemplating to gradual industrialization. They also aired the fashionable idea of sending a mission to study collective farming in the USSR.[23]

Politically, the conference opened by making it clear there was no question of African independence. Regarding the immediate future, there was a somewhat confused debate between neo-assimilationists (led by a Martinique-born governor, Raphael Saller) and those who like Laurentie were beginning to envisage some form of federal solution. But this was largely a question of emphasis; all governors agreed in demanding greater scope to express the distinct 'personality' of their own territories, all assumed that power would remain, if not in French hands, at least in those of men thoroughly assimilated in culture and political outlook. Although some still regarded 'federalism' as a dangerous word, de Gaulle told the American press in July that he envisaged 'un système de forme fédérale'; and later in the year (contradicting those who held 'self-government' to be an un-French concept) he spoke of France's aim 'à mener chacun de ses peuples à un développement qui lui permette de s'administrer et plus tard de se gouverner soi-même'.[24] But exactly how this lengthy process was to be initiated was reserved for debate by the Constituent Assembly which French electors would choose after the Liberation. Brazzaville had made it clear that the African colonies would be represented there by more than their former single Deputy; but developments in North Africa were creating doubt as to how effective this representation would be.

Colonial reformers, formulating new plans in Algiers, were soon under pressure from settlers and reactionary administrators who intended to restore the foundations of French control in the Maghreb. Although Morocco and Tunisia, because of their Protectorate status, were excluded from the jurisdiction of the Constituent Assembly, French citizens resident there successfully claimed the right to elect representatives. Algeria, on the other hand, already formed, constitutionally, part of the French Republic. In 1944 a committee established by de Gaulle proposed a comprehensive twenty-year programme of social and economic reforms, as a necessary prelude to fuller political assimilation; meanwhile Algeria would have twenty-six members in the Constituent Assembly. Settler pressure however ensured that these would be chosen by two separate electorates, or 'colleges'. One consisted solely of French citizens – essentially, of 400,000 voters of European descent, though now diluted by some 60,000 Muslims: an Ordinance of 7 May 1944 had taken up the approach of the abortive Blum-Viollette Bill of 1937 by extending full citizenship to sixteen categories of Muslims who had distinguished themselves in the life of the territory. The remaining 1,350,000 adult Muslim males formed the 'Second College' which would return the remaining thirteen Deputies, though in practice their elections were always subject to administrative supervision and interference, and often to ballot-rigging. Thus, although the French reformers (unlike the British) were permitting direct African participation in debate about the future of the empire, it was far from certain how effective their voices could be.*

NOTES AND REFERENCES

1. C.O.267/673/32285, Jardine to Dawe, Personal and Secret, 15 Oct. 1939
2. Myron Echenburg, '*Morts pour la France*: the African Soldier in France during the Second World War', JAH 26,1985 p. 364
3. B. Lanne, 'Le Tchad pendant la guerre', *Les chemins*, pp. 443f, cites Eboué's figure of 1844 recruits to 1 July 1940, compared with Chad's target of over 6000 in the mobilization plan. (AAEF 3B 2376, Reste

*For the representation of Black Africa, see below, pp. 80-1.

Circular, 24 March 1939). For suspension of labour recruitment in the other colonies and proposed reductions of quotas, AAEF 3B 2375, Boisson to Mandel, 318, 13 Dec. 1939

4. AAEF 3B,2379, Sicé to Governors, 20 Nov. 1940, announces the posting of all Balali clerks out of Brazzaville; cf. Sicé to Governor Chad, 72, 20 Dec. 1940; F. Eboué, *Circulaire générale sur la politique indigène en AEF*, (Brazzaville, 8 Nov. 1941)

5. Boisson's policies, often simplified by his critics, may be studied in a collection of his speeches and directives, *Contribution à l'oeuvre africaine* (Rufisque, 1942). See also his introduction to A. Villard, *Histoire du Sénégal* (Dakar, 1942)

6. CAB 66/32 WP (42) 601, American Influence in West Africa, Memo by Stanley, 22 Dec. 1942

7. PREM 3/502/5 Swinton to Churchill, Tel.547,13 Dec. 1942 cf. R. W. Graham, 'American Imperial Interests in West Africa during the Second World War', paper presented to SOAS Conference, May 1984

8. CO 847/23/47181/1943, Pan-African Policy

9. B. Awoonor-Renner, *This Africa* (London, 1943)

10. Moyne to Amery, 26 Aug. 1941, quoted W. R. Louis, *Imperialism at Bay, 1941–1945, The United States and the Decolonization of the British Empire* (Oxford, 1977) pp. 126–7; PREM 4/42/9 Eastwood to Martin, 1 Sept. 1941

11. Hansard, Commons, 391, 13 July 1943, 142ff

12. CAB 66/59 WP(44)738 C.O. Paper on International Aspects of Colonial Policy, 14 Dec. 1941

13. Louis, *Imperialism at Bay*, pp. 192–6; K. Harris, *Attlee* (1982) pp. 170, 211

14. Arthur Marwick, 'The Impact of the First World War on British Society', *Journal of Contemporary History* III, 1968, pp. 60–3

15. C.O.847/17/47135/39 Note of a Meeting at the Carlton Hotel, 6 Oct. 1939. See also A. H. M. Kirk-Greene's Introduction to Hailey's Report, *Native Administration and Political Development in British Tropical Africa* (1942: reprinted Nadeln, 1979)

16. C.O.967/13 Schedule of Subjects for Consideration and Action Taken: revised 7 April 1942

17. P.P. 1940–1, VIII Cmd 6299, Circular Despatch by Moyne, 5 June 1941

18. C.O.847/21/47100/1/1941, Discussion between Moyne, Hall, Hailey and others, 18 March 1942

19. C.O.967/57 Sir Arthur Dawe's Memorandum [July 1942] and Mr Harold Macmillan's Counter-Proposals [15 Aug.] C.O.847/23/47181 Cranborne to Attlee 22 July 1943. cf. N. J. Westcott, 'Closer Union and the Future of East Africa, 1939–1948', JICH X 1981 pp. 67–88

20. Cf. J. D. Hargreaves, *The End of Colonial Rule in West Africa* pp. 29–36

21. CAB 65/44, War Cabinet Minutes 152, 21 Nov.: 173, 21 Dec. 1944

22. C. R. Ageron, 'De Gaulle et la Conférence de Brazzaville', in G. Pilleul etc. *L'entourage et Général de Gaulle* (Paris, 1979) pp. 243–51

23. République française, Ministère des Colonies, *Conférence Africaine Française: 30 janvier 1944–8 février 1944* (Paris 1945)

24. Ageron, 'L'entourage ...' pp. 250–1

CHAPTER FOUR

The Mobilization of African Discontents, 1939–1947

LINKAGES WITH THE ARAB WORLD

The one African country where political nationalism seriously threatened the Allied war effort was Egypt. The collaboration required from King Farouk's ministers under the Anglo-Egyptian Treaty of 1936 was essential to the defence of the Middle East; but many Egyptian politicians denied the legitimacy of that treaty, and received support among army officers, students, Muslim fundamentalists, and the growing population of impoverished workers and peasants. Some favoured a German victory. In February 1942, after the loss of Benghazi, the Resident Minister, Oliver Lyttelton, had to deploy British troops to keep Farouk in line; this increased the bitterness of young radicals, whether trained in Islamic brotherhoods or British universities. Although Britain retained control throughout the war, by 1945 her continued military presence was widely challenged. Some politicians, aspiring to leadership in a united Arab world, concentrated much fury against British policy in Palestine; others were most angered by her refusal to accept Egypt's historically based claim for hegemony in the Nile valley.

The Sudan, legally a condominium of Britain and Egypt, was in practice governed by officials responsible to the British Foreign Office, convinced that this vast and diverse country welcomed their just and efficient rule. But when in 1942 a flying visit from Sir Stafford Cripps gave the young patriots who had been inspired by the Indian example to found the Graduates' General Congress an opportunity to invoke the Atlantic Charter and demand the right of self-determination, the government felt obliged to respond, if only to pre-empt the Egyptians; they accelerated Sudanization of public services and established a central Advisory Council (for the Muslim North only). The Civil Secretary acknowledged that further steps towards self-government would follow at a pace largely dictated 'by events in Egypt and the Arab States of the Middle East.'[1] But the Advisory Council was boycotted by the Graduates' Congress and by a major Muslim brotherhood, the Khatmiyya; these formed the basis for a political party, the *Ashiqqa*, which looked towards Cairo for support. The British therefore patronized the *Umma* party led by Sayid [Sir] 'Abd al-Rahman al-Mahdi, head of the other major Sufi brotherhood. The government also countered Egyptian claims by emphasizing their responsibilities towards the non-Muslim peoples of the southern provinces; a conference at Juba in 1947 began to draw this remote region into the political process. Some of the least politically conscious peoples of Black Africa thus became involved in developments geared to the volatile politics of the Arab world.

France's North African dependencies had always been part of that world, and during the 1930s various new political organizations had reflected growing anti-colonialism among both French- and Arabic-speakers. Until the war all remained pretty securely under police control; but military defeat brought new interventions from outside. General Franco gave discreet encouragement to nationalists in French Morocco, hoping to re-unify the Sultanate under Spanish patronage; Germany's occupation of Tunisia in 1942–43 provided the occasion for Habib Bourguiba, leader of the proscribed *Néo-Destour*, to return from detention in France; the American occupation stirred hopes of eventual freedom. Apart from radical forms of Islam infiltrating from the Middle East, the Muslim rulers whom France had perforce maintained in her two Protectorates provided a focus for patriotic opposition. The deposition of Moncef Bey by the returning French helped to unite different nationalist groups to demand an independent Tunisia within a united Arab Maghreb. In Morocco Sultan Mohamed V, encouraged by Roosevelt's visit and by subsequent correspondence, gave discreet encouragement to the *Istiqlal*, an independence movement founded in December 1943.

Algeria still lacked any comparable national focus; lip-service paid by the Third Republic to assimilationist principles had diverted some Muslims from trying to establish a new ethnic identity. De Gaulle's reform of 1944 had removed formal barriers to the full enfranchisement of practising Muslims, but any approach to decolonization on such lines was programmed for self-destruction; even those *colons* willing to share power with Algerians would never allow them to achieve a majority. During the war those moderate

Algerians who had once hoped for emancipation through genuine assimilations, such as the French-speaking pharmacist Ferhat Abbas, began to talk of building an Algerian nation within the French Union, and drew nearer to the radical *Parti du Peuple Algérien* founded by Messali Hadj in 1937. Frustrated in their claims for equality, and radicalized by wartime hardships, many Algerians began to talk of independence: this was among the slogans with which the people of Sétif, near Constantine, celebrated Victory Day on 8 May 1945. When the police tried to seize their banners fighting broke out, followed by violent attacks on settler families; over a hundred Europeans were murdered, and others robbed, wounded or raped. There followed the bloodiest repression seen in Africa since the colonial 'pacification'. Muslim victims were numbered in thousands; hopes of solving Algeria's problems through Franco-Muslim partnership were fatally damaged; and anti-Western feeling throughout the Arab world received a new stimulus.

NATIONALIST STIRRINGS IN WEST AND EAST AFRICA

The repercussions of the violence around Sétif extended more strongly through North Africa and the Middle East than into tropical Africa. Where nationalist movements could be identified here they mostly still seemed to depend on relatively narrow elites; liberal imperialists in France and Britain remained confident of controlling their development, provided that the planned reforms could be quickly implemented. Although some trade union and political leaders had been able to exercise influence in proportion to their capacity to assist or impede the war effort, few could demonstrate consistent and extensive popular support. Wartime mobilization had greatly broadened the horizons within which many Africans could perceive the life of their own communities; but even those who now regarded themselves as Nigerians as well as Yorubas, Tanganyikans as well as Manyema, Congolese as well as Balali, were rarely aspiring to an independent nation-state.

Consciousness of belonging to a wider society, it must be remembered, grew not only through the hardships and suffering of conscript soldiers and labourers but also out of the opportunities for personal achievement and financial gain which the war brought to some farmers, contractors, artisans and servicemen. Demobilized soldiers were not, on the whole, burning to liberate their countries from colonial rule; their enlarged consciousness often embraced disciplined loyalty to the empire, and campaign medals were cherished possessions. Many, like Corporal Waruhiu Itote, returned with memories of inter-racial comradeship as well as of discrimination, keen appreciation of the value of military order and discipline, and a new sense of solidarity with their fellow-subjects; not all went on, as Itote did, to join trade unions, or political organizations like the Kenya African Union.[2] Ambition was as likely to focus on initiating improvement in the home village, on using a gratuity to set up in business, even on applying techniques of jungle warfare to the trade of illicit diamond mining.[3]

Africans educated in the languages and ideas of their colonial masters were certainly formulating political objectives for their countrymen, and devising new methods of pursuing them within colonial structures. In West African capitals lawyers and journalists could apply their old techniques of constitutionalist rhetoric backed by litigation in increasingly favourable conditions, as when Danquah's sophisticated footwork forced the pace of reform in the Gold Coast. But accelerating progress along paths charted by the rulers did not constitute a real challenge to colonial authority. Neither in Freetown nor Accra did these constitutional reformers seem capable of harnessing the human energies which the war had released among the population at large. As late as September 1948 an American assessment of the role which anti-colonial nationalisms were then beginning to play in the global confrontation between American and Soviet power concluded that in Africa, beyond the Mediterranean coasts, they 'had not yet attained critical proportions.'[4]

In 1945 nationalism seemed most advanced in Nigeria. The Nigerian Youth Movement, founded in Lagos in 1934 to demand better opportunities for higher education, established some twenty branches in provincial towns, and after Azikiwe returned to Nigeria in 1937 his *West African Pilot* forcefully advocated Nigerian self-government within the British empire. When Oliver Stanley reviewed the political outlook after touring West Africa in 1943, it was Azikiwe whom he considered 'the biggest danger of the lot'.[5] In 1944 'Zik' became General Secretary of a new party, the National Council of Nigeria and the Cameroons (NCNC). Although such objectives as 'imparting political education to the people of Nigeria with a view to achieving self-government' sounded fairly modest, the NCNC made serious attempts to secure a national constituency. Its constitution encouraged the affiliation of trade unions and other voluntary associations, including the 'tribal unions' of Lagos, bodies of fellow-countrymen in regular communication with their home towns in the provinces. Igbos were noted both for concern for the progress of their immediate kinsmen and home-towns, and for shared pride in Zik's achievements; life in Lagos fostered stronger common sentiments of belonging to a primary nation with a shared 'moral economy' than had ever existed in Igboland itself. But though strongest among Igbos, one of the NCNC's prime objectives was 'imparting political education to the people of Nigeria with a view to achieving self-government', and it made serious attempts to secure a national constituency. Among its leaders was Michael Imoudou, a Yoruba trade unionist, who during 1945 had led a strike of railway, postal and other government workers. Its solidarity showed how wartime hardships had increased class-conscious militancy; after forty-four days the strikers secured a Commission of Inquiry which justified their claim for a 50 per cent cost-of-living allowance.

Yet the NCNC could not concentrate Nigerian discontents with an effectiveness approaching that which the Indian National Congress was currently achieving. Its immediate aim was to win the support of frustrated and discontented people throughout the country, especially educated men in the lower grades of the public service, whose collaboration the British would need to implement their new development policies. A perfect issue on which to base such a nationalization of discontent was provided by the mishandling of what Andrew Cohen and the colonial reformers intended to be a progressive new constitution. By 1943 a reforming governor, Bernard Bourdillon, had persuaded Stanley to over-rule conservative officials who wished to use the Emirates of the Muslim North as a brake upon Nigeria's political development, and Bourdillon's more authoritarian successor Sir Arthur Richards somewhat reluctantly agreed that Northern representatives (indirectly elected through Native Authorities, in the cautious spirit of Lord Hailey) should participate in a central Legislative Council. But whereas Bourdillon had been careful to maintain friendly relations with Azikiwe and other Lagos politicians, Richards treated them with contempt, failing to consult them about the constitution or to demonstrate that an African majority in the legislature, even including a large bloc of Northern Muslims, was a genuine political advance.[6] This maladroit handling of constitutional reform presented Azikiwe and his colleagues with open targets for criticism, and greatly facilitated a grand recruiting tour of Nigeria, in which Azikiwe and Imoudou were joined by Herbert Macaulay, the veteran manager of Lagos politics, in 1946.

But it remained doubtful whether the nationalist fervour of the NCNC leaders would be capable of uniting the different local centres of discontent, or of weakening the loyalty which most Northern Muslims still owed the Emirs and their British counsellors.

In eastern Africa too many whose immediate political concern was with the improvement of local communities were becoming conscious of wider contexts. In Uganda and Tanganyika as well as Kenya there was much mistrust of settlers who were advocating a 'closer union' of British East Africa in hope that it would eventually pass under their control. Although Mathu's nomination to the Kenya Legislative Council was followed in 1945 by a similar appointment in Tanganyika, these lonely figures offered a weak counterpoise to larger groups of articulate Asian and European Members. Official ideas about eventual decolonization seem to have assumed the continuance of institutionalized multi-racialism even in Uganda, which had few European settlers. Constitutional draftsmen applied their principle of partnership through a political arithmetic which gave less weight to population figures than to subjective assessments of what the three main racial groups would offer the infant nations. Europeans would bring scientific and technological expertise, and mature political wisdom; Asians, commercial enterprise and lesser technical skills; Africans had little more to offer than their labour. Even those who realized how little the resulting constitutions were compatible with democratic principle might excuse them on the pragmatic ground that settlers whose confidence had grown so rapidly during the war might otherwise turn to South Africa for support.

The African masses, it was assumed, might still prove malleable. Despite signs of increasing political consciousness among groups of civil servants, traders, teachers, workers and peasants, such explicitly national leadership as was offered by the West African intelligentsia was rarely evident. Riots in Buganda in 1945, and again in 1949, revealed the growth of 'populist' attitudes among peasant farmers and other commoners, directed against members of the chiefly hierarchy as well as the British policies which sustained them; but the expressed goal was 'the rule of democracy' within the Kabaka's kingdom, rather than throughout the protectorate of which it formed a privileged part.[7] In Tanganyika a broadly-based African Association, founded in 1929, achieved new vitality between 1944 and 1948, claiming 1780 members in 39 branches, and the Swahili newspaper *Kwetu*, edited by a Ganda immigrant, began to use the word *uhuru* (in the sense of 'freedom' rather than of national

73

independence).[8] But the British policy of developing self-government at local rather than national levels seemed to have better prospects in East Africa than in the west.

In Kenya too the British preached multi-racialism; Governor Sir Philip Mitchell, an outspoken paternalist, intended to hold the future in trust for the Africans against both the political ambitions of euphoric European settlers and the dynamic capitalism of Asian businessmen. Africans however were becoming less willing to accept the passive status of wards (and the lack of respect often shown by other races), or to accept as their spokesmen chiefs who depended largely on official patronage. Even before the war the Kikuyu Central Association, binding its members by the traditional method of secret oaths, was making substantial headway in Rift Valley and Central provinces, and beginning to form alliances beyond Kikuyuland; after 1940 it was proscribed as potentially subversive. Mitchell hoped to identify more constitutionally-minded African spokesmen in the Kenya African Union (KAU), founded in 1944, but the KCA's influence continued to grow; many Kenyans hoped that Jomo Kenyatta, returning in September 1946 with international prestige as Pan-African and author, would be accepted as their spokesman. When Mitchell, echoing Hailey's priorities, offered Kenyatta an apprenticeship in administrative responsibility rather than a political platform in the Legislative Council he reinforced the (largely unjustified) impression that colonial 'trustees' would always give preference to the interests and prejudices of their own countrymen. Leaders of Kenyatta's generation were in any case now being challenged by articulate ex-soldiers, frustrated entrepreneurs and prospering farmers. In the absence of a national political forum, the various welfare and improvement associations, co-operative unions, independent churches and secret societies to which such men devoted much creative energy began, with varying degrees of force, to express radical dissatisfaction with the colonial order.

COMING CONFLICTS IN SOUTHERN AFRICA

The most mature political movements of Black Africans, though condemned to remain for decades the least effective, were in the Union. In 1936, when the government removed from the common electoral roll the ten thousand Africans of Cape Province who still retained the vote, an All African Convention was founded, aiming 'to act in unity in developing the political and economic power of the African people.' More important, Smuts's wartime rhetorical promises of postwar freedom encouraged a revival of the African National Congress under Dr A. B. Xuma, a physician educated in Scotland and the USA. Congress called for an Africanization of the Atlantic Charter through extensions of political rights, more equitable distribution of land, and erosion of the hated pass laws which limited Africans' freedom of movement. But little happened; the contrast between Smuts's international liberalism and his failure to relax his oppressive regime at home led younger radicals, including the law students Oliver Tambo and Nelson Mandela, to organize a Youth League, whose pressure aimed 'to impart to Congress a truly national character'. 'National character' here implied a stronger appeal to racial solidarity; some Youth Leaguers criticized Xuma's readiness to co-operate with the white-led Communist Party and with the passive resistance campaigns which events in India inspired among South Africa's 300,000 Asians. Other forms of militancy were fostered in the impoverished migrant labour force which industrial growth required. At the peak of a mine-workers' strike in 1946 74,000 men were out; but without ultimate success. For if Black South Africans showed greater strength and sophistication, at this time, than their brothers to the north, they faced an incomparably stronger and more ruthless state machine. Very few white South Africans were willing to contemplate any relaxation of control, despite the studied ambiguities with which Smuts answered reasoned appeals from the ANC.

As the economic and political influence of the Union expanded northwards, so did African perceptions of what it might mean. Even before wartime industrialization southern Africa was becoming a single labour market, with its centre on the Rand and subsidiary poles of attraction in the mines of Northern and Southern Rhodesia. In the High Commission Territories of Basutoland, Bechuanaland and Swaziland, in Mozambique and Nyasaland, thousands of men had experienced life in the racially stratified society of the Union, and observed the strategies by which Africans tried to soften or evade its severities. The influence on trade unionism and politics in the Union of Nyasas educated by Scottish missionaries is well known, Clements Kadalie's ICU providing the great example; but there are early indications of a reverse traffic in ideas, with the return of migrants influenced by the ANC. Other reflections of practical Pan-Africanism included the northward spread of Union-based African churches, missionary, Ethiopian, or Zionist, and the experiences of men who like Joshua Nkomo travelled to the Union for education at levels not yet available in their own countries.

But if aspirations for freedom were often sharpened by knowledge of the Union, they originated in conditions within the northern territories themselves. Workers in the Northern Rhodesian copper mines did not need to be told cautionary tales from the Rand. In March 1940, when white miners took advantage of wartime demands to strike for improved pay and privileges, Africans at two mines followed suit with notable solidarity, making it very clear that resentment of industrial colour-bars, and of the racial arrogance which enforced them, counted for as much as material hardship. 'Cannot a slave, too, speak to the master?' their strike notice rhetorically demanded. After seventeen strikers had been killed the men returned to work, and won some improvements through a British Commission of Inquiry; but the companies refused to abandon the colour-bar, and perspicacious officials feared a coming 'struggle between the races'.[9]

Rising expectations and heightened perceptions of racial injustice gradually led African clergy, teachers and government employees in Nyasaland and Northern Rhodesia towards political protest. Even before the First World War former pupils of the missionaries had formed local 'Native Associations' to bring grievances and petitions, respectfully but firmly, before often distrustful officials. The Nyasaland African Congress founded in 1944 was essentially a development from such bodies, although its first President, Levi Mumba, had known Kadalie in the Union.[10] In Northern Rhodesia too the Welfare Associations formed from the 1920s pursued limited and practical aims; when the Colonial Office established consultative councils during the later war years many rural Africans at first found these acceptable channels through which to press for more equitable racial partnership under their British trustees. But the prospect of being handed over to the rule of the white residents had a radicalizing effect. When settler spokesmen after the war began to press for responsible government, the most deferential community leaders were alarmed; and their fears were greatly intensified by renewed talk of union with the strongly entrenched settler regime south of the Zambezi.

In Southern Rhodesia the white population believed that decolonization had substantially taken place in 1923, in their favour. The settlement of that year formalized the large degree of internal self-government already enjoyed by the 35,000 Europeans; thereafter Africans could no longer appeal to London against colour-bars, pass laws, or the grossly uneven distribution of land, and their activities had to be adapted to the politics of survival under an administration and police-force controlled by settlers. As in the north they formed local associations and welfare societies; but these had to deal with officials who, however benevolently paternal their intentions, were themselves identified with the social structure of colonial exploitation. In constitutional theory, Africans would acquire the vote as they acquired more education and property; but in 1948 only 258 Africans were registered in the electorate of 47,000, and it was clear that number would not be allowed to increase substantially. Nevertheless the Bantu Congress founded by clerks and clergymen in 1934 still appeared willing to work deferentially within the system.

There were signs that this apparent tranquillity was superficial. Peasant hatred of the regime was being generated by the interacting effects of evictions carried out to accommodate a large postwar wave of immigrant settlers and by the government's increasingly rigorous conservation measures, enforced to meet ecological problems which were largely caused by the inequitable distribution of land. The ICU, which from its base in Bulawayo led significant strikes in 1945 and 1948, was extending its influence in rural Matabeleland; among Mashona peasants radicalism grew more slowly but no less surely.[11] Some Native Commissioners began to warn about the growth of 'nationalism and communism'. But most white Rhodesians and new immigrants remained euphorically confident in their manifest destiny to build a new Dominion, in which their ascendancy would be happily accepted by a docile African majority.

Political debate among Rhodesians, never very profound, centred on the frontiers of this new Dominion. While many were content to seek full independence within present boundaries, perhaps in closer relationship with the Union, Dr Godfrey Huggins, Prime Minister since 1933, favoured amalgamation with Northern Rhodesia and Nyasaland, which could respectively contribute a booming copper industry and a reservoir of capable workers to the economy of a central African Dominion. But such a scheme was likely to mean extension of the racial attitudes and laws of Southern Rhodesia to the detriment of Africans in the northern Protectorates, and was therefore ruled out by a British Commission in 1938. Two years later Hailey confirmed this danger with judicious under-statement:

the most characteristic feature of the attitude of Southern Rhodesia towards issues of native policy has in the past been a certain unwillingness to recognize the implications of the fact that the native is an integral part of the Colony.[12]

But during the war, though Huggins agreed to put the case for amalgamation on ice, it was powerfully voiced by Roy Welensky, rising leader of the white labour aristocracy of Northern Rhodesia; and postwar immigration increased the pressure for Britain to relax its control of a region with obvious potentiality for economic growth (see Table 1). The dangers which these pressures might present to African interests were eventually to provide the catalyst needed to convert the various discontents of the northern Protectorates into effective nationalist movements.

Table 1 The European and African populations of Southern Rhodesia, Northern Rhodesia and Nyasaland, 1938–50 (Source: P. P. 1950–51 XXVI Cmd 8234. Central African Territories: Geographical, Historical and Economic Survey, 1951).

	S. Rhodesia	*N. Rhodesia*	*Nyasaland*
European population: 1938	61,000	13,000	1900
1946	83,000	22,000	2000
1950	129,000	36,000	4000
African population: 1950	1,960,000	1,849,000	2,330,000

FRENCH AFRICA AFTER BRAZZAVILLE

Although Frenchmen often claimed to be applying universal constitutional principles to the government of their Black African empire, the governors at Brazzaville knew that the needs of their several colonies varied greatly; and wartime experience had increased differentiation. In Senegal (always recognized as a special case) Vichy had destroyed the bridgehead of *citoyen* privilege secured by Diagne; this made educated leaders more conscious of common interests with urban workers, Muslim farmers and ex-servicemen. After the army in December 1944 killed thirty-five repatriated prisoners of war who were expressing grievances over pay, the Socialist lawyer Lamine Guèye undertook the defence of surviving protest leaders: this tragic episode created bitterness in the soldiers' homelands throughout AOF.[13] Meanwhile in the Dakar conurbation expansion of import-substitution industries during the war brought increased over-crowding and squalor; in 1944 a plague epidemic claimed 812 victims.[14] This immigrant labour-force was still largely unorganized; but the railwaymen, with encouragement from the *Confédération générale du Travail* in France, were establishing strong trade unions, which from October 1947 organized a particularly resolute five-month strike throughout AOF.[15] Within the 'Bloc' of African organizations formed to contest elections after the Liberation the initiative still lay with cultured *évolués* like Guèye and Leopold Sedar-Senghor, a Catholic poet and philosopher who had lived in France since 1933. But it was clear that such men, on whom French assimilationists placed great hopes, would have to take account of deep social movements, not only in Senegal but throughout AOF.

In the Ivory Coast, one of France's more promising colonial economies, the political initiative was taken by African farmers required to make unfair contributions to wartime production campaigns. European planters, though they produced only 25 per cent of the colony's coffee and 5 per cent of its cocoa, demanded preferential allocations of the labour recruited by administrative coercion, notably from the heavily-populated regions of Upper Volta. In 1944 the wealthier African farmers, for a time members of a common association with the Europeans, broke away to establish a *Syndicat Agricole Africain*, which attacked the use of forced labour by Europeans and aimed to attract labour by offering better wages, or share-cropping arrangements. The leader was Felix Houphouet-Boigny, a Baule chief who before becoming a successful coffee farmer had trained as an 'African doctor' in Dakar; he won support from André Latrille, a progressive Gaullist governor who had presented a forthright condemnation of the forced-labour system to the Brazzaville conference.[16] By voicing the widespread African hatred of forced labour Houphouet was standing up for African rights as well as defending the class interests of emerging capitalist farmers; in the election of 1945 he was able to use the *Syndicat* as a base for demanding that the new Republic should honour the promises of Brazzaville. The *Parti Démocratique de la Côte d'Ivoire* (PDCI) which he founded in 1946 quickly became a well-organized political party with support in many sections of the population with grievances against colonial rule.

The French mandated territory of Cameroun also contained a small but influential population of European settlers (3210 in 1944). Worried by the danger of retrocession to Germany, they had been enthusiastically Gaullist in 1940; their reward was British financial support, which enabled them – with intensified use of forced labour – to maintain prices and expand production. In September 1945 they euphorically invited settlers from Ivory Coast, AEF, and elsewhere to a meeting in Duala; this grandiosely named *États-Généraux de la Colonisation française*, dreaming of French settler colonies like

South Africa, demanded greater control over African labour, and encouragement for French immigration. But Africans too had advanced under Gaullist rule: since the foundation of JEUCAFRA in 1938 controls over political associations and trade unions had been gradually relaxed. While the *États-Généraux* deliberated there were manifestations against its blatant racialism, led by railwaymen striking for wage-rises to meet increased living costs and by unemployed migrants receiving no wages at all. On 24 September the demonstrators clashed violently with armed settlers, and several dozen Africans were killed. This was the starting-point for the eventual emergence of a distinctly Camerounian radical nationalism.[17]

Other French colonies avoided such sharp confrontations in 1945; either conflicts of interest were less stark or African opposition was less well organized. In Congo, for example, the followers of Matswa were successfully kept away from electoral politics. Only in Madagascar had some nationalists, supported by clandestine societies among the dominant Merina people, set sights on independence; to them only did the Brazzaville declaration seem a challenge rather than a promise. Even so, the promised African participation in constitution-making meant that 1945 saw intensive electoral activity in each territory. France's centralized structures, intended to strengthen control from Paris, had the paradoxical effect of synchronizing African reactions and stimulating political activity even in the more 'backward' colonies.

Officials of the Colonial ministry, faced with the unfamiliar duty of consulting African opinion, were uncertain how to proceed. S. M. Apithy, a young Dahomean expatriate appointed to a consultative committee alongside Senghor, was astonished to find an official draft classifying all the Black African colonies as suited to a *politique de domination*.[18] Eventually it was agreed that AOF with Togo should have ten representatives in the French Constituent Assembly, AEF four, Madagascar four, and Cameroun two: but that they should be elected by the 'dual college' system.* In each constituency (usually two neighbouring colonies) one member represented holders of French citizenship under prewar legislation (which, except in Senegal, meant a few hundred expatriates); the other would be chosen by an electorate cobbled together locally out of twelve categories of *notables évolués*. In Ivory Coast, for example, the First College had

---

*Algeria's twenty-six representatives were also divided between two 'colleges'; French residents in Tunisia and Morocco gained five representatives.

3630 voters, almost all French: the second consisted of 30,500 Africans (including 101 women), less than 1 per cent of the population.[19] Nevertheless, even this oligarchical franchise permitted the election of some authentic African spokesmen. In Senegal Guèye was returned by African urban voters in the First College, Senghor (supported, notwithstanding his Catholicism by leading *marabouts*) by the Second. Houphouet was successful in Ivory Coast, despite the efforts of some administrators and their clients. Where officials more successfully encouraged rural populations or ethnic minorities to form 'patron parties' amenable to their guidance, this sometimes led to the return of rather moderate patriots. But there was a small but audible voice from Black Africa as well as from Muslim Algeria in the assemblies which undertook to write a constitution for both France and her colonial empire.

De Gaulle's Provisional Government, while primarily concerned to maintain the unity and restore the power of the empire, had decided to move towards the liquidation of formal colonial status within the framework of a new French Union, to be 'freely consented to' between the indivisible French Republic and a number of 'Associated States'. Morocco, Tunisia and Indo-China would thus achieve internal autonomy (though many Frenchmen, including powerful Army officers, did not intend this to become complete or genuine); but control of their foreign policy and defence, and substantial economic leverage, would remain concentrated in Paris. The Black African colonies would become 'Overseas Territories' within the supposedly indivisible Republic, whose constitutional status was still in process of evolution; the immediate increase in their liberties, though real, would be subordinated to the needs of French policy. Moves in the direction of decolonization had been necessitated by American pressure as well as by the re-appraisals of colonial reformers; the new French Union was clearly intended to fortify France against such pressure in future – to increase rather than diminish her international strength. To combine decolonization with consolidation was not inherently impossible (the Soviet Union had succeeded); but it required the metropolitan state to exercise stronger control over agents still interested in maintaining colonial relations than the Fourth Republic was ever able to achieve. Even while the Constituent Assemblies were still sitting, conflicts developed in Indo-China which would reveal basic weaknesses in the new design.

Nevertheless, the constitutional debates of 1946 offered the representatives of Black Africa opportunities to make important gains through tactical co-operation with French politicians. Of the three dominant parties, both Socialists and Communists hoped to find allies for themselves among the new colonial representatives; the MRP (which strengthened its position after a referendum in France rejected the first draft constitution) was more sympathetic to the settler lobby of the *États-Généraux*. To consolidate support from the Left the African Deputies had to suppress aspirations to anything more than local autonomy, emphasize their desire for full cultural and political assimilation, and concentrate on securing equal rights of citizenship and abolition of the Dual College system.[20] Their most important successes lay beyond the strictly constitutional debates: a *Loi Houphouet-Boigny* of 11 April 1946 outlawed all forms of forced or obligatory labour, and on 7 May the first *Loi Lamine Guèye* abolished the legal distinction between subjects and citizens on which the hated *indigénat* had rested.

The constitution itself, as adopted on 28 October 1946, proved more disappointing, especially for North Africans. Algeria's representation in the National Assembly was raised to thirty Deputies, but the Dual College was retained, and also applied to membership of the Algerian Assembly set up in September 1947. Liberal imperialists declared that, though there could be no collective self-government, individual rights would be safeguarded[21]; but in practice Second College elections were subject to blatant administrative interference and ballot-rigging and the substantial legislative powers devolved to the Assembly were used to block offically proposed reforms in local government and in the status of the Arabic language. Messali's PPA, banned after Sétif, was reconstituted as the *Mouvement pour le Triomphe des Libertés Démocratiques* (MTLD), still more firmly committed to demand independence; in 1947 some of its younger members formed an underground organization which began to acquire arms with a view to insurrection.

Relatively speaking, Black Africa fared better. Although the Dual College was retained in AEF, Madagascar and Cameroun, the representation of AOF was raised to thirteen Deputies, all elected on a common roll. The French governors who continued to wield the powers of state within each colony were now to be advised by elected assemblies; and these detailed provisions were declared *susceptibles d'évolution* (i.e. they could be changed by law or decree without recourse to constitutional amendments). One may wonder how many French politicians fully shared Pierre Cot's declared intention 'de mettre un terme au régime colonial';[22] but they had at least accepted a considerable relaxation of colonial autocracy.

In the colonial empires of the lesser powers the war brought less political pressure, even where the need for reform might have seemed greater. After the Italian empire had been decolonized by Allied armies, Haile Selassie returned to Addis Ababa in their baggage train; his restoration appeared to be initially welcome to most of the peoples of Ethiopia, though this would not be the case when he asserted his claim to succeed the Italians in Eritrea. The Belgians, under little American pressure and with Kimbangu safely in gaol, felt no compulsion to do more than update their policies of social and economic paternalism. In the African empires of the Iberian neutrals, opposition to the increasingly intensive exploitation of African labour still took the traditional forms of emigration and tax-evasion. The small political movement formed by a few Portuguese *mesticos* and *civilisados* during the 1920s had largely been controlled or extinguished by Salazar; it was still what an historian of Angola calls 'the silent generation.'[23]

Viewed on a continental scale, then, the forces of African discontent mobilized by the war hardly seemed to threaten their rulers with early ejection. Compared with its predecessors of the 1920s, the Fifth Pan-African Congress which assembled in the Manchester district of Chorlton-on-Medlock in October 1945 seemed to have lost in continentality what it had gained in radicalism. Although the honoured presence of W. E. B. DuBois (now aged 77) and of Garvey's first wife provided continuity with transatlantic Pan-Africanism, the meeting was organized by those expatriates from British colonies who, influenced in one way or another by Communist contacts, had gathered round George Padmore. A solid nucleus was provided by trade union delegates from Black Africa and the Caribbean who had attended the recent inauguration of the World Federation of Trade Unions; among students and other African residents in UK who attended were Obafemi Awolowo, J. E. Appiah, and Dr Hastings Banda. Apart from one Togolese visitor, all participants were anglophone; such activists from French colonies as might have attended preferred to await the Constituent Assembly in Paris. Many of the Congress resolutions had a sharp anti-imperialist edge; Kwame Nkrumah, back from ten years in the USA, demanded 'complete and absolute independence' for West Africa.[24] But any colonial rulers who read about this distant assembly felt little cause to tremble. Where liberal imperialists were offering opportunities for constructive engagement in reform, local African leaders were eager to respond; the initiative still rested with those who sought a slow and controlled decolonization.

NOTES AND REFERENCES

1. Newbold to Sandars, 24 Nov. 1941, quoted P. Woodward. *Condominium and Sudanese Nationalism* (1979) p. 34
2. Waruhiu Itote, *'Mau Mau' General* (Nairobi, 1967) Chs 3, 4, 5; cf. D. Killingray, 'Soldiers, Ex-Servicemen and Politics in the Gold Coast, 1939–1950' JMAS, XXI, 1983
3. P. Greenhalgh, *West African Diamonds* (Manchester, 1985) p. 172
4. U.S. Central Intelligence Agency, Research Reports, Africa 1946–76. Microfilm Reel 1. 'The Break-up of the Colonial Empires and its Implications for U.S. Security', 3 Sept. 1948, p. 6
5. C.O.554/132/33726/5 Discussions with Stanley, 27–8 October 1943
6. J. E. Flint, 'Governor versus Colonial Office: an Anatomy of the Richards Constitution for Nigeria 1939 to 1945', Canadian Historical Association, *Historical Papers* 1981
7. 'The Advent of Populism in Buganda', D. A. Low, *Buganda in Modern History* (1971) pp. 148–51
8. J. Iliffe, *A Modern History of Tanganyika* (Cambridge, 1979) pp. 377–80
9. R. I. Rotberg, *The Rise of Nationalism in Central Africa* (Cambridge, Mass, 1966) pp. 168–78
10. Roger Tangri, 'Inter-war "Native Associations" and the formation of the Nyasaland African Congress', *Transafrican Journal of History*, I, 1971, pp. 84–102; B. Pachai, *The History of the Nation* (1973) pp. 231–2
11. T. O. Ranger, *Peasant Consciousness and Guerrilla War in Zimbabwe* (1985), Ch. 3 & 4
12. Hailey, *Native Administration and Political Development* (1979 edition) p. 335
13. M. J. Echenberg, 'Tragedy at Thiaroye: the Senegalese Soldiers' Uprising of 1944' in P. Gutkind etc., (ed.) *African Labor History* (1978); *idem* 'Morts pour la France . . .' JAH 26 1985 pp. 363–80
14. Denise Bouche, 'Dakar pendant la deuxième guerre mondiale: Problèmes de Surpeuplement' RFHOM LXV 1978 pp. 423–78
15. J. Suret-Canale, 'The French West African Railway Workers' Strike, 1947–8' in Gutkind, *African Labor History*. Sembène Ousmane's novel, *God's Bits of Wood* (1960), though not a historical source (the author was in France in 1947–48) suggests how the strike radicalized attitudes.
16. ANSOM A.P.2201/4 Rapport sur le régime du travail indigène, 8 Jan. 1944. I owe this reference to Mr Dev Moodley
17. R. A. Joseph, *Radical Nationalism in Cameroun* (Oxford 1977) Ch. 2
18. S. M. Apithy, *Au Service de mon Pays* (Paris, 1956) p. 14
19. J. N. Loucou, "Les premières élections de 1945 en Côte d'Ivoire", *Annales de l'Université d'Abijan* I,4 1976 pp. 7–10
20. Extracts from the *Journal Officiel* of 19–20 Sept. 1946 are translated in J. D. Hargreaves (ed) *France and West Africa* (1970) No. 55
21. Governor-General Naegelen, 1948, quoted M. Kahler, *Decolonization in Britain and France* (Princeton, 1984) p. 178
22. P. Isoart, 'L'élaboration de la constitution de l'Union française: les Assemblées Constituantes et le problème colonial', *Les Chemins* p. 24
23. R. Pelissier, *La Colonie du Minotaur: Nationalismes et Révoltes en Angola (1926–61)* (Paris, 1978) pp. 235–9

24. George Padmore (ed) *Colonial and Coloured Unity: History of the Pan-African Congress* (1947; 2nd ed 1963)

CHAPTER FIVE
Colonialism Transformed, c.1945-1949

A NEW INTERNATIONAL CONTEXT

In Africa, unlike Eastern Asia, it was by no means clear that the war had fatally weakened the colonial empires. In 1945 major decisions about the postwar order were being taken by a three-power directorate in which the British Empire participated along with the USA and the USSR. Yet, even before the plenitude of American military and economic power had been demonstrated by her use of atomic weapons and her abrupt termination of Lend-Lease, British policy-makers acknowledged that there was no parity of strength. The Deputy Under-Secretary of the Foreign Office wrote:

> ... because we are numerically the weakest and geographically the
> smallest of the three Great Powers, it is essential that we should increase
> our strength in not only the diplomatic but also the economic and
> military spheres. This can clearly best be done by enrolling France and
> the lesser Western European Powers, and, of course, also the
> Dominions, as collaborators with us in this tripartite system.[1]

Too obvious to stress was the intention also to derive international advantage from the collaboration of the colonies, and from established positions of imperial strength in Egypt and the Middle East. This assessment, though prepared for a Conservative Minister, was not altered in essentials when revised for the guidance of Ernest Bevin, Foreign Secretary in the Labour Government elected in July 1945.

Labour took office with a set of principled attitudes towards foreign and colonial affairs rather than any alternative policy. Hostility to imperialism and aspirations to promote universal peace and fraternity were tempered by an instinctive patriotism which had been reinforced by experience of policy-making within the wartime coalition. The 1943 Labour Party Conference had watered down a radical 'Charter of Freedom for Colonial Peoples' in favour of a policy statement which, by subordinating self-government to long-term economic and social planning and local government reform, reflected the newly emerging liberal imperialist consensus. The Fabian Colonial Bureau was establishing itself as 'the research organization for the creation of a Labour colonial policy' by working in symbiosis with the Colonial Office itself;[2] George Hall, the new Colonial Secretary and his very active deputy Arthur Creech Jones had in effect been co-opted into the policy-making elite. Both had come to colonial affairs as trade unionists anxious to improve the conditions of African workers; and Creech Jones, (who had tutored Kadalie in 1926, and later served on the Elliot Commission) was unusually well informed about and sympathetic to African aspirations for self-government. But neither regarded that as an immediately practical objective. When Creech Jones addressed a Fabian meeting on 'Labour's Colonial Policy' after his promotion to succeed Hall in October 1946, he might have been speaking to Cohen's brief.[3] As for his senior and more influential Ministerial colleagues, few had given African questions much thought, and not all who had felt wholly benevolent.

On wider issues of foreign policy there were sharper disagreements, both public and private, within the party. Experience as Churchill's deputy had to some extent adjusted Clement Attlee's internationalism to embrace more concrete appreciations of national interests. For the Indian sub-continent, of which Attlee had personal experience, he had no doubt that independence had become necessary as well as just. Africa and other parts of the colonial empire Attlee viewed more dispassionately, weighing both moral obligations and strategic and economic advantages against the cost to an impoverished Britain of political and military commitments in 'deficit areas'. But he treated the advice of diplomatists and Chiefs of Staff more critically than the resolutely patriotic trade unionist he had appointed to the Foreign Office. Ernest Bevin at once threw his weighty authority behind Orme Sargent's objective of restoring the British empire to equal and independent status within the three-power directorate.[4]

But if Bevin was never ashamed to refer to the British Empire with pride, he was imagining a new sort of empire, reconstructed under the fraternal guidance of a British big brother. As a member of the Advisory Committee established under the 1929 Colonial Development Act Bevin had convinced himself that there need be no contradiction between developing colonial markets to increase employment for British workers and improving the material conditions of African life. His interpretation of liberal development theory seems to have been that the accelerated growth of the exchange economy would, if properly guided by a tutelary state, lead to the emergence of democratic African leaders prepared to work with British trade unionists to build progressive societies. The limited extent to which such an outlook implied innovation rather than continuity in British policies first became evident in the Middle East.[5]

Bevin never doubted that Britain should maintain and strengthen her position in that region, not merely to secure oil supplies and strategic communications, but to sustain her claim to remain one of the three world Powers. Where he differed from some advisers was in seeking to exercise influence through collaboration with independent Arab governments, rather than by direct military interventions such as had been necessary in Egypt in 1942. He also expressed a strong preference, which he was not often able to implement, for partners with real popular support, based on 'peasants not pashas'. He did however accept the need to retain strong military forces within the region. This meant that Bevin was under continuous pressure from potential Egyptian partners who wished not only to bring British forces in Egypt down to the levels permitted by the 1936 Treaty, but to negotiate a new treaty reducing those levels still further. Since it became increasingly clear that the British army could no longer count on alternative bases in Palestine, it seemed vital to maintain a military presence in Cyrenaica: and, even more, to resist the claim which the Soviet Union presented in September 1945 to be granted trusteeship over Tripolitania.

It is beyond the scope of this book to consider how far this Russian move (or her disquieting behaviour in Turkey and Iran during the last months of the war) represented deliberate threats to the British Empire, how far Bevin's responses, by confirming Stalin's suspicions, may themselves have precipitated the Cold War. But the Tripolitanian request certainly increased fears of Russian plans, not only to dispute British hegemony in the Middle East, but to advance into Africa. Molotov was alleged to have said that the USSR believed herself entitled to an African colony, and to have added, 'if you won't give us one of the Italian colonies, we should be quite content to have the Belgian Congo'. This (possibly semi-facetious?) remark seems to have persuaded Bevin and Secretary Byrnes that 'what the Russians really wanted was uranium' and the eventual 'destruction of the

British Empire'[6]; and also to have turned Bevin's mind towards tropical Africa.

Early in 1946 the political and financial costs of maintaining large armies in the Middle East in face of Arab hostility led Attlee to suggest a possible withdrawal of land and air forces to 'a line of defence across Africa from Lagos to Kenya.' Bevin's imperial imagination was fired by this idea, not least because it might attract a larger South African contribution towards 'our manpower, financial and industrial requirements'. Apart from purely strategic aspects, 'a thorough development of the Middle East trade area, particularly in the belt extending from West Africa to East Africa, could offset the cost of retaining the small defence commitment in the Mediterranean'; Bevin therefore proposed an inter-departmental committee to study 'the political, industrial, commercial and strategic implications of developing East and West Africa, and the development of a Lagos–East Africa trunk road.' The Chiefs of Staff regarded Kenya as too distant from the Mediterranean for anything more than a reserve base, but attention was given to reviving the wartime African Line of Communication as a permanent part of Imperial strategy. In September 1947 construction work began on a large storage depot on the Mombasa–Nairobi railway, though this was abandoned in 1950 after fruitless expenditure of £2,000,000.[7] Meanwhile more would be heard of Bevin's new interest in developing African resources in the cause of Imperial strategy during the economic crisis of 1947.

While these reassessments of Imperial strategy were threatening to draw Britain's African colonies into the early confrontations of the Cold War, other linkages between international and colonial policy were being established within the United Nations Organization. While its Charter, as agreed in outline at Yalta, did not provide for that general internationalization of colonies which Wilson and Roosevelt had envisaged, it did set up new mechanisms of accountability. In territories placed under international Trusteeship, these appeared quite formidable. Administering states undertook, among other things,

> To promote the political, economic, social and educational
> advancement of the inhabitants of the Trust Territories, and their
> progressive development towards self-government or independence as
> may be appropriate to the particular circumstances of each territory and
> the freely expressed wishes of the people concerned ... (Article 76b)

Their discharge of this undertaking was to be supervised (except in the case of 'strategic' territories, none of which lay in Africa) by a Trusteeship Council, composed equally of colonial and non-colonial powers and responsible to the General Assembly. Besides receiving comprehensive Annual Reports this body was empowered to receive petitions, interview petitioners, and send Visiting Missions – openings which some African politicians quickly learned to exploit.

Trusteeship, however, only applied where formal agreements had been concluded: in practice, to some former mandates and some former Axis territories. One African mandate was excluded: Smuts and his successors refused to place their South West African dependency under Trusteeship and, without legal authority, ruled it as in most respects part of the Union. Trusteeship status had, for the time being, little effect in the Belgian territory of Ruanda-Urundi; but African leaders in Tanganyika became aware that a new political resource was available, and those in the divided territories of Togo and Cameroons soon found opportunities to play off their French and British rulers.

The disposal of Italy's African empire raised more immediate problems. Haile Selassie, restored as Emperor of Ethiopia in 1941, was as a founder member of UNO able to advance his claim to take over the Italian colony of Eritrea when British Military Administration withdrew. In 1950, despite evidence of substantial opposition from Eritrean Muslims, the General Assembly agreed to a federation with Ethiopia, which was later to prove extremely uneasy. The problem of Somalia was even more complicated: the nineteenth-century partition had divided the Somali, a pastoral people with strong consciousness of a common culture, between five different governments. The British, who from 1941 occupied all Somali territories except Jibuti, suggested unification under their own Trusteeship; but though this had some attraction to the educated patriots of the Somali Youth Club it was rejected by Ethiopia (determined to regain possession of important Somali pasturelands) and by the other Powers. This left the way open for a brief rehabilitation of Italy's colonial credentials: as the Cold War developed the western allies hoped that a foreign policy success might prevent the young Republic moving nearer the communist camp. In 1949 the General Assembly approved a ten-year Italian trusteeship over her former colony.

The most serious international conflicts were over Libya. In Cyrenaica the British relied on collaboration with Muhammed Idris, head of the powerful Sanusiyya brotherhood, to justify continuing control over the military bases they had established. The French were anxious to retain control of the Saharan province of Fezzan. Tripolitania was the bone of contention. All the western powers resisted the Soviet claim to Trusteeship, but the French were almost equally alarmed by the possible influence of Britain, deeply distrusted as patron of the Arab League, on the borders of their North Africa empire; when their own claim to Tripolitania was rejected they endorsed that of Italy. A Bevin–Sforza plan of April 1949 proposed Britain as trustee for Cyrenaica, Italy for Tripolitania, and France for Fezzan; but the proposed time-limit of ten years, too short for the French, was too long for the Arabs and their allies in the UN. Rejection of this partition eventually led to recognition of an independent Libyan monarchy under Idris in December 1951 – a solution which allowed Britain and the USA to retain military bases, but one more acceptable to the people of Cyrenaica than to the urban population around Tripoli.[8]

The General Assembly's interest in colonial problems extended beyond its constitutional responsibility for the disposal of the Italian empire and the supervision of Trusteeship. Of its fifty-one original members, eleven came from Asia or Africa and twenty from Latin America; some of these were immediately anxious to 'erect an equally rigorous system of accountability'[9] on the basis of the somewhat general 'Declaration regarding Non-Self-Governing Territories' which formed Chapter XI of the Charter. During the 1947 session India secured majorities (but not by the requisite two-thirds) in favour of extending Trusteeship not only to South-West Africa but to other colonies; of giving the Assembly extended rights under Chapter XI; and of obliging South Africa to defend its treatment of its Indian population. And during the later 1940s, as the number of independent Asian states increased in counterpoint to the development of the Cold War, governments in Britain and France became increasingly anxious to make colonial policy conform to their diplomatic priority of creating an international front against communism.

Although in the immediate postwar years the Soviet Union had neither the intention nor the means to establish a presence in Black Africa, the danger that communists might fill any vacuum left by disintegrating empires continued to modify American anti-colonialism. As early as December 1944 events in Iran were leading American officials to conclude that 'the continuance of the British Empire in some reasonable strength is in the strategic interests of the United States.'[10] Fears of a great postwar expansion of American business, backed by the American state, were not immediately fulfilled in Africa, where US interests were largely concentrated in areas of mineral wealth, with Liberia and the Union the only significant recipients of investment.[11] Under President Truman anti-colonialism was more muted than under Roosevelt. As the State Department's perceptions of the postwar world changed, they became more favourable towards colonial regimes prepared to offer sufficient satisfaction to moderate nationalists to forestall the danger of communist penetration. That danger seemed strongest in the French empire, especially in North Africa. By June 1947 Secretary Marshall was somewhat naively urging the French, in order to avert the danger of driving Arabs towards the communist camp, to

> approach leading Nationalist elements with constructive, concrete and long-range plans which will guarantee gradual but sure evolution towards something comparable to Dominion status within French Union.[12]

The relations of the French Communist Party with African nationalists were complicated by their participation, until May 1947, in the tripartite coalition government. Heirs to the Jacobin tradition of French nationalism as well as to Leninist faith in the industrial working class, many Communists approached African problems with a heavy paternalism similar to that of their bourgeois partners. Good Stalinists were reluctant to entrust African nationalists with direction of their own Communist Parties, let alone their own governments; hence their Ministers shared responsibility for the Sétif massacre, as well as for the fatal refusal to discuss independence for Viet-Nam in 1946. But such responsibilities lay heavily on some consciences; one contributory factor to the break-up of the coalition in May 1947 was disquiet about bloody reprisals recently undertaken against rebellion in Madagascar.

Madagascar was represented in the Constituent Assemblies by two doctor-politicians who, rejecting the Brazzaville programme as inadequate, claimed autonomy as an Associated State within the French Union, and founded the *Mouvement démocratique de la rénovation malgache* (MDRM). Some local leaders in peripheral areas, fearing Merina domination, founded the more moderate *Parti des déshérités de Madagascar*, with encouragement both from administrators and from communists who equated disinheritance with a proletarian vocation. Neither party seems adequately to have expressed deep populist aspirations for 'the total independence of the Malagasy fatherland', which a French High Commissioner later recognized as underlying the remarkable wartime growth of secret societies.[13] These aspirations were heightened by signs of a settler offensive inspired from South Africa. On the night of 29 March 1947

French forces and foreign settlers in many parts of Madagascar sustained fierce and well co-ordinated attacks; France was faced with a second colonial war, which she could not control until July nor finally conclude until late 1948. Rebel propaganda raised hopes of foreign intervention – but by American or British forces, not Russians. Communist Ministers reluctantly acquiesced in the arrest of the MDRM Deputies (though they disavowed the rebels), the removal of their Parliamentary immunity, and the launching of savage campaigns of repression and reprisal. The number of Malagasy dead ran well into five, possibly six, figures; the French lost 350 soldiers (many of them Senegalese) and some 200 civilians. Yet colonial authority was eventually restored with surprisingly little international publicity; and the French government, purged of its communist members, was encouraged to pursue its attempt to reconquer Indo-China.

To secure the American support on which their Indo-China campaign became increasingly dependent in the later 1940s French politicians had to equate the preservation of their Union with resistance to Soviet and Chinese communism. This created difficulties for many Black African Deputies who, on their arrival in the Constituent Assembly, had chosen to ally with the French Communist Party. In most cases this decision was 'a measure of efficacity, not the defence of an ideology'[14]; they needed guides and patrons in the unfamiliar political world of Paris, and so long as the Communists remained in the coalition their alliance seemed highly serviceable. Yet even in 1946 it brought dangers. Leading African Deputies, worried by the colonial backlash of the *États-Généraux*, summoned a Congress to Bamako in October with the aim of uniting their various local parties into a *Rassemblement Démocratique Africain*. This move, encouraged by the Communist Party, was accordingly opposed by Moutet and his Socialist colleagues, and by colonial administrators who feared the effects of African unity under such patronage. Although the RDA was duly launched under Houphouet's leadership, half the Black African Deputies elected to the National Assembly, led by Senghor and Guèye, refused to join. When the Communists left the government, and the Overseas Ministry passed into MRP hands in November 1947, the constituent parties of the RDA were left exposed to strong administrative harassment.

In Europe 1947 was a year of material hardship, and the French government, struggling to deal with Communist-backed strikes and demonstrations as well as the wars in Indo-China and Madagascar, began to feel paranoid about Africa. On 1 August Moutet, reviewing some fragmentary intelligence reports, wondered whether they represented

> premonitory symptoms of a vast enterprise of disintegration in our Overseas Territories, which is tending, following Indo-China and Madagascar, to create new fronts of agitation and conflict.[15]

During the following winter the great West African railway strike strengthened hypotheses of an international conspiracy between nationalists and communist strategists of the Cold War, and confirmation was provided by an African tour of Raymond Barbé, dogmatic colonial 'expert' of the French Communist Party. At a mass meeting in Abijan on 20 October 1948, Barbé called for direct action throughout the empire against the French government and its American paymasters; and Houphouet himself, from the chair, expounded the Stalinist thesis that 'the world is divided not into two blocs but into two camps, that of the oppressors and that of the oppressed.'[16] It is hardly surprising that in the same month a new Governor of the Ivory Coast, Laurent Péchoux, was instructed to use the power of the colonial state to break the RDA. The international confrontation was strengthening the *colons* and other opponents of colonial reform.

Although the tide of reaction was running less strongly in London, both British and French governments wished to present a common front of enlightened colonialism to the world. Colonial officials had been discussing co-operation since 1945, but discovering divergences over both methods and motives of reform. Whereas Cohen and Poynton hoped to win African support by co-ordinating measures of practical benefit in both empires, from environmental control and public health to cross-border trade, the French were more concerned to win international approval for existing policies. The British Foreign Office too saw co-operation in Africa as helping to create a third international power-bloc; their attempts to present an Anglo-French front in the UN over such questions as the future of the two Togolese Trust Territories tended to increase African suspicions of the colonial reformers' good faith.[17] Indeed by 1947 the Foreign Office were urging that the search for a common African policy should be extended to other states – Belgium, Portugal, South Africa – whose policies were hardly consistent with the liberal ideals with which Cohen and Creech Jones hoped to win the confidence of African nationalists. At the same time the British Government felt overwhelmingly tempted to try to solve an acute economic crisis by planning colonial development on an Imperial scale, rather than through the decentralized approach of the Colonial Office, which attempted to secure local consultation and co-operation in identifying African needs. In this respect at least Britain's practice began temporarily to resemble French traditions she affected to despise.

NEW IMPERIAL DYNAMICS?

Experience during the 1930s had convinced most Europeans that economic progress, in Africa or at home, would require the state to take a more active role in economic planning. The smaller powers, under less international pressure to show results, still intended that their plans should be financed by colonial governments, borrowing where necessary in international markets, with the costs borne essentially by African tax-payers. Salazar had initiated plans for the Portuguese empire in the 1930s, but they were not translated into large programmes in Africa until 1953. In Belgian Congo, where the war had greatly stimulated mineral production, a plan envisaging expenditure of some £183,000,000 was adopted in 1948. This placed some emphasis on developing African peasant agriculture, and on welfare services: notably absent was provision for higher education. No transfer of political responsibility to African hands was yet contemplated; and Belgian parliamentarians, so long as they were not expected to vote funds, took little interest in African affairs.

In both France and Britain, however, governments understood that if they were to use their African empires to strengthen their international influence they would have to commit resources of their own. In Jean Monnet's Plan for French recovery, the development of primary production in the empire formed an integral part; besides improving African living standards, this was to contribute to the French Union's balance of payments.[18] Morocco and Tunisia received loans to execute programmes largely formulated in Paris; plans for rural development and education in Algeria were directly financed from metropolitan funds. The reconstituted Ministry of Overseas Finance at last received funds to match the plans for the *mise en valeur* of Black Africa which had been accumulating since Sarraut. Their objectives had evolved since the war; the Fourth Republic, like the British Labour Party, gave high priority to the advancement of African welfare through *équipement sociale*. Following the welcome abolition of forced labour and the *indigénat*, Africans were promised improvements in education, health and welfare services at all levels. For the elite more scholarships became available in France, and in 1949 existing colleges in Dakar were formed into an Institute of Higher Education, which in 1957 became the eighteenth French university.

So far as economic policy was concerned, less was new; one leading scholar judges that unimplemented plans of Vichy had set more radical objectives.[19] The old ideal of centralized planning of 'complementary economies', with the colonies supporting established French industries by providing minerals and selected raw materials and foodstuffs, changed only gradually. A new Investment Fund for Social and Economic Development (FIDES) was fairly generously endowed with funds from which it made grants to support development plans drawn up for (rather than by) the Overseas Territories. Between 1946 and 1956 FIDES devoted some 18 per cent of its funds to 'social expenditures', a similar amount to production (largely agriculture), and 64 per cent to a general heading of 'infrastructure' – meaning, in most cases, improved transport designed to facilitate exports by African farmers, foreign companies, or multinational mining enterprises. FIDES expected these expenditures to be matched by contributions from colonial budgets, at a level initially set at 45 per cent; this could either be borrowed (at favourable rates) from another French fund, the *Caisse Centrale de la France d'Outre-Mer*, or raised directly from African tax-payers.[20] Critics of these arrangements, in a territory where their support of aluminium manufacture did lead to a notable increase in Gross National Product, conclude that they were used 'as a means of employing Camerounian financial resources as investment capital for French industrial and commercial enterprises.'[21]

French investors were indeed increasingly ready to promote industries in the colonies, whether to provide consumption goods for regional markets or to process local materials previously exported to France. Marseille's analysis of French investments in the colonies during the postwar years shows that a decline in their total value was combined with a sectoral shift towards industrial enterprises, and a regional one towards tropical Africa. He attributes this to the declining influence, within the world of colonial business, of those representing traditional French industries, and to growing perceptions of benefits obtainable from investment in colonial industry. Apart from such obvious attractions as cheap labour, leading figures in the *Union coloniale* like Paul Bernard argued (initially with reference to Indo-China) that opening entrepreneurial opportunities to the aspirant middle classes might divert them from political agitation and show them the advantages of continued association with France. Readjustments of economic relations were thus to precede – and possibly pre-empt – the relaxation of political control.[22]

These tendencies do not mean that the French government, or French society generally, were psychologically prepared for the end of empire. If some leaders of French capitalism were beginning to see Africa in a new perspective, plenty of smaller enterprises and individual families still saw familiar types of future prospects for themselves. Between 1945 and 1960 the French population of Senegal increased from 16,432 to 38,000[23]; there were comparable increases elsewhere. Interactions between the changing perceptions of colonial reformers, of the varied interest groups, and of those concerned to restore France's position in the world were complex and frequently contradictory; if in the last resort it was international considerations which tended to prevail, these did not always point in the same direction. French attempts to reconstruct relationships were still coloured by old imperial ideologies or myths. The franc zone developed as a powerful means of planning, from Paris, the general direction of an imperial economy. While some FIDES projects promoted industrial diversification, the old concentration on a few cash crops was encouraged by the *caisses de compensation* set up in 1948 and intended, like the British Marketing Boards, to stabilize farmers' incomes. Increases in Africans' political representation gave them little control over policy or administration; the new Territorial Assemblies were required to vote substantial salary increases for a bureaucracy whose rate of expansion greatly exceeded the rate of Africanization. Substantial sections of the population, whose collaboration was particularly important to France, did derive real benefits from the postwar reconstruction of the French Union; but the most important motor of reform remained the drive to re-establish French power in the postwar world.

Domestic revival, reconstruction and reform as a basis for a strong world presence were equally clearly the priorities of postwar Britain; it was soon apparent that her allocation of resources for nation-building in Africa, however generously intended, would not be adequate to satisfy wartime aspirations. An impoverished Britain, with a Labour government committed to revive the country's military power as well as to improve the living standards of its working class, could reasonably claim that in the circumstances of 1945 a ten-year allocation of £120,000,000 for colonial development and welfare was not ungenerous. (As a proportion of GDP, expenditures during this period would exceed those in later, more affluent, times.) Yet British grants could be no more than pump-primers for extended development plans to be financed mainly by colonial tax-payers. In any case, benefits were not perceived immediately. The capital goods, building equipment and technical skills required were scarce, and colonial needs rarely secured priority from Treasury planners; actual disbursements from CDW funds in 1945–46 and 1946–47 were respectively £4.6m and £3.7m.[24]

In return for such allocations, colonial subjects were still required to support, in various ways, the 'imperial economy' which wartime expediencies had brought into being. Controls over colonial trade, notably through the various Marketing Boards, and over colonial borrowing, were maintained and strengthened. The British Treasury, until 1947, drew more revenue from taxes paid by British companies in Africa than did most colonial governments. Most importantly, the wartime depletion of currency reserves had necessitated the transformation of the sterling area into 'a tight-knit currency union', within which allocations of dollars were strictly controlled from London.[25] In principle this control was exercised in the common interest of all participants: but whereas Australia, Egypt or India could make effective representations about their needs, colonies depended on allocations by Britain. Although African colonies held only a small part of Britain's huge sterling debt (in 1945 roughly £100m each for East and West Africa out of a total of £3650m)[26], they were still being required to forgo imports of desirable American goods so that the Labour government could execute and improve upon the Coalition's pledges to create a British welfare state. Membership of the sterling area could bring compensating advantages, notably favoured access for members' exports to sterling markets; but for dollar-earners like the Gold Coast the sacrifices far out-weighed the benefits received from CDW funds. Indeed as a prosperous colony the Gold Coast came low in the CDW queue, its total receipts amounting to little over £4m, and many Gold Coasters were well aware of this imbalance.

The Fabians, most confident of all colonial reformers in the enlightenment of their prescriptions, soon realized that not all Africans shared their confidence. In April 1946, hoping to break 'the vicious circle of misunderstandings and recriminations', the Colonial Bureau invited some sixty overseas students and others to a weekend conference at Clacton-on-Sea. Their guests were not mollified by measured expositions of Labour's good intentions with regard to economic planning, trade union development and constitutional reform. An anonymous West Indian commented shrewdly on the inherent ethnocentrism of most progressive politicians; Kwame Nkrumah boldly recited the programme for 'complete and absolute independence' which he had formulated for the Pan-African Congress.[27] Rita Hinden, the Bureau's formidable secretary, was deeply hurt by this continuing 'misunderstanding'; when her close associate Creech Jones became Colonial Secretary in October she suggested that some dramatic gesture, such as a conference of African Legislative Councillors, might help to recapture African confidence. Her proposal was studied at length by an official committee under the Parliamentary Under-Secretary, Ivor Thomas, which duly produced an important series of policy papers for discussion, in the first place, by a conference of African governors in November 1947.[28]

Two of these papers are of central importance to students of British decolonization: they have been called a 'blueprint' which laid down 'that within a generation most of the major African countries would be self-governing within the Commonweatlh'.[29] A discussion of 'General Political Development of Colonial Territories' was originally drafted by the Deputy Under-Secretary, Sidney Caine; Andrew Cohen prepared a more detailed study of 'Constitutional Development in Africa'. However these constituted something less than a blueprint for something less than universal independence. Caine explicitly contrasted the strong trend towards 'local self-government' with the tendency developing since the war for national sovereignty to be everywhere constrained by international obligations and agreeements; he envisaged decolonization as a progressive 'substitution of counsel for control' within a Commonwealth community where only the larger colonies could expect to achieve 'full Dominion status'. Cohen's paper began by laying down rigorous conditions for that achievement:

> In West Africa internal self-government cannot be achieved until
> territorial unity has become a reality, sufficient numbers of Africans
> have emerged qualified by their training and character to manage their
> own affairs on a territorial scale and the political leaders have become
> representative of and responsible to the people.

In East Africa it would presumably be necessary to wait longer, until

> The Africans have developed to a stage where they can play their full
> part with the immigrant communities in the government of the
> territories.

During the intervening period Cohen proposed, not a blueprint, but a flexible policy over several decades:

> ... in the Gold Coast, the territory where Africans are most advanced politically, internal self-government is unlikely to be achieved in much less than a generation.

These memoranda showed an intelligent perception that, even if radical expatriates like Nkrumah still lacked direct contact with the African masses, they were voicing widespread frustration with life under colonial control. If Caine's emphasis on 'local self-government' reflected justifiable caution in identifying discontent with nationalism, there was no intention to limit reform to parish-pump politics (desirable though parish pumps would seem in many villages!) In a famous despatch to African governors on 25 February 1947 Creech Jones identified local government reform as the key to his comprehensive programme of 'political, social and economic advancement'. The new structures were seen not only as a means of planning local priorities democratically (a word deliberately chosen to reflect Fabian ideology), but as cases on which pyramids of representative institutions were to be constructed – more rapidly than Hailey had envisaged in 1942, if not so rapidly as would in fact prove to be necessary. Cohen's bench-mark of a generation for attainment of full internal self-government was regarded as feasible for Nigeria as well as the Gold Coast; but other colonies were distinguished on grounds of economic viability, political maturity, or ethnic complexity. Extended periods of nation-building seemed necessary everywhere.

The Colonial Office hoped that these measured statements of policy, once endorsed by the governors, could be communicated to the proposed conference of Legislative Councillors in 1948 as a comprehensive programme which would restore confidence in British intentions. But their emphasis was modified by two developments of later 1947. One was the critical reaction of the governors, once assembled in November, to the 'dry theoretical ideas' of Caine and Cohen. This was voiced most cogently by Sir Philip Mitchell of Kenya, supported by most of his colleagues from eastern Africa and also by Arthur Richards, growing steadily more reactionary since his ennoblement as Lord Milverton. Gubernatorial objections inevitably slowed or stultified the implementation of new policies in particular colonies; they also blurred the presentation to Africans, by insisting that 'representative' should be substituted for 'democratic' as the criterion for local government reform.[30]

Still more important were constraints imposed on economic policy by the sterling crisis of the preceding summer. In 1946 the United States Congress had authorized a loan to Great Britain on condition that within a year sterling should be made freely convertible. When this moment arrived on 15 July 1947 the British economy proved totally unprepared to take the strain; convertibility had to be suspended after forty days' erosion of currency reserves and the sterling area was obliged to revert to policies of strict austerity under the direction of Sir Stafford Cripps. During the governors' conference Cripps renewed an appeal, already contained in a Colonial Office circular, for help from colonial governments in correcting the imbalance of sterling–dollar exchanges. Immediately further restrictions were to be placed on imports, both of American consumer goods and of steel and other scarce commodities required for development; these implied increased taxation to control demand-inflation, and further delays in such timid projects for industrialization as the Colonial Office had accepted. Cripps further called for expansion of dollar-earning exports, even at the risk of depressing prices and reducing returns to the farmers; controls over colonial import and export programmes were greatly tightened, with the result that by 1952 accumulated balances of the African colonies (held in London and invested there on their behalf) provided over 20 per cent of the Sterling Area's reserves.[31] As a corollary to this, ultimate responsibility for colonial development programmes was transferred to the new planning staff established within the Cabinet Office under Sir Edwin Plowden; in the longer run too it seemed that the priorities of development as perceived in particular colonies were to be subordinated to those of the wider imperial economy. Temporarily at least there would be little substitution of counsel for control.

Even before the sterling crisis Ministers who shared Bevin's faith in a natural harmony of interests between British workers and their colonial subjects had begun to look to Africa for help in reviving the imperial economy and maintaining British food rations. Since Stanley's time the Colonial Office had been contemplating establishing Development Corporations which would establish productive and eventually profitable enterprises overseas, though without clarifying how the interests of colonial subjects should be balanced against the pressure for financial viability. From 1946 other Ministries became interested in such schemes in the context of a perceived crisis of world food production. Despite this multiplicity of good intentions, the Labour government was led by its domestic priorities into policies through which, in the sober judgement of an economic historian, 'Britain exploited those dependencies that were politically unable to defend their own interests in more ways and with more serious consequences than at any time since colonies were established.'[32]

Socialist enthusiasm for large-scale planning, and the Food Ministry's concern about oil-seed supplies, focused in 1946 on a suggestion by a senior member of the United Africa Company for mechanized groundnut production in thinly-populated areas of Tanganyika. There was great ideological and technocratic enthusiasm for a scheme which promised to promote 'development' at the same time as producing food, despite warnings about the ecological environment, the likely costs of production and transport, the availability of labour at the appropriate seasons, and the ultimate benefit to Tanganyikans. By 1951 experience had proved the validity of such warnings, and a scheme in which some £40,000,000 had been invested was reduced to one of 'experimental development' (at which level it eventually achieved some modest success). The Colonial Development Corporation, established in 1948 at the same time as the Overseas Food Corporation, had a hardly more successful beginning; a large poultry farm in the Gambia failed to produce either eggs for the British housewife or notable benefits for Gambians.[33]

Even where development expenditure was more effective, one effect was to link the fortunes of African producers more closely than before with those of the British imperial economy. Cripps and Bevin believed as firmly as any Victorian liberal in the mutually beneficial effects of the international division of labour. Some British investments did bring great benefits to some Africans, above all those best able to take advantage of new opportunities for education and public employment. But much development was increasing long-term dependence, making African economies *more* vulnerable to depressions of the 70s and 80s than they had been in the 30s. Yet Labour Ministers so readily accepted the view that the development of Africa's economic resources should be pushed forward rapidly in order to support the political and economic position of the UK that the Secretary to the Cabinet needed to remind them that their policies 'could be said to fall within the ordinary definition of imperialism'.[34]

Pressure on African resources was increased because the economic crisis coincided with the intensification of the Cold War. In January 1947 Attlee had finally accepted the insistence of Bevin and the Chiefs of Staff on maintaining a strong military presence in the Middle East, and in the same month Ministers secretly agreed to proceed to develop atomic weapons. A Moscow meeting of Foreign Ministers in March and April saw four-power co-operation in Germany under increasing strain, though it did not finally collapse until they reconvened in London at the end of the year. Increasingly the USA was assuming leadership of a western bloc. In March President Truman took over Britain's self-assumed responsibility for supporting Greece and Turkey against communist pressures, and on 5 June 1947 Secretary Marshall offered American support for a concerted European Recovery Programme. Both these initiatives, inspired essentially by anxiety about the power balance in war-weakened Europe, were presented to the American Congress and public as necessary to prevent the spread of international communism; the rapid escalation of an ideological Cold War intensified American interest in supervising the evolution of nationalist movements in the empires of their allies.

Bevin for his part hoped to use the economic respite afforded by Marshall Aid to remodel his dream of a third international force based on alliance between the British and French empires. He insisted on excluding the colonies from direct involvement in the Marshall Plan, so as not to reduce Britain's own share of the assistance, nor 'whet American appetites in the colonial empire'.[35] Despite continuing American pressure for universal free trade Bevin urged study of a possible Commonwealth customs union, and an intensive drive to increase exports of African raw materials: 'we must free ourselves from financial dependence on the United States of America as soon as possible. We shall never be able to pull our full weight in foreign affairs until we do so.' In September he told the French Premier Ramadier that by co-operating in Eurafrican enterprises Britain and France might eventually achieve a world status 'equivalent to that of Russia and of the United States.'[36] African resources of strategic minerals Bevin regarded as particularly important, even though experience was already showing (for example over proposals to produce aluminium in the Gold Coast)[37] that the UK could no longer provide the heavy capital investment needed to develop the resources she controlled.

During the first quarter of 1948 Labour's Paymaster-General, the economist H. A. Marquand, toured eastern Africa from the Sudan to Cape Town, evidently intending not only to identify difficulties impeding existing development projects but to form some general appreciation of how Africa might assist Bevin's hope of redressing the international balance. His conclusions were an impressive synthesis of some fashionable theses: the need to instruct African farmers and to counter the perceived menace of soil erosion; the link between social and educational improvement and economic growth; the desirability of concentrating investment (and allocations of scarce supplies) on such large projects as inter-territorial railways, power generation in the Rhodesias, irrigation control in the Nile basin. Applauded by Attlee, Marquand's report was fed into a Working Party on comprehensive colonial development which Cripps had established under his chief planner, Edwin Plowden.[38]

It was not only economic resources that Africa was expected to contribute to the Cold War effort. During the autumn of 1947 Field-Marshal Montgomery, Chief of the Imperial General Staff, also toured the continent; on return he submitted a report to Attlee calling, in his own distinctive style, for a 'Master Plan' to involve Africa in resisting the communist menace. Creech Jones had little difficulty in exposing the Field-Marshal's highly simplified approach to economic development and his failure to comprehend the need to secure African co-operation or the political dangers of close association with the Union; (though his warnings did not prevent Montgomery, next October, exhorting the conference of African legislators to unite against communism under 'the great Dominion in the South'). But the Colonial Secretary did accept the need 'to strengthen the position of Western Europe internationally by building up the economy of Africa and linking Africa more closely with this country and other countries of Western Europe.'[39] This aim was also emphasized by Bevin in a series of powerful papers, approved by the Cabinet in January 1948, which proposed reacting to Soviet hostility by organizing some form of Western Union, backed by the resources of the Commonwealth. Bevin was still hoping in this way

> ... to develop our own power and influence to equal that of the United States of America and the USSR. We have the material resources in the Colonial Empire, if we develop them, and by giving a spiritual lead now we should be able to carry out our task in a way which will show clearly that we are not subservient to the United States of America or to the Soviet Union.[40]

Bevin's commanding political authority enabled him to impose these imperial priorities over any concern for primary African interests which might have been voiced by Creech Jones, his former Parliamentary Private Secretary. But in the political climate of the Cold War, attempts to yoke the colonies to the cause of European revival were acceptable even to Bevin's left-wing critics. In April 1947 the 'Keep Left' group of Labour MPs declared that 'the future of European Socialism depends on the success of our combined colonial policies in the African continent', suggesting co-ordinated action not only to reduce Europe's dependence on the New World for foodstuffs and raw materials, but to secure 'manpower for the defence of Africa'. One year later Ian Mikardo was suggesting 'a joint British-French-Belgian-South African-Egyptian planning and development of the greater part of Africa', to be based on multiple replications of the Tennessee Valley Authority.[41]

In the double context of the Cold War and of African development, the continental role of South Africa seemed as crucial to Mikardo as to Montgomery. For Britain she remained one of the few major customers with whom there was a favourable trade balance; her gold production provided essential backing for Sterling Area reserves; her resources of uranium and other minerals might prove vital for military industries; and the Royal Navy's base at Simonstown was central to any 'Master Plan' for regional defence. When George VI toured South Africa with his family in 1947 these British interests still seemed reconcilable with Smuts's ambitions to become a major regional power within a strong Commonwealth. But in May 1948, as the Commonwealth began to adjust uncomfortably to its reinforcement by new Asian members, Smuts was defeated in a General Election. The new Nationalist Prime Minister, D. F. Malan stood for white supremacy in a more extreme and uncompromising form than Smuts (who had manifested sufficient mild symptoms of liberalism to encourage the ANC in its constitutionalist course); his government included Nazi sympathizers hostile to any British connection; and it inherited Smuts's ambitions for northward expansion. These latter features worried British politicians otherwise prepared to condone the internal brutalities of *apartheid*; but they did not remove the need for collaboration. In August 1951 the British and South African governments jointly convened a regional defence conference in Nairobi, attended by the colonial powers and by American observers, which prepared contingency plans for wartime co-operation throughout eastern and southern Africa.[42] Although South African opposition to the arming of Africans precluded an alliance, British Ministers remained eager to retain Nationalist goodwill.

This anxiety led the Commonwealth Relations Office consistently to advocate appeasement: in United Nations debates about the treatment of Indians and the future of Namibia, and in the affairs of Basutoland, Bechuanaland and Swaziland: three territories, administered through the British High Commission but economically dependent on the Union. While maintaining their refusal to transfer these countries to South African rule without evidence of African consent, British officials were led into some uncomfortably contorted postures, especially when in September 1948 Seretse Khama, the young Chief-designate of the Bangwato of Bechuanaland, married a British bride. When eventually in 1950 the Commonwealth Relations Office decided to exile not only Seretse but his uncle Tshekedi, who as regent Chief opposed the marriage as subversive of tradition, the issues were complex; but the decisive factor was neither the custom nor the wishes of the Bangwato but the reaction to inter-racial marriage of the majority of white South Africans. Recognition of a chief who had so flagrantly violated white South African folkways, it was feared, would not only make Malan's government more determined to secure political control of the three High Commission Territories, but might lead Afrikaners even more intransigent than Malan 'to exploit colour feeling in order to sever the tie with Great Britain'.[43] Such a threat to Britain's international interests was judged serious enough to over-ride any arguments on Seretse's behalf based merely on considerations of justice or human rights. Labour Ministers certainly faced an intractable problem; but their attempts at constructive procrastination worried many of their supporters and stimulated the formation of a new liberal pressure-group, the Africa Bureau.

British dreams of reinvigorating the old Commonwealth as a constructive force in the international power-balance, conceived precisely when its 'spiritual' consensus needed to stretch to embrace new members, now seems to have been doomed to frustration. Hopes of using Britain's depleted resources to direct the nation-building process in dependent territories were also over-ambitious. As Plowden's planners addressed the problems of colonial development they became all too aware both of continued shortages of equipment, supplies and finance and of contradictions between imperial priorities and African needs. Though investments in African nation-building continued they were no longer driven by hopes of creating a new sort of imperial power. In March 1949 a new planning committee in the Foreign Office rejected the aim of re-establishing Britain, even if sustained by colonies, Commonwealth and a French alliance, as a third power commensurate with the Soviet Union and the USA. British policy, it was concluded, must henceforth be based on co-operation with the USA within the North Atlantic treaty signed in April 1949.[44] Her best hope was to maintain senior status among America's allies, through a 'special relationship' guaranteed by possession of her own atomic weapons. To emphasize that status

British troops were sent to fight alongside Americans in the Korean war in July 1950 – an additional commitment for the hard-pressed Chiefs of Staff, who could no longer draw on the Indian Army as imperial reserve.

An even clearer indication of British dependence on America had come during the summer of 1949 when the Sterling Area's gold and dollar reserves, despite the relief afforded by Marshall Aid, again began to fall rapidly. In late August the Cabinet reluctantly approved a 30 per cent devaluation of sterling against the dollar, and heavy cuts in public expenditure. Since Washington agreed in return to adopt expansionist policies, whose effect was later enhanced by the boom induced by the Korean war, the result was indeed to ease the pressure on sterling (and so to remove any immediate incentive to pursue the option of closer integration with Europe). Devaluation imposed new hardships on the colonies (whose currencies, unlike the French African franc in 1948, were automatically devalued also); but its eventual success did weaken the drive for quick exploitation of African resources. Early reports on the groundnut scheme weakened the enthusiasm of Bevin and Mikardo alike for large technocratic corporations, and more realistic appreciations of costs and benefits began to emerge from Plowden's planning staff. But the greater freedom which economic recovery permitted arrived too late for the Labour government.

THE SECOND COLONIAL INVASION

So were the good intentions of Labour Ministers and colonial officials towards the African colonies largely frustrated by the constraints of the postwar years. While Africans were being consulted about reforms in their government, far-reaching decisions affecting their immediate conditions of life were being taken on their behalf by the imperial authorities. Centralized planning was hard to reconcile with progressive devolution of responsibility. Creech Jones's conference of African Legislative Councillors, which finally met in November 1948, did have some apparent success in inspiring African confidence. 'The idea of an African union linked to a union of western Europe has found an echo in the local assemblies', a French observer reported. J. B. Danquah proclaimed, to the delight of his Fabian friends, that 'this offer of mutual confidence in place of distrust and suspicion must mean just one thing – a change of heart in the Imperial Colonial Office.' But to African colleagues Danquah was rather more sceptical; indeed during the conference itself he had questioned whether the contribution Africans were being required to make to the Sterling Area had been justly determined.[45] The changing emphasis in Labour's development policies had not gone unnoticed in Africa.

Whatever may be thought of the justice with which the costs and benefits of British development policy were distributed, the general effect was to draw more Africans into more direct contact with agents of the colonial state than ever before. Young British graduates and ex-servicemen were recruited in hundreds, with every expectation of a lifetime career in colonial administration, and instructed in the new doctrines of good government in a series of university summer schools. Specialists were recruited to implement new policies for agricultural production and marketing, to provide new social and medical services, to work in fisheries or education. To many Africans they seemed the agents, not necessarily unwelcome, of a 'second colonial invasion', intruding into the affairs of local communities which older forms of native administration had left, except in tax-collecting seasons, in relative tranquillity.[46] New drives for agricultural or environmental improvement, even when more realistically planned than the groundnuts scheme, involved more of those attempts to direct the lives of peasant farmers which had begun during the erosion scare of the '30s. Schemes for co-operative enterprise and community development made participants more aware of other decisions affecting their lives which were being taken far beyond local control. Larger projects to improve transport, power or water supplies mobilized labour forces with expectations of their own.

While drives for development brought these new European forces into Africa – even more conspicuously in the French and Belgian empires than in the British – some of the agents were Africans themselves. The progressive Africanization of public services was an important part of the Colonial Office strategy of nation-building. But since it was invariably asserted that this must not be achieved by dilution of the 'standards' which the colonizers had defined for themselves, the process could not come to maturity until the new University Colleges, that central feature of British policy, began to produce graduates during the 1950s. Before this few candidates appeared suitable for the senior services in eastern Africa (Sudan excepted), and the progress in the west was slow. In 1948 a British Commission thought the 98 senior government posts held by Africans out of a total of over 1300 in the Gold Coast represented 'a fair increase'; but proportionately it represented little advance on the 1925 figure of 27 out of 500, and it fell far short of the expectations which Guggisberg had held out at that time.[47] How far the effectiveness of the second occupation would be increased by more rapid Africanization remained to be seen.

What is clear is that educational expansion, the necessary preliminary to a transfer of power within the colonial state, was the feature of development which aroused the greatest African enthusiasm, and the highest expectations. There were more expectations than could be quickly satisfied. Each colony continued to produce large plans for more places in primary, secondary, technical, pedagogical and university education. Proportions, both existing and projected, among these levels varied greatly. Many administrators thought that Higher Education received too high priority from Colonial Office planners, especially when they realized how heavily those planners had underestimated the costs of a modern university. But that view was rarely shared by Africans, who saw university degrees as master keys to national progress as well as to personal ambitions. At every level of the educational pyramid queues of disappointed aspirants began to form; 'school-leavers', persons judged to have proceeded as far as their country's resources would allow, began to be seen as a potential social problem.

By 1948 then it was clear to anyone who had not perceived this already that the process of development would create new sources of discontent and frustration, and that these could not be satisfied or contained within the framework of improved local government. The new demands which imperial governments had begun to impose on their African subjects could only increase this social volatility. As the next chapter will show, the range, depth and gravity of African discontent still varied greatly between the various colonies; but it seems that few of the legislators invited to endorse British policies during the 1948 London conference can have fully appreciated the social pressures latent within their own countries. In some areas Africans were already beginning to force the pace of reform, and soon they would be threatening to seize the political initiative, not only in the Islamic countries of the Mediterranean but in tropical colonies also.

NOTES AND REFERENCES

1. F.O.371/50912, 'Stock-Taking after VE-Day.' Memo by Sir Orme Sargent, 11 July, revised 31 July 1945

2. P. Pugh, *Educate, Agitate, Organize* (1984) pp. 188-95 On domestic bipartisanship. cf. P. Addison, *The Road to 1945* (1975)
3. A. Creech Jones, *Labour's Colonial Policy* Fabian Society: Colonial Controversy series No. 3, 1947
4. R. Smith & J. Zametica, 'The Cold Warrior: Clement Attlee reconsidered, 1945-7' *International Affairs* 61, 1985, pp. 237-52; C. John Kent, 'International Dimensions of British West African Policy, 1939-1949', Ph.D thesis, University of Aberdeen, 1986. These paragraphs, among others, owe much to discussions with John Kent.
5. Wm Roger Louis, *The British Empire in the Middle East, 1945-51* (Oxford, 1984); Alan Bullock, *Ernest Bevin: Foreign Secretary 1945-1951* (Oxford, 1983) pp. 113-15
6. Louis, *Middle East*, pp. 270-1, quoting Dalton's diary, 5 Oct. 1945: V. Rothwell, *Britain and the Cold War* p. 252, quoting Pierson Dixon diary 10 Feb. 1946
7. K. Harris, *Attlee* (1982) p. 299, quoting Dalton diary 9 March 1946; CAB 131/1 DO(46) 10 Minutes of Cabinet Defence committee 5 April 1946; cf. Bullock, *Bevin*, pp. 239-46; Louis, *Middle East*, pp. 15-20, 108-10; P. Darby, *British Defence Policy East of Suez* (1973) pp. 36-8
8. Louis, *Middle East* pp. 265-306; P. Guillen, 'Une menace pour l'Afrique française: le débat international sur le statut des anciennes colonies italiennes', *Les chemins* pp. 69-81
9. Sir Hilton Poynton in K-G, p. 17
10. FRUS, 1944, Vol. V, p. 486, Memo by Wallace Murray, 19 Dec. 1944
11. P. Duignan & L. H. Gann, *The United States and Africa: A History* (Cambridge, 1984) pp. 300-2
12. FRUS, 1947, Vol. V, pp. 686-9; Marshall to Caffery, Top Secret 10 June 1947
13. de Coppet, July 1947, quoted J. Tronchon, *L'insurrection malgache de 1947* (Paris, 1974) pp. 144-5
14. G. Lisette, *Le Combat du Rassemblement Démocratique Africain* (Paris, 1983) p. 166
15. ANSOM, A.P. 2255/1, V. Secret Note by Moutet for Ramadier, 1 Aug. 1947
16. Report, Service de la Sûreté de la Côte d'Ivoire, 21 Oct. 1948: Damas, pp. 560-4
17. M. Michel, 'La co-opération inter-coloniale en Afrique Noire, 1942-1950: un néo-colonialisme éclairé?' *Rélations Internationales* 34, 1983, pp. 155-71; Kent 'International Dimensions ...' Chs XII, XIV
18. Présidence du Conseil: Commissariat-Général du Plan de Modernisation et d'Équipement. Rapport ... sur le Plan ... Réalisations 1947-9 et Objectifs 1950-52. (Paris, 1949) pp. 118-32
19. J. Marseille, *Empire colonial ...* pp. 347-49
20. T. Hayter, *French Aid* (1966); pp. 35-9; J. Suret-Canale, *Afrique noire, Occidentale et centrale: De la Colonisation aux indépendances 1945-1960* Vol. I (Paris, 1972) pp. 103f
21. R. A. Joseph, *Radical Nationalism in Cameroun* (Oxford, 1977) pp. 105-14
22. J. Marseille, 'Une approche économique et financière de la décolonisation: l'évolution des bilans des entreprises coloniales', *Les chemis* pp. 167-71: cf. his *Empire colonial ...*, *passim*

23. Rita Cruise O'Brien, *White Society in Black Africa: the French of Senegal* (1972) p. 275
24. Morgan, II, p. 84; IV, pp. 10–11
25. N. J. Westcott, 'Sterling and Empire; the British Imperial Economy 1939–1951' (Seminar paper, Institute of Commonwealth Studies, London, 20 Jan. 1982): A. E. Hinds, 'Sterling and Imperial Policy, 1945–51', JICH XV 1987 pp. 148–69
26. H. A. Shannon, 'The Sterling Balances of the Sterling Area, 1939–1949', *Economic Journal* 60 1950 pp. 532, 550
27. Fabian Colonial Bureau: Controversy Series No 1 *Domination or Co-operation?* (1946) For a vivid fictional account by a participant, Peter Abrahams, *A Wreath for Udomo* (1956) pp. 64–77
28. CO 847/36/47328 Hinden to Creech Jones 21 Oct. 1946 and subsequent papers.
29. Ronald Robinson in K-G p. 179; cf. his 'Andrew Cohen and the Transfer of Power in Tropical Africa, 1940–1951' in M-J & F. For embellishments of Robinson, CHA VIII pp. 43, 341. A better analysis of these memoranda is R. D. Pearce, *The Turning-Point in Africa* (1982) pp. 167–75. Various drafts of the memoranda are in CO 847/36/47238; I use the versions submitted by the Committee on 22 May and approved by Attlee on 11 June 1947
30. Pearce, *Turning-Point* pp. 177–82. For a French view of the governors' conference, ANSOM, AP 2224/4 Massigli to Bidault 22 Jan. 1948
31. CO 847/36/47328 Speech by Cripps 12 Nov 1947. cf. Y. Bangura, *Britain and Commonwealth Africa* (Manchester, 1983) pp. 40–5; also Morgan II, pp. 4–9; Jane Bowden, 'Development and Control in British Colonial Policy, with reference to Nigeria and the Gold Coast, 1935–48', Ph.D thesis, University of Birmingham, 1980, Ch. VII
32. D. K. Fieldhouse, 'The Labour Governments and the Empire-Commonwealth', in R. Ovendale (ed) *The Foreign Policy of the British Labour Party, 1945–51* (1984) p. 95. P. S. Gupta, 'Imperialism and the Labour Government of 1945–51' in J. M. Winter (ed) *The Working Class in Modern British History* (Cambridge, 1983) is rather more charitable. For detailed evidence on this subject, Morgan, Vol. II
33. Morgan, II, Ch. 5, 6 M. Cowen, 'Early Years of the Colonial Development Corporation: British State Enterprise Overseas during late Colonialism', AF.AFF 83 1984 pp. 63–75; W. Rendell, *The History of the Commonwealth Development Corporation* (1976) Ch. 1, 2 For comparable French failures, Suret-Canale, *Afrique Noire* III,i, pp. 122–4
34. PREM 8/923, Norman Brook to Attlee, 14 Jan. 1948
35. FO 800/444, Bevin to MacNeil (at UN) Top Secret 17 Oct. 1947
36. FO 800/444, Bevin to Attlee, Secret, 16 Sept. 1947; V. H. Rothwell, *Britain and the Cold War* (1982) pp. 448–9, quoting note of Bevin-Ramadier talks, 22 Sept. 1947; cf. Kent, 'International Dimensions ...' pp. 524–6; Bullock, *Bevin* pp. 491–2 cf. Gupta, *Imperialism and the British Labour Movement*, p. 306, quoting Dalton diary, 15 Oct. 1948
37. R. W. Graham, *The Aluminium Industry and the Third World* (1982) Ch. V.
38. PREM 8/923, Report by Marquand on his Visit to Africa, 2 April 1948
39. PREM 8/923, Montgomery to Attlee, 19 Dec. 1947; FO 800/435, Memo by Creech Jones, Top Secret, 9 Jan. 1948; cf. J. B. Danquah to UGCC, in

H. K. Akyeampong, *Journey to Independence and After* Vol. I (Accra, 1970) pp. 87–8

40. CAB 129/23,CP (48) 6: Memo by Bevin, 'The First Aim of British Foreign Policy', 4 Jan. 1948: cf. Bullock, *Bevin* pp. 513–18

41. *Keep Left* by a Group of Members of Parliament, May 1947, p. 44. Ian Mikardo, *The Second Five Years: A Labour Programme for 1950* Fabian Research Series No 124, April 1948 pp. 2–3

42. FRUS, 1951, V (1982) pp. 1224–28, Jooste to Acheson, 11 July 1951

43. Baring to Liesching, 11 July 1949, quoted C. Douglas-Home, *Evelyn Baring: The Last Pro-Consul* (1975) pp. 182–5: cf. CAB 129/40,CP (50)138, Memo by Gordon-Walker, 26 June 1950; R. Hyam, 'The Political Consequences of Seretse Khama: Britain, the Bangwato and South Africa', HJ 29 1986 pp. 922–47

44. FO 371/76384, Strang to Bevin, 22 March 1949 (final version 9 May); A. Adamthwaite, 'Britain and the World, 1945–9: The View from the Foreign Office', *International Affairs* 61 1985 pp. 228–31

45. ANSOM A.P.2224/4 J. de Raymond to Coste-Floret, 20 Oct. 1948; J. B. Danquah, *Friendship and Empire* F.C.B. Controversy Series No. 5, May 1949, p. 8; Danquah to UGCC, 8 Nov. 1948, in H. K. Akyeampong, *Journey* p. 80

46. D. A. Low & J. Lonsdale, 'Towards the New Order, 1945–1963', HEA III (1984) esp. pp. 12–16

47. Report of the Commission of Enquiry into Disturbances in the Gold Coast (Colonial No 231, 1948) p. 30; R. E. Wraith, *Guggisberg* (1967) p. 229

CHAPTER SIX

Pressures for Independence, c.1948-1953

During the postwar years both British and French governments were faced with growing contradictions between their intention to substitute counsel for control in relationships with their African dependencies and more urgent incentives to use the economic and military resources of those dependencies to strengthen their international influence. Their need provided Africans who could establish credentials as spokesmen in the colonial dialogue with opportunities to insist that the political independence of their countries provided the only acceptable basis for collaboration. Events in Asia, where independence was relatively successfully conceded to India, Pakistan, Burma and Ceylon but bitterly contested in Indo-China and Indonesia, seemed posthumously to justify Roosevelt's insistence on the importance of that word. In face of insistence from African leaders and of international pressures colonial reformers in London, if not yet in Paris, had to suppress their persistent doubts as to whether international sovereignty and universal suffrage represented viable or desirable objectives for every colony. A crucial struggle to secure control over the process of decolonization took place in the Gold Coast, where British colonial reformers at times lost the initiative to a new type of political party which mobilized African discontents on a platform of populist nationalism. Because Nkrumah's success had wide repercussions, this confrontation will be examined at some length. After 1951, careful distinctions between different stages of local autonomy, and between self-government and independence, became increasingly irrelevant, at least in colonies where there were no powerful immigrant minorities. But much constitutional ingenuity was still applied in vain searches for alternative goals in colonies where expatriate interests could exert influence in the metropolis.

NKRUMAH: THE CHALLENGE OF POPULIST NATIONALISM

As Cohen noted in 1947, liberal imperialists regarded the Gold Coast as an ideal pilot/state for their decolonization strategy. The country (or at least its southern provinces) enjoyed a relatively prosperous commercial economy, thanks to the enterprise of its cocoa farmers, with consequently high levels of schooling and health services; and in 1944 Alan Burns had secured enthusiastic support from a long-established political elite for the first stage of a measured constitutional progress. But by January 1948, when Burns was succeeded as governor by one of the Colonial Office planners, Sir Gerald Creasy, the reformers seemed to have been over-confident. Because of delays in drafting the necessary Statutory Instruments the constitutional changes approved in 1944 had not been implemented until 1946, by which time they no longer appeared quite so progressive. Personal relations with African leaders, in which Burns took much pride, had been soured by his bitter quarrel with Danquah over a so-called 'ritual murder case' in Akim Abuakwa.* Still more important, the colonial administration, depleted and exhausted by its wartime duties, was failing to identify, still less to satisfy, rising expectations in many sections of society.

With the wisdom of hindsight it is not difficult to identify grievances. Continuing controls on foreign trade frustrated aspiring businessmen denied import licences, demobilized drivers unable to use their gratuities to buy lorries, market women who saw the big companies diverting supplies to their own retail stores. Educational expansion failed to satisfy young people halted by hurdles they believed themselves competent to pass. Ambitious countrymen found that local government reform could strengthen, rather than limit, the power of their chiefs. Farmers' Associations who knew the fallibility of agricultural experts rejected their instructions to 'cut out' cocoa trees infected with swollen shoot. Such tensions made Gold Coast society even more volatile than during the agitations of the '30s. When on 28 February 1948 the commander of a small police detachment in Accra fired on a procession of protesting ex-servicemen, killing two,

---

*Burns and his officials believed that the funeral ceremonies of Ofori Atta I in 1944 included a human sacrifice. Despite certain gaps in the evidence, eight men were tried for murder and condemned to death. Danquah, a kinsman of the royal family, showed great forensic and political skill in prolonging the processes of appeal; eventually he involved British MPs in what he regarded as a defence of human rights but Burns as a frustration of natural justice. Eventually four of the accused had their sentences commuted by Burns, one died in prison, and three were executed in March, 1947. See A. Burns, *Colonial Civil Servant* (1949) pp. 219–39

widespread rioting and looting in the city spread to three other towns, including Kumasi; eventually twenty-nine people were killed and well over two hundred injured. A governor with more experience outside Whitehall might have restored order at less cost; but in the long perspectives of colonial or African history this was a tragedy of moderate dimensions. To Fabian optimists in London it nevertheless seemed a traumatic warning.

But a warning of what? In the fraught atmosphere of early 1948 many feared the long arm of the recently founded Cominform. Only a few days earlier communists had overthrown a coalition government and seized power in Czechoslovakia; they were waging civil war in Greece and were on the point of doing so in Malaya (the only colony which brought more dollars than the Gold Coast into the Sterling Area). A few shreds of circumstantial evidence allowed Labour ministers to jump to the conclusion that the communist conspiracy had reached West Africa. The respectable bourgeois Africans who had formed the United Gold Coast Convention (UGCC) to expedite progress towards self-government had recently engaged as General Secretary Kwame Nkrumah – Pan-African activist, trouble-maker at the Fabian conference, and a man who during his twelve years abroad had read widely and mixed freely with American and British communists.

Nkrumah was no communist. His passionate political creed owed as much to Mazzini and Marcus Garvey as to Marx, and is best characterized as populist nationalism. He had certainly consorted with Marxists of both Stalinist and Trotskyite persuasion, who had enlarged his political vocabulary; but orthodox class analysis provided unreliable guidance for political activity in the Gold Coast. Nkrumah did however know that thousands of Africans, beyond those reached by traditional elite politics, would respond to clear and simple demands for political freedom for their continent. And what he *had* learned from the communists was the potential strength of a political party, centrally directed and disciplined, which could identify needs and establish roots in towns and villages throughout the country. On 20 January he had presented the UGCC with detailed proposals to do just that. But on 28 February they were still little more than proposals. Nkrumah had not made the Accra riots; but the government's response helped to make Nkrumah.

Once the colonial reformers understood that they were not facing a Kremlin conspiracy, they determined 'to remove the causes of discontent which alone would make a Communist *putsch* conceivable'.[1] Since little could be done immediately to provide more development capital or consumer goods, this implied political initiatives. At Colonial Office prompting Creasy appointed three Scottish Fabians of limited African experience – a lawyer, a trade unionist, and an agronomist – 'to enquire into and report on the recent disturbances in the Gold Coast and their underlying causes; and to make recommendations on any matter arising from their enquiry'. The Commissioners discharged this wide remit speedily, visiting the Gold Coast from 7 April until 9 May and submitting a comprehensive report one month later. Hardly an aspect of government policy escaped their criticism, usually severe, and they concluded that 'in the conditions existing today in the Gold Coast a substantial measure of reform is necessary to meet the legitimate aspirations of the indigenous population'.[2]

This recommendation did not imply any early transfer of power: on the contrary, the commissioners declared that:

His Majesty's Government ... has a moral duty to remain until

(a) the literate population has by experience reached a stage when selfish exploitation is no longer the dominant motive of political power, or

(b) the bulk of the population has advanced to such a stage of literacy and political experience as will enable it to protect itself from gross exploitation, and

(c) some corresponding degree of cultural, political and economic achievement has been attained by all three areas now part of the Gold Coast.[3]

These conditions seem more rigorous than those implied by Cohen a year before; yet some visible initiative seemed urgently necessary to satisfy political expectations created by the riots. The Colonial Office decided to engage a wider African leadership in practical dialogue. Fears of a communist offensive in Africa were still strong in London, and stimulated a review of police, intelligence and security services throughout the empire; but this review quickly showed that the red alarm in the Gold Coast had been premature. Nkrumah had already been released, along with the other five UGCC leaders who had been exiled to the Northern Territories, in the belief that his influence could be neutralized while they were being reconciled. Instead of adopting the Watson Commission's uninspiring suggestions for constitutional reform, Creech Jones referred the whole question for detailed study by a Committee composed exclusively of forty African notables.

This initiative appeared to succeed; in August 1949 the report of Justice Coussey's Committee broadly endorsed the Colonial Office approach to the gradual transfer of responsibility. In the form in which the proposals were finally implemented[4] eighteen of the fifty-six members representing Asante, Togoland and the Colony in the new Legislative Assembly were to be chosen by Provincial Councils, based upon the reformed structure of local government; the nineteen representatives of the less politically active Northern Territories would be elected by a special Council somewhat similarly constituted. The remaining southern members would be chosen by adult male suffrage – a revolutionary innovation in Black Africa; but only in five urban seats would it be exercised directly. In each of the thirty-three rural constituencies the final selection lay with delegates elected to special electoral colleges. Only three British officials retained *ex officio* seats in the Assembly and in the Executive Council, which was to include eight Ministers chosen from the Assembly. These would assume overall responsibility for groups of government departments; but control of finance, defence and external affairs, together with ultimate reserve powers over the whole constitution, remained with the governor.

While this careful political arithmetic reflected British constitutional thinking, the accelerated pace was liable to alter the expected effects. No graduate of the new University College could be ready to serve as Minister, or train as Permanent Secretary. Cohen, recognizing that political advance in West Africa was going to be 'more rapid ... than the capabilities of the peoples would justify on merit', became anxious to increase public investment through agents like the Colonial Development Corporation, so that 'as the West African territories get greater political freedom they should be more closely linked to the UK economically, both for their own advantage and ours'.[5] But the Labour Government was less willing than the Fourth Republic to invest more heavily in colonial development. Constitutional advance would to some extent be a substitute for economic assistance; yet they were not yet ready to transfer power over a colony so vital for the health of sterling, and still regarded as strategically important.[6] Hailing Coussey's Report as 'a victory for moderate opinion', Creech Jones persuaded the Cabinet on 13 October that 'a very considerable degree of African participation in the control of policy' had become inescapable; but there were two significant reservations in his endorsement of Coussey. He rejected as premature proposals that the new Assembly should elect a Leader, who would then nominate his fellow-Ministers: and that the Executive Council thus constituted should become collectively responsible to the Assembly.

> I do not believe, [Creech Jones ruled] that the institution of a Leader of the House would work effectively in the absence of an established and well-tried party system, by which I mean a system where through usage over a period of years parties have become generally accepted as necessary parts of the constitutional machinery of the country. In this sense there is not as yet a party system in the Gold Coast ...[7]

But already Nkrumah had begun to prove him wrong.

Creech Jones's emphasis on the crucial importance of party for the development of parliamentary government reflected a current British orthodoxy which would find authoritative exposition in Lewis Namier's Romanes Lecture for 1952.[8] Disciplined parties, organized to discover and express the common intentions of a national electorate, were the necessary condition of effective parliamentary sovereignty; in their absence legislatures must remain closed arenas for bargaining among groups representing local or sectional interests, or factional 'connections'. In such conditions the Crown [sc. Governor] not only could but must retain a decisive voice in choosing Ministers and so in directing policy. The historical rehabilitation of George III could only encourage the Fabian Ministers of George VI to cherish the remaining 'influence of the Crown'.

But Nkrumah had also learned the importance of party, from other teachers. While senior members of UGCC were debating the merits of bi-cameralism in the Coussey Committee, their General Secretary was creating a political machine under his own leadership, which for a time appeared to mobilize all the most vigorous elements in the country. Nkrumah strengthened contacts with Asante farmers and Sekondi railwaymen; 'Ghana Colleges' enrolled people blocked on the educational ladder; a new Accra newspaper, the *Evening News*, exhorted the discontented to unite against imperialism. Finally in June 1949 the Committee on Youth Organization, formed as a militant spearhead of UGCC under Nkrumah's leadership, turned into the Convention Peoples' Party (CPP), with wide support in the south, and a proclaimed commitment to Positive Action to secure 'Self-Government NOW'.*

It does not seem that Nkrumah had yet devised a clear strategy for achieving self-government, or closely studied the Indian experience

---

*Since at the 1945 Pan-African Conference Nkrumah had demanded 'complete and absolute independence', and his plan for the UGCC in January 1948 defined the aim as 'Self-Government or National Independence', this formulation seems to represent a tactical withdrawal: because 'self-government' was still a more familiar concept to West African electors or because it offered better hope of verbal compromise with Britain? Not until August 1956 did Lennox-Boyd abandon attempts to substitute for independence 'the more re-assuring words ... [full] self-government within the Commonwealth'. (CAB 129/83 CP(56)204, Memo of 24 Aug. 1956).

which he liked to evoke. Someone who had was Reginald Saloway, one of the few Indian civil servants to transfer to Africa in 1947. In December Saloway, with the approval of an experienced new governor, Sir Charles Arden-Clarke, established the first personal contact between Nkrumah and a senior British official. Both men seem to have been unexpectedly well-impressed; Nkrumah noted Saloway's warnings against facile Indian analogies, and his assurances that 'the constitutional road' was genuinely open.[9] Nkrumah was not yet identified as the inevitable successor. In January the CPP's attempt to launch 'Positive Action' with a general strike collapsed, without martyrs, before an incomparably better-prepared response by the reformed security forces; Nkrumah was tried, convicted and imprisoned; and Arden-Clarke sensed an opportunity to fill a 'political vacuum' by rallying 'moderate opinion' in favour of the new constitution.[10] But there was no vacuum; the CPP, unlike the UGCC 'moderates', was already well organized to follow the 'constitutional road' of manhood suffrage. During 1950, as local CPP leaders provided indispensable assistance to officials in their unprecedented task of registering an African electorate, Arden-Clarke achieved a realistic appreciation of the party's strength and seriousness. On 9 February 1951 it became clear that the CPP had won 34 of the 38 elective seats; although this was less than an overall majority of the Assembly there was no doubt that party politics had effectively arrived. Assuming approval from Creech Jones (himself engaged in a less successful election campaign) Arden-Clarke summoned Nkrumah from prison and invited him, as Leader of Government Business, to nominate colleagues for ministerial office.[11]

In Britain's postwar crisis, good order in the Gold Coast and continued access to its dollar-earning resources were essential. The option of securing these by force alone was politically unacceptable; the constitution, intended to win the collaboration of 'moderate opinion', had in fact delivered a CPP majority; all that remained was to make the best of Nkrumah's willingness to give an extended interpretation to 'Self-Government NOW'. In retrospect the six years of dyarchy which followed seems a protracted transition, but it was far shorter than Cohen or Watson had expected. The Colonial Office, recognizing that Hailey's hope of entrenching reformed Native Authorities in the new constitutional structure could not be achieved in the Gold Coast, conceded control of local government to CPP Ministers in 1952. During these six years rising cocoa prices stimulated by the Korean war increased government revenues by over

50 per cent, and so provided Ministers with means to distribute benefits to their constituents, their party, and in some cases to themselves; this made them more ready to accept advice from British officials about methods of administering a modern state. 'He is being educated by *us*,' wrote one of them.[12] The syllabus was not ideologically neutral; in the words of one of Nkrumah's mentors, 'it took the form of imposing upon the people and government of Ghana the forms, legalities, shapes, safeguards, committees, and above all the objectives, procedures, morals and moralism of British parliamentary democracy'.[13] In return for Arden-Clarke's endorsement as heir-apparent Nkrumah agreed to follow the Colonial Office to the end of the 'constitutional road'; it proved unnecessary to test the strength of the CPP in a revolutionary struggle.

Oliver Lyttelton, the forceful industrialist and former Guards officer who in 1951 became Churchill's Colonial Secretary, seems at first to have been less than happy with this bargain. In June 1952 he visited Accra and in his bluff way tried to 'bring home ... a certain number of home truths' to Nkrumah and his colleagues; but Arden-Clarke persuaded him that 'if the government of the Gold Coast is to continue to be by consent, constitutional changes are inescapable'. When proposals arrived Lyttelton advised the Cabinet that 'their rejection would bring to an end settled government by consent, and forfeit the goodwill towards the United Kingdom and the desire to retain the British connection which are common to all parties in the Gold Coast'.[14] In February 1954 he reported reassurance on two critical issues. One was the fear of Ministerial corruption; a judicial Commission, established after the Minister of Works had admitted receiving £2000 from a contractor for 'election expenses', had found no evidence of corruption among other senior Ministers. Still more welcome was the Gold Coast Cabinet's new attitude to communism. They had agreed, Lyttelton reported,

(i) to ban the entry of all Communist literature into the Gold Coast ...
(ii) to exclude any European with Communist sympathies from the public service and to exclude any African with Communist sympathies from a certain number of Departments like the Administration, the police, and the Department of Education.
(iii) to confiscate the passports of the few Gold Coast Communists who wish to travel behind the Iron Curtain.[15]

Once Nkrumah had won another election in 1954, Lyttelton's successor Lennox-Boyd somewhat reluctantly accepted December 1956 as target-date for 'full self-government within the Commonwealth'.[16]

The main challenges to Nkrumah's claim to inherit the political kingdom now came from within. From 1954 his government faced growing opposition, especially in regions outside its southern power-base: in the North, and particularly in Asante, new generations of 'discontented aspirants' feared exclusion from the benefits of independence.[17] But the cocoa boom provided the CPP with substantial resources for public improvement and private patronage; the security services of the state were now working on their side; and the message of populist nationalism – that possession of the political kingdom would allow *all* the peoples of Africa to progress and prosper – still had wide appeal. Conservative Ministers, worried by the growing opposition, delayed the drive to independence by requiring Nkrumah to face the test of a third election; but when the CPP won another victory, on a reduced poll, the Cabinet approved legislation which made Ghana an independent state within the Commonwealth on 6 March 1957. One Minister, Duncan Sandys, expressed an old Tory view of trusteeship by suggesting delay to re-open the possibility of a federal constitution; but his colleagues, conscious of an approaching Suez crisis, were unwilling to prolong their responsibility.[18] Imperial trusteeship, with its attendant burdens, was going out of fashion. As Nkrumah insisted, Ghanaian independence was not a mere merit award for a 'model colony', but a turning-point in the history of the continent. Africans elsewhere soon signalled their agreement.

TOWARDS INDEPENDENCE: SUDAN AND NIGERIA

In the early 1950s only two other British territories were clearly identified as comparable to the Gold Coast in readiness for early independence under African rule: both were large and complex countries where historic conflicts had been temporarily contained within colonial boundaries. Nigerian independence seemed to follow naturally, though by no means simply, from that of Ghana; in the Sudan progress towards independence preceded, may indeed have helped to reinforce, Nkrumah's demand.

Constitutional progress in the Sudan continued to be stimulated by nationalists in Egypt. While officials primarily concerned with British relations with the Arab world sought a treaty with Egypt which would deal with the Sudan as well as the Suez base, other members of the Foreign Office, in their role as paternalist administrators and trustees for the Sudanese people, insisted on preserving the right of the latter to self-determination. At the United Nations Britain fended off Egyptian pressure by claiming her own duty to 'keep the ring until such time as the Sudanese are in a position to take over the control of their own country, and to decide for themselves their international status'.[19] In 1948 she established the first Legislative Assembly covering the whole country: as its powers were limited and its members chosen by a mixture of nomination, indirect, and direct election it was boycotted by the Ashiqqa party, which continued to look to Egypt for support. But constitutional progress continued, and was accelerated: internal pressure apart, this was the best response to Egyptian criticism. The army officers who overthrew Farouk in 1952 were most interested in securing British withdrawal from the Canal zone; in February 1953 General Mohammed Neguib accepted the right of the Sudanese people to self-determination after a short period of self-government, and the Foreign Office obliged its apprehensive Sudanese officials to accept this. Internationally supervised elections did give a majority to the National Unionist Party (successors to the Ashiqqa); but, having progressed so far, Sudanese politicians decided that independence might be more advantageous than union with Egypt. On 1 January 1956 Sudan became a Republic, outside the Commonwealth though retaining good relations with Britain. Serious tensions within the new state – between North and South, between Islamic and secular concepts of nationality – had not been resolved, had indeed in some ways been increased by British attempts to do so. The timing of independence, however, had not been determined by any notional 'readiness' of Sudanese society but by the needs of British Middle Eastern policy.

Nonetheless the Sudan was cited as a precedent during Cabinet discussions of Ghanaian independence[20], and in the even more complex process of nation-building in Nigeria. In 1946 the aftermath of the strike, of Richards's authoritarian handling of constitutional reform, and of the NCNC recruiting tour seemed to have turned Nnamdi Azikiwe from an able political journalist into a formidable threat to Britain's West African constitutional strategy. 'Under a quiet and unassuming manner he conceals a passionate hatred of the British', Richards believed. 'On several occasions he has revealed paranoiac tendencies'. His trade union ally Imoudou seemed 'an agitator of the Hitler type'. But Richards was coming close to paranoia himself; the Communist contacts of which he accused the NCNC were either imaginary or superficial, and its leaders were still far from achieving nation-wide support, even among the urbanized populations whom Richards feared.[21] The size and cultural complexity of Nigeria made it far more difficult than in the Gold Coast to build a mass party, even on the plausible platform of populist nationalism.

In the first place, the NCNC had no common ideology. In 1946 young radicals anxious to fight colonial rule by direct action founded a 'Zikist' movement within the party; but they denied that this represented a personality cult, and Azikiwe's own relations with this militant tendency remained obscure. More serious was the long-familiar temptation for 'nationalist' politicians to emphasize ethnic identity and ethnic rivalries. Igbos, and other peoples of the south-east, took pride in the success with which they had grasped their broadening educational opportunities during the twentieth century; this made the Yorubas, who had long regarded themselves as educationally advanced and politically mature, fear that Igbos might dominate the centralized Nigerian state sought by the NCNC. In 1945 a group of mature students in London founded the *Egbe Ọmọ Oduduwa*, a society which aimed to approach Nigeria's cultural and political development through closer study of Yoruba experience; their leader, Obafemi Awolowo, published a book advocating a federal Nigeria built upon autonomous 'national groups'. In May 1948, when many West Africans had been stirred by the news from Accra, some prominent Lagos Yoruba established the *Egbe* in Nigeria, convening a conference at Ile-Ife under the presidency of the chief who symbolized the spiritual unity of all children of Oduduwa, the Yoruba ancestor-god. Violent clashes between Yorubas and Igbos in Lagos followed, giving warning of conflicts to come.

But the most serious obstacle to nationalist unity was the historic division, as in Sudan in some ways exacerbated by British administrative policies, between the southern provinces and the Muslim-dominated North, which contained over half Nigeria's population and covered three quarters of its territory. The social control of the Muslim aristocracy originally entrenched by the *jihads* of the early nineteenth century had in many ways hardened under British over-rule. Although the extreme conservative school of British administrators, who wished to establish 'Native States' free from any interference by southern politicians, had been decisively defeated,*

---

*Not all may have recognized defeat. As late as 1956 Brian Sharwood Smith, Governor of the Northern Region, is said to have suggested that Lennox-Boyd should work for an independent North: 'like Jordan – Muslim and friendly'. (J. N. Paden, *Ahmadu Bello*, 1986, p. 222).

some officials still encouraged powerful Emirs in their hostility towards southern nationalists. Such meetings as the 1946 NCNC delegation was able to hold in northern towns were largely attended by immigrant clerks and traders from the south, or by the substantial non-Muslim minorities encapsulated within the Region. Only a few Muslim school-teachers showed much interest in Nigerian politics, and the declared aims of the first political organization which they founded in December 1949, the Northern Peoples' Congress (NPC), were to enhance the authority of the natural rulers and assist them to enlighten the commoners. Nkrumah, of course, faced retarded national consciousness in the northern Gold Coast, but not such a powerfully active and cohesive force.

Despite nationalist suspicions, the British government did not intend to use that force to prevent eventual self-government, or to create a Jordan or Pakistan. Their aim was, by devolving powers from Lagos, to build structures within which Nigeria might move to independence as a strong federal state; and to ensure that, despite its educational backwardness, the North should enjoy the full influence to which its population entitled it within that state. But it was assumed that – despite the existence within its boundaries of important non-Muslim peoples like the Tiv, and Muslim polities distinct from the authority of Sokoto, like Borno – the North would remain a single entity whose leaders would be entitled to a dominant position within independent Nigeria. This crucial assumption may reflect a deliberate intention to exercise some form of neo-colonial control through conservative Emirs, though it can also be explained by sheer administrative inertia in face of the difficulties of dismembering a political formation to which Emirs and officials were almost equally attached. But whatever the hidden agenda, British policy was to maintain Nigeria as a unity. One official, not displeased that the formation of the *Egbe* seemed a rebuff to Azikiwe, nevertheless deplored 'the element of separatism which cuts across what I conceive to be our traditional policy of the unification of Nigeria', and feared it might set a bad example to the North.[22] And if Richards may have emphasized divisions among Nigerians as a means of weakening the NCNC, such tactics were rejected by his successor, Sir John Macpherson, and by the new Chief Secretary Hugh Foot, a Cornish radical whose sincere commitment to African progress impressed all who met him.

From his arrival in Nigeria in 1947 Foot worked hard to win the personal trust of political leaders and to engage Nigerians from all parties in concrete programmes of improvement. In March 1948 the

Legislative Council meetings were held in Kaduna, to emphasize Northern responsibility in Nigerian affairs; 'the trend of the debates', Foot reported, 'indicated that the thinking leaders of Nigeria are moving rapidly to the conception of a federal state'.[23] Soon afterwards Azikiwe was appointed to a Commission with the important and popular task of expediting Nigerianization of the public services; the opening of University College, Ibadan, later that year confirmed the improvement in career expectations for the young. In August Macpherson, prompted by events in the Gold Coast, took the initiative in announcing a review of the Richards constitution; but instead of establishing a Coussey-like committee Foot persuaded the Nigerian members of the Legislative Council to proceed 'by way of village meetings and divisional meetings and provincial meetings throughout the country'.[24] Debate of this sort was highly esteemed in the political cultures of southern Nigeria, and large sections of the future electorate were drawn into direct dialogue with the colonial government.

That the humane good sense of Macpherson and Foot had kept the political initiative in British hands was confirmed in November 1949, when police opened fire during an industrial dispute at the government's Enugu colliery and killed twenty-one miners. Although this was a human tragedy on the scale of Accra, its political consequences were relatively minor. Macpherson appointed a Commission, including two Nigerian members, with relevant expertise; this discounted alarmist rumours of communist influence, criticized the conduct of the police, and made practical recommendations to improve the conduct of industrial relations.[25] Although the shooting had been followed by riots in four east Nigerian towns, and attempts by Zikist radicals to politicize the unions, Azikiwe himself strongly condemned their attitudes; and in 1950 after an attempt to assassinate Foot, the Zikist Movement was banned with little public dissent.

By 1951 Foot's consultations culminated in a somewhat contentious 'General Conference', whose recommendations had effects which Nkrumah had avoided in the Gold Coast: the restraining influences of chiefs and local notables from West and North provided constitutional checks against the rise of populist nationalism. But if some NCNC leaders felt cheated, they could never have emulated the success of the CPP in a country which contained such diverse political cultures. The Macpherson constitution formalized the political identity of the three existing Regions, giving each an Assembly based on complex systems of indirect election and manhood suffrage, and an Executive Council, with Nigerian Ministers taking over responsibility for such major functions as education, development planning, and local government. The British decolonizers had managed their consultations so well that Macpherson and the Colonial Office were able, without arousing strong adverse comment, to disregard a Conference recommendation that Federal and Regional Ministers should be elected by their legislatures, and to emphasize that Governors retained continuing responsibilities for good government. It was, wrote Macpherson, 'impracticable to leave to the hazard of popular election the choice of men for office requiring ability, integrity and tact' – and still practicable publicly to uphold the values of constitutional balance against those of popular sovereignty.[26]

But even if there was no Nigerian CPP capable of enforcing its choice of Ministers at federal level, natural majority parties quickly emerged in each Region. In the East it was the NCNC; in the West the Action Group, political heir to the *Egbe Ọmọ Oduduwa*, achieved a less secure supremacy; in the North the NPC developed as an avowedly regional party, sustained by the power of the Muslim aristocracy. The central legislature and executive were constituted by delegations from each Region; but it was soon clear that the real gains in patronage and power had fallen to those who controlled the Regional executives, and that united action at the centre was difficult to achieve. Following conflicts in the Federal Council of Ministers, Lyttelton somewhat petulantly informed the British Cabinet in May 1953 that

> the collapse of the cumbrous constitution established under the auspices of the Labour Government has provided an opportunity of according a larger measure of autonomy to the 14 million Moslem inhabitants of the Northern Provinces who were more favourably disposed to this country than the Southern Nigerians.[27]

He therefore convened a constitutional conference in London on 30 July.

Lyttelton seems to have found Nigerian politicians not uncongenial, and his own 'frank and brutal' approach went down better than many expected. At one point the conference seemed near breakdown, and Lyttelton prepared a Cabinet paper which, presumably because of its hard words, is still withheld from public scrutiny; but eventually, after a further session in Lagos, Nigerians were led to accept compromises in order to ensure continued constitutional progress.[28] Substantial powers were reserved to a remodelled federal government, but the most important changes were to extend the autonomy of the three Regions, each of which was authorized to request full internal self-government from 1956. It is not clear how quickly Lyttelton intended the independence of Nigeria to follow.

In June 1948 an official publication defined the goal of British policy as 'to guide the Colonial territories to responsible self-government within the Commonwealth'.[29] With three major African countries proceeding more rapidly in this direction than formerly expected, possible difficulties in the application of that policy began to appear. One problem was how to decide when the process of guidance could be judged complete. While Africans, often quoting British mentors, increasingly claimed self-government as their natural right, British mandarins regarded it as a skill which it was their duty to impart through prolonged apprenticeships. The Watson Committee, for example, had proposed very exacting conditions of 'preparedness'. But most such discussions remained interesting exercises in political theory; as the Cabinet Secretary warned Attlee in July 1950, criteria of administrative competence or political maturity usually proved elastic under political pressure.[30]

A more serious obstacle to a smooth procession towards self-government was the problem of the 'viability' of small or poor colonies which Moyne had discerned in 1941. In 1949 a committee of distinguished academics, diluted at Attlee's suggestion by 'practical administrators' and two MPs, was appointed to consider whether alternative constitutional goals for such territories might be devised. After two years' work the Committee's modest but 'un-English' proposals failed to carry conviction with colonial governors, let alone with African nationalists.[31] The problem would eventually be solved by default; when in the 1960s it became expedient to abandon such colonies, criteria of viability would prove equally elastic.

A third difficulty, perceived by Attlee as early as 1947, was also inconclusively addressed by this committee: that of incorporating an indefinite number of self-governing states into the loose and personalized structures of the Commonwealth. Until the Second World War, most Englishmen had regarded that body as an association of pale-skinned governments, sharing many common characteristics of culture, language and race, with sufficient community of interest to make close political and economic collaboration at least theoretically attainable. It seems that the Commonwealth Relations Office of 1947 did not unreservedly welcome Nehru and Jinnah into this white man's club; certainly many politicians and officials were taken aback when they realized that the Colonial Office would eventually be sponsoring an indefinite number of further applications. One immediate reaction was to suggest some form of two-tier Commonwealth, within which African governments which failed to meet those undefined criteria of political maturity and viability might be accommodated. But in 1954 another committee of officials under Norman Brook considered the political embarrassments which would follow any attempt to offer Nkrumah's Ghana second-tier status; and Conservative Ministers, if not wholly persuaded by Brook's rhetorical optimism about the economic, political and military prospects of an expanding multiracial Commonwealth, accepted full Ghanaian membership as unavoidable. The awkward questions of what limits should be set to this enlargement, and what effect new African members would have on the position of South Africa, were once again deferred.[32]

While these issues of principle were being inconclusively discussed at the highest levels of government, the Colonial Office continued to conduct much current business on the assumption that on independence African colonies *would* be able to remain within the Commonwealth. From 1948 it was assumed that the third West African colony, Sierra Leone, should be guided constitutionally in the same direction as the Gold Coast and Nigeria, if more slowly. The first step was to break a local deadlock by rejecting claims to entrenched political privileges being made on behalf of the Krio community – though this included many empire loyalists with talents and training which might have made them natural partners in any 'neo-colonial' plan of decolonization. But the ageing leaders of the National Council of Sierra Leone (with whom Wallace-Johnson was now uneasily allied) displayed unyielding legalistic particularism in their relations with the spokesmen who were beginning to emerge from hitherto rather somnolent rural areas in the Protectorate, and in 1951 the Colonial Office lost patience and imposed its own constitution. The Legislative Council was reconstituted with an African majority, composed largely of chiefs chosen by the new District Councils; and Ministers nominated by the Sierra Leone Peoples' Party began to assume departmental duties. Even in the Gambia the responsibilities of elected Councillors were extended, though full independence for a population equivalent to that of a small British city was as yet expected by nobody.

In eastern Africa progress on the lines envisaged in 1947 was more tentative. Some believed that here the problem of creating viable entities might be solved by the closer union of neighbouring colonies; but on what basis such unions might be attempted, and into whose hands power might eventually be transferred, were highly contentious issues.

BRITISH EAST AFRICA: SETTLERS, IMPROVERS AND FREEDOM FIGHTERS

At the 1947 governors' conference Sir Philip Mitchell had voiced the opinion of his colleagues in East Africa that their region was so different from West Africa that Cohen's decolonization strategy was not only premature but wholly inappropriate. Mitchell saw his primary duty to Kenya Africans as the promotion of improvement in their social and economic conditions; this would require continuing inflows of European settlers and European capital, as well as a gradual, discreet, recovery by the colonial state of powers which the settlers had acquired during the war. Reforms in local government were judged far more important than extended African representation in Legislative Councils; the few black faces present there seemed to symbolize the isolation of African constitutionalists rather than any prospect that they would eventually inherit real power.

Certainly more Africans were worried about land than about representation, nowhere more so than among the Kikuyu people of Kenya. Early in the century European settlers had secured titles to lands which, even if not then under cultivation, were part of the Kikuyu patrimony. Post-war European immigration, combined with African population growth, increased pressure to reduce the cultivation and stock rights of the 200,000 squatters who had remained on these lands as a conveniently accessible labour force. At the same time discontent was also caused by well-meaning attempts, under postwar development plans, to improve agricultural productivity in the African reserves. The more commercially-minded peasant farmers (many of whom were also government-appointed chiefs) having shared in wartime prosperity, were often willing collaborators in attempts by zealous colonial improvers to reduce cattle-stocks, enforce veterinary controls, or counter soil erosion by elaborate terracing. But many improvements were labour-intensive, and the additional labour was often not provided willingly – especially when, as with short-based forms of terracing, it appeared that the experts had over-estimated its cost-effectiveness to the poorer farmers who were required to do the work.

The political elite who had formed the KAU aimed to become the central channel through which such popular discontents were expressed. Like Nkrumah, Jomo Kenyatta regarded himself as a natural leader of frustrated aspirants – harassed farmers, returning soldiers, ambitious students – but it seems he might have been initially satisfied to act as the government's accredited African conscience within a developing constitutional framework. But if Mitchell was to hold the settlers in check, he could not associate too closely with African populists. By 1947 the KAU was widely regarded as ineffective, both in Kikuyuland and the Highlands and among the growing impoverished proletariat of Nairobi and Mombasa. Following a dock-strike in the latter town a militant African Workers' Federation was formed under Kikuyu leadership, and in 1950 there were violent clashes during a strike by low-paid workers in the capital. Leaders of the old underground KCA were already trying to unify Kikuyu resistance by secret use of traditional oaths, but their influence was now being eclipsed by younger militants – ex-servicemen of the so-called 'Forty Group', squatters displaced by settler expansion, and most notably the Nairobi trade unionists Fred Kubai and Bildad Kaggia, who took over and radicalized the KAU. A new central committee, administering a much stronger oath to larger numbers of Kikuyu, became a dominant power in the Nairobi locations, and rapidly extended its popular support in Central Province and among squatters in the Highlands. By mid-1952 outbreaks of arson, cattle-maiming, and personal violence, predominantly directed against Kikuyu supporters of official policies, were so widespread that the administration was losing control over much of Kikuyuland; after delay caused by a change of governor a State of Emergency was declared in October. During two years of intensive military operations in the forests, followed by five of serious guerrilla warfare, the British government found itself faced with an elusive enemy known by the name of Mau Mau.

Historians still find it difficult to understand the nature of this insurrection, which in the obscurity of its origins and the apparently indiscriminate direction of its violence most closely resembles the Madagascan revolt of 1947. European contemporaries, sickened by the nature of oathing ceremonies as well as the bloody atrocity of many attacks, spoke angrily about its 'bestial atavism'. Anthropologists, seeing that the violence was a product of present grievances rather than of any atavistic past, interpreted Mau Mau as 'not a reversion to ancient rituals but a regression deriving power from the breach of universal taboos'.[33] Later commentators gave more weight to the political and social context of revolt; by 1960 even an extremely hostile official historian could see Mau Mau as 'the violent manifestation of a limited nationalistic revolutionary movement'.[34] Some African writers hailed it forthrightly as a struggle for national liberation; but since participation was largely confined to Kikuyu (with the neighbouring Embu and Meru) – and since nearly 2000 African civilians were killed, as against thirty-two Europeans and twenty-six Asians[35] – such a view raises problems about the nature of the modern Kenyan nation. Perhaps the least unsatisfactory way to slot Mau Mau into typologies of insurrection is as a tribally-based peasant revolt originally formed on the fringe of a nationalist movement.

It is not easy to see what objectives the leaders of Mau Mau hoped to secure; what they did in fact indirectly achieve was a profound re-orientation of British policy. The 'Imperial factor' returned to Kenya in the shape of the British army, whose commanders worked with Governor Baring to co-ordinate political and military responses to the revolt. In order to win African confidence and provide a wider basis for future economic development, the government hastened the adoption of new agricultural policies, designed to encourage the influence of enterprising yeoman farmers with secure titles to land and African businessmen desiring orderly capitalist development. Kenya was still seen as a multiracial society, but with considerable changes in its racial balance. Despite their services during the Emergency the settlers had become more of a liability than an asset in Britain's Imperial balance-sheet; although some of them were slow to understand this, their hopes of inheriting power were doomed. Moreover, British tax-payers began to take more interest in a colony where control was costing money, and lives of National Servicemen. The security forces had won some of their victories only by methods of terror and counter-violence which began to attract political criticism in the UK.

These conflicts in Kenya tended to overshadow political developments in other East African territories during the postwar years. Pursuing its search for large and viable units, the Colonial Office in 1948 created an East African High Commission to control certain common services, with a Legislative Assembly drawn from the three mainland territories; originally Europeans, Asians and Africans were to have equal representation, and when Kenya settlers secured a revision in their favour African fears were everywhere sharpened. The islands of Zanzibar and Pemba, where British authority rested on treaties of protection with an Arab Sultanate, were necessarily excluded from this association. Here the ruling Arab oligarchy appeared to retain sufficient support among the African majority for the British to proceed, without too much fear of communal conflict, towards such measures of self-government as seemed appropriate for a community of under 300,000 people. But in Tanganyika and Uganda Africans became increasingly anxious about what terms of 'partnership' the British rulers of East Africa might have in view.

Although the European community in Tanganyika did not have the self-confidence or cultural coherence of the Kenya settlers (many of them were of German or Greek origin), a more closely united East Africa might have helped them to consolidate their power. Under Governor Edward Twining (1949–58) they benefited from the political arithmetic of parity: from 1952 20,000 Europeans, 80,000 Asians and eight million Africans each had ten representatives in a Legislative Council still controlled by an official majority. In retrospect it seems curious that, less than ten years before independence, the Colonial Office should expect African acquiescence in such privileges for the 'immigrant' communities. But the emerging political consciousness of most Africans still seemed largely focused on local horizons – on expanding co-operative enterprise to take advantage of rising export prices, on criticizing the attempts of colonial reformers to restructure local government or direct the course of agricultural improvement, on resisting new European settlement around Mounts Kilimanjaro and Meru. It seemed reasonable to hope that local improvers would recognize the advantage of encouraging Europeans and Asians to invest their capital, enterprise and technical skills in the country's development.

In an attempt to deflect these local leaders from nationalist politics, the government in 1953 forbade its employees to join the Tanganyika African Association. Nevertheless in that same year Julius Nyerere, a young graduate of Edinburgh University, became President of that still somewhat diffuse body, and began to turn it into a party of populist nationalism analogous to Nkrumah's CPP. He enjoyed a few advantages. Tanganyika's trusteeship status gave Nyerere access to a platform at the UN, which kept Tanganyika before the eyes of the world and Nyerere before the eyes of Tanganyikans. And internally, the very heterogeneity of the African population made it less difficult to create a national consciousness out of seeds planted among the various 'primary nations'; no single ethnic group threatened to dominate, and the Swahili language provided a *lingua franca* free from implications of favouritism. In 1954 the African Association was transformed into the Tanganyika African National Union

(TANU), and under its able President began the work, not of demanding an immediate transfer of power which Nyerere knew he was not ready to receive, but of preparing the country for independence under an accredited national leadership. But it was not, at that time, clear how quickly such a programme might mature.

In Uganda the settler problem arose only indirectly, through fears of incorporation in some East African union; but relationships among African primary nations were more complex. Postwar reformers concentrated on local government, and on creating Provincial Councils which might eventually send representatives to the centre; meanwhile the Legislative Council was still constituted by racial arithmetic, with nominated representatives of 47,000 Asians and 6600 Europeans out-numbering (or from 1950 equalling) those of five million Africans. But not all centres of provincial politics had the same degree of historic identity; the kingdom of Buganda, while providing the base from which Christianity, western commerce and colonial control originally penetrated the country, had secured privileges which now became an obstacle to the colonial reformers' view of Uganda's future. In 1952 Cohen himself became governor, eager to guide the country towards self-government as a unitary parliamentary democracy; when Mutesa II, the sophisticated Kabaka, tried to withdraw Buganda from the jurisdiction of the central government, Cohen deported him. As in Sierra Leone, the British in their eagerness to establish a broadly representative successor government seemed ready to abandon traditional collaborators. But the Baganda formed not a diffuse 5 per cent but a compact 17 per cent of Uganda's population; among commoners as well as traditional elites Mutesa's defence of historic rights and privileges, as well as his evident distrust of the Conservative government's intentions as regards East African federation, found a good deal of support. In 1955 'King Freddie' was reinstated, receiving guarantees of a considerable degree of autonomy for Buganda in return for accepting integral participation in the future Ugandan state.

But the progress of that state towards self-government was complicated, even after ideas of East African federation had been finally dropped. Mutesa and his chiefs were still not truly reconciled to merging into a unitary Uganda, and continued to defend their own institutions. But now political consciousness developed rapidly among other peoples. Since 1952 a Uganda National Congress had been trying to establish itself as a national movement, calling like Nkrumah for 'self-government NOW'; in Buganda it drew some support from 'democratic populists' of the Bataka party, and elsewhere

133

acquired followers by identifying and espousing local causes. However this could be a divisive method, and Congress failed to establish truly national credentials. Whereas in Tanganyika the process of constitutional change would promote national unity through the activities of TANU, in Uganda it often intensified particularisms, and so prepared for future conflicts. Once the British government made it clear that Uganda could achieve self-government without a fight, contention as to how the powers of government should be distributed became increasingly acute.

SETTLER PRESSURE IN CENTRAL AFRICA

Although a few Conservative supporters in Great Britain had keenly supported the idea of an East African union under white leadership, the best prospects for any such extension of settler rule lay further south. In Southern Rhodesia pressure for independence came not from Africans but from a confident and expanding white community, whose belief that they had already been effectively decolonized in 1923 had been confirmed by the British government's failure to use its right to disallow certain legislation. From 1948 attitudes within Malan's government, as well as a tide of northward migration, suggested a growing danger of Southern Rhodesia's incorporation into the Union. Some liberal imperialists came to believe that the only alternative to an eventual extension of apartheid beyond the Limpopo might be to accept the closer union of Central Africa which these whites desired, while insisting on constitutional guarantees for African rights. The importance of Rhodesian mineral resources to the Imperial economy, the apparent absence of African political movements capable of inheriting power, and the lack of resources or will to impose stronger Imperial control, combined to make the notion of transferring power to liberally-minded settlers committed to inter-racial justice intellectually attractive, if not very realistic.

Closer union of the Rhodesias and Nyasaland, it was widely assumed, would be more efficient economically and administratively, though the likely distribution of benefits was rarely analysed. The main difficulty was the clear aim of most supporters to create a state in which white people would remain supreme, even if they asserted their supremacy rather less starkly than those ungentlemanly Afrikaners. Racial partnership, Huggins revealed in a celebrated indiscretion, would resemble that of horse and rider. African spokesmen in

Northern Rhodesia and Nyasaland quickly revealed deep misgivings, though these were less strong in Southern Rhodesia, where white supremacy already existed. But Huggins and Welensky, elected leaders of the settlers in south and north, used their access to the British government to preach the moral and material attractions of creating a new Dominion, whose African subjects would gradually receive wider political rights in proportion to their social and cultural progress. Labour Ministers, judging that the ascendency of these authoritarian paternalists might be less prejudicial to African interests than that of Malan, began to move to meet their desire for union on the compromise ground of Federation.

Arguments for Federation were marshalled in mid-1948 by H. N. Parry, a South African-born official of the Commonwealth Relations Office who had been appointed Secretary to the recently established Central African Council.[36] Besides the evident political attractions of creating a viable state under leadership sympathetic to the aims of Imperial policy, the economies of the three territories seemed neatly complementary: Northern Rhodesian copper could underwrite the enterprise of Southern Rhodesian settlers, and the resulting flows of capital and immigrants could provide resources for 'the moral and social advancement of Africans'. For British Ministers, the question was how far resources accumulated in Rhodesia *would* in fact be so applied. Creech Jones, supported by the judgement of Hailey and of missionaries and scholars who knew the region, was sceptical. Most of Huggins's constituents regarded Africans as Peter Pan children, entitled perhaps to controlled doles of parental favour but unlikely ever to achieve responsible adulthood; some post-war immigrants were even less liberal. Many who supported Federation as a road to independence did so precisely because it would exclude the danger of Black power which was now raising its head in West Africa. Some Labour Ministers sympathized, their racial prejudices proving stronger than their democratic principles; others knew that they had no power to impose the Gold Coast pattern. After the 1950 election Cohen decided that a multiracial federation was the most practicable way to continue the process of substituting consultation for control in Central Africa; and he tentatively persuaded James Griffiths, the deeply democratic trade unionist who became Colonial Secretary when Creech Jones lost his seat in 1950, to move in this direction. A committee of officials from the three territories and from the UK, chaired by G. H. Baxter of the CRO, concluded conditionally that a federal scheme would be the best form of 'closer association'; and in September 1951 Griffiths and Patrick Gordon-Walker of the CRO (who had returned from an African tour much worried by expanding South African influence) attended an inter-governmental conference at Victoria Falls.

For British Ministers the crucial issue was the risks of transferring power over Africans in Northern Rhodesia and Nyasaland into the hands of elected European settlers. It was not enough to insist that responsibility for African education, health, agriculture, local government, and other areas of 'Native Policy', would remain with the two Protectorate governments, and so ultimately with the Colonial Office; activities of the federal government would also impinge on African interests in many ways, and most African spokesmen doubted the effectiveness of the safeguard offered them – an African Affairs Board under a Federal Minister for African Interests. In 1949 a Nyasaland physician practising in Britain, Dr Hastings Banda, with Harry Nkumbula of Northern Rhodesia, prepared a memorandum expressing widely-held fears. Huggins and Welensky desperately sought more favourable African voices, but failed to convince Griffiths that the federal plan could be approved at that time. But shortly after the Victoria Falls conference the Labour Government was defeated in an election, and Lyttelton became Colonial Secretary.

As General Manager of the British Metals Corporation in the 1920s, Controller of Non-Ferrous Metals in 1939, and Chairman of Associated Electrical Industries since the war,[37] Lyttelton well understood the Imperial importance of the Copperbelt (which the post-Korea boom was bringing to its highest prosperity); as son of Joseph Chamberlain's successor at the Colonial Office he shared the illusion that liberally-minded British settlers could offer Africans a middle course between the conflicting nationalisms of Nkrumah and Malan. With a convinced Federalist at the Colonial Office, the new Parliament was easily persuaded. Welensky had already organized a powerful lobby which played on the assumption of conservative paternalists that white men could better judge the true interests of Africans in the world of modern capitalism than could Africans themselves. True, Fabian socialists and some Scottish churchmen continued to voice the growing fears and suspicions of articulate Africans; one important though unintended effect of the Federal proposal was to accelerate the growth of broadly-based African Congress movements in Northern Rhodesia and Nyasaland. But other Labour supporters were tempted by the argument that institutionalized multiracialism offered the best hope of development in countries where British trusteeship had not been notably progressive. There was much philosophizing about the political morality of race relations: surely proposals which the most reactionary third of Southern Rhodesian whites rejected as too liberal could not be wholly bad? Even though the safeguards proposed for African interests became somewhat eroded during a series of conferences boycotted by representative Africans, Parliament approved the establishment of the Federation of Rhodesia and Nyasaland in September 1953.

Under the successive Federal premierships of Huggins and Welensky, and that of Garfield Todd in Southern Rhodesia, some attempts were made to prove that Africans could benefit from their enforced partnership, and that the white minority would prove a worthy legatee of imperial trusteeship. By alleviating minor African grievances, Federalists hoped to encourage the gradual growth of a deferential African middle class willing to enter a political arena governed by European rules. The British government attached particular importance, and some financial support, to a University College in Salisbury, which it hoped would become both a model and a training-ground for multi-racialism; the sixty-eight full-time students admitted in 1957 included seven African men, one African woman, and one Asian. But there was only limited progress in reducing the prevalence of racial discrimination and insult, or the stark differentials in wages and working conditions on which European trade unions insisted, and none at all in removing the fundamental injustice of the Southern Rhodesian land settlement. Some extremely elaborate exercises in electoral arithmetic were introduced into both Federal and territorial constitutions, but none promised more than the slow access of privileged Africans to strictly controlled rations of political influence. As Lyttelton later reluctantly agreed, 'the Europeans sat still ... and made no progressive, or at least too hesitant, moves to engage Africans in a further share of the Government'.[38]

So the few African representatives in federal and territorial legislatures, dependent on white patronage for such influence as they might occasionally exercise, commanded little confidence among populations increasingly aware of what was happening elsewhere in Africa. From 1951 the essentially moderate leaders of the old Northern Rhodesian welfare societies united in their own African National Congress: not a strong or racial body at first, this grew in strength by articulating those fears of increasing settler power which were becoming widespread at both territorial and federal level. In Nyasaland too, where the ANC dated from 1944, local conflicts assumed wider significance in the climate of insecurity which Federation had created; both Protectorates saw a series of strikes, riots, boycotts, and other protests. In Southern Rhodesia, where Federation brought some minor improvements to middle-class Africans, there was less evident unrest; but from 1957, when constitutional amendments were enacted despite formal objections by the African Affairs Board, fears grew that the constitutional review which the British Government had fixed for 1960 would complete the transfer of power into settler hands. The ANC of Southern Rhodesia was reconstituted and Joshua Nkomo, hitherto a rather lonely spokesman of moderate protest, found himself drafted to the presidency of a more militant body. As the Conservative government in Britain appeared to maintain its confidence in the good intentions of Rhodesian whites, the growing evidence of African dissent increased the misgivings which their missionary and Labour critics had voiced since 1953. The rather uneasy political consensus which British politicians had achieved about methods of decolonization began to come into question.

CHANGING COURSE IN *AFRIQUE NOIRE*

Britain's readiness to adapt her policies to nationalist pressures in West Africa had consequences not only for her own East African dependencies but for neighbouring French colonies. As has already been noted, 1947 saw the beginning of a general hardening of French policy. The government of Robert Schuman, facing rebellions in Indo-China and Madagascar as well as intensified Cold War in Europe, began to identify colonial nationalism with international communism, thus inducing increased American support in Asia. And these developments, following France's wartime eviction from Syria and Lebanon, increased the determination of settlers and soldiers in North Africa to make no concessions to Arab nationalism. Only in Tunisia was there perceptible, but slight, movement towards local autonomy. The promised reforms in Algeria were largely aborted, while in Morocco the Sultanate began to emerge as a possible focus of resistance. After riots in Casablanca in April 1947 (not apparently politically inspired) were bloodily suppressed with the use of Black African troops, Sultan Mohamed V made a speech in the international city of Tangier which appeared to call for the unification of Morocco within the Arab world, and to offer veiled encouragement to the Istiqlal. The French response was to replace a reforming Resident, Erik Labonne, with the authoritarian General Juin, who quickly made it clear that independence for the Maghreb was not on any French agenda.

In Black Africa, that word was not even on the agenda of African politicians, who were therefore allowed to enjoy a little more freedom of action, while reaping advantages from the French programmes of social and economic development. Between 1947 and 1951 the West African territories claimed an average annual growth of Gross National Product of 13.8 per cent;[39] and although much of the benefit accrued to foreign firms and expatriate officials, members of that African elite whose collaboration might open the way to a gradual decolonization of relationships within the French Union also received a share. But this did not have the desired political consequences. Such gratitude to France as the beneficiaries experienced was offset by their increasing awareness of claims and grievances of their own constituents. Political parties formed to contest elections inevitably took up the causes of their strongest potential supporters – trade unionists in Guinea, farmers in Ivory Coast, Sufite orders in Senegal, Muslim reformers in French Soudan. Simultaneously the leaders became conscious of common interests with one another, and with Africans elsewhere.

Such Pan-African tendencies were not confined to those parties which had joined the RDA, nor to the railwaymen who showed such inter-colonial solidarity during the strike of 1947-48. The prize exhibit of French assimilationists was Leopold Senghor, the Senegalese philosopher and poet whose mastery of the French language qualified him to help draft the constitution of the Fourth Republic. But when in 1948 Senghor edited an anthology of French poetry by Black writers, heralded by Jean-Paul Sartre as 'the only great revolutionary poetry of our time', this was immediately recognized as a manifesto of *négritude*, a call to Black people to look to their own cultural resources. In a key text Senghor's friend Aimé Césaire, Communist Deputy for Martinique, challenged western emphases on material achievement by exalting the intuitive values of suffering peoples 'who never invented anything, never explored anything, never subdued anything'.[40] But this by no means implied their continuing passivity; Senghor was re-orienting his political as well as his cultural activity. In the same year he resigned from the French Socialist Party, which had shared governmental responsibility during the railway strike, to form the *Bloc Démocratique Sénégalais* (BDS). By alliances with *grands marabouts* of both Muridiyya and

Tijaniyya orders the new party secured widespread, if often passive, support in rural Senegal for Senghor's elegant ideas of a distinctively African socialism.

Such rebellions against French cultural and political tutelage were inevitably encouraged by the progress of populist nationalism in British Africa. In February 1948 the French Foreign Ministry, worried by reports of a planned Pan-African Congress in Lagos as well as by pressures at the UN, suggested developing their *entente* with Britain by a thorough exchange of political intelligence, and a common publicity campaign to convince world opinion of meritorious colonial developments under way. The Red Scare triggered by the Accra riots made British diplomatists sympathetic, despite fears of appearing to 'gang up' with less enlightened colonialists.[41] But it was as a nationalist, not as a communist, that Nkrumah challenged French policy; by 1949 his example was leading members of the RDA, in private, to envisage possibilities of independence for the first time.[42] Henri Laurentie, retiring as Political director of the Overseas Ministry, noted that neither France nor Britain would be able to satisfy the legitimate economic expectations of Africans, and suggested to Cohen that they might try through inter-colonial co-operation to initiate some alternative pan-African initiative from above. Failing this, pressures from inside and outside would lead to 'the anarchic emancipation of Africa, which would necessarily bring with it at least a partial loss of authority both for Britain and for France, and the disorderly intervention of the United States into the continent'.[43] But French and British priorities continued to diverge; it was too late to undo the damage which the protagonists of the nineteenth-century partition had inflicted on Africa, and on themselves.

French policy seemed most vulnerable in the Ivory Coast, both because Houphouet's PDCI was the strongest local section of the RDA, and because many Ivoirians had kinsmen in the ebullient Gold Coast. Nkrumah, himself a son of the Nzima borderland, visited Abijan in September 1948, where he was reported to have conferred with Houphouet before travelling to meet other RDA leaders in Guinea.[44] But even before these contacts, or Barbé's fraternal mission, a tough administrator, Laurent Péchoux, had been promoted Governor with instructions to break the RDA. Already the French had reduced Houphouet's influence by detaching Upper Volta as a separate colony and ensuring a favourable election result there in June 1948; they now attacked his supporters in the Ivory Coast proper, intervening heavily in local rural politics as well as in the towns. Péchoux's *chef de cabinet* warned his British neighbours that the RDA aimed at 'a Communist Ivory Coast in a Communist *Union française*', and was trying systematically to undermine the public confidence on which all colonial authority depended.[45] The socialist High Commissioner Béchard agreed that the RDA, 'following the trail of the *Mouvement de Rénovation Malgache* and of the Viet Minh' had become 'a fundamentally anti-French and xenophobic movement'.[46]

So 1949 was a year of violent 'incidents' in the Ivory Coast. Administrators, cheered on by racialist settlers, used the security forces to settle disputes between the RDA and its local opponents, which their own evident partiality had often provoked. But resistance continued to grow. By January 1950 more than fifty Africans had been killed, and over three thousand gaoled, in a series of strikes, boycotts and demonstrations which challenged colonial authority far more seriously than the 1948 disorders in the Gold Coast. The climax came in February with a ban on RDA meetings throughout Africa. Houphouet himself escaped arrest only through his immunity as a member of the French parliament – a benefit of assimilation denied Nkrumah and other anglophone leaders.

Yet in 1947 the National Assembly *had* lifted the immunity of the Malgache Deputies; the breadth of support for the RDA was leading the French to make more careful distinctions among nationalists. A rapid enquiry by two colonial inspectors emphasized the urgent need to recapture the confidence of Ivoirians; their report emphasized the bitterness with which the people still recalled the forced-labour system, their gratitude to Houphouet for its abolition, and the extent to which the authorities had lost touch with their subjects. Meanwhile the National Assembly despatched its own Commission of Enquiry, with Gabriel Lisette (an Antillais who represented Chad as an RDA Deputy) as Secretary; this assembled a mass of interesting testimony, though its promised analysis of events never followed.[47] By July 1950, when René Pleven became Prime Minister, he realized that the new order he believed he had helped institute at Brazzaville was in danger of collapse.

So the French gradually withdrew from this dangerous and unnecessary confrontation. Soon after Pleven took office his colonial adviser, P. H. Siriex, was approached by Raphael Saller, an important intermediary in Franco-African relations. A Frenchman from Martinique who was present at Brazzaville as Governor of Jibuti, Saller successively became Pleven's *chef de cabinet* and Director of Development Planning in the Ministry of Overseas

France; since 1948 he had represented Guinea in the French upper House, and now claimed to speak on behalf of African parliamentarians outside the RDA. (He would later become one of Houphouet's Ministers in the Ivory Coast). Saller's message was that the African traders and planters who had founded the PDCI were becoming frightened by the confrontation, and would be able to persuade Houphouet, against opposition from Secretary-General Gabriel d'Arboussier, to break the RDA's compromising alliance with communism. Pleven, and President Auriol, thereupon encouraged Houphouet to negotiate a rapprochement with the new Overseas Minister, François Mitterand. Measures against the colour-bar and electoral reforms were introduced; Mitterand took Houphouet under his wing during a visit to the Ivory Coast, and posted Péchoux off to Togo; in return the RDA changed its parliamentary affiliation from the communists to the UDSR, a small party to which both Pleven and Mitterand belonged. France's change in course, primarily motivated by the evidence of popular support for the RDA, was thus facilitated by a temporary conjuncture of domestic politics.

It also signalled a greater readiness to distinguish between African nationalism and international communism. Having used anti-communist arguments to enlist American support against the Viet Minh, Frenchmen found Americans showing an uncomfortable eagerness to combat communism in other colonies. Robert Delavignette, the colonial reformer who had succeeded Laurentie, feared that the USA might take advantage of France's weakness in Asia to 'intervene in Africa by means of economic investments which will lead to political control',[48] and resolved to keep the decolonization process there under French control. When in September 1950 an American delegation led by Assistant Secretary of State George McGhee catechized French officials about the Red peril, they were assured that the social basis for communism in Black Africa was weak and that France had the situation well in hand. The answer to the danger of nationalists being led to accept communist leadership, the political director of the Quai d'Orsay declared, was

> to persuade the native groups (a) that their aspirations for self government [can] be realized within the framework of the French Union, and (b) that their best interests, materially and otherwise, lie in close co-operation with France.[49]

Although independence still seemed unacceptable, experience since Brazzaville had brought French officials to recognize that there was something to be said for the Anglo-Saxon conception of 'self-government' – particularly if government was to be exercised by men as sympathetic to a capitalist economy and a French connection as Houphouet and the rising Ivoirian bourgeoisie had now become.

Following this tactical re-regrouping, the French appeared to be more fully in control of their West African colonies than their British neighbours. A former Colonial Office official who had turned to academic study of French practice noted in 1950 that, in the absence of any attempt to encourage representative local government, old authoritarian structures and methods remained largely unchanged.[50] Even in the Ivory Coast, official pressure and fraud deprived the RDA of one of its two seats in the parliamentary election of 1951, and in more remote colonies like Mauritania, Niger and Chad local commandants, through their chosen collaborators, still had effective control of election results. But elsewhere the French faced new African leaders with authentic power-bases, notably Sékou Touré, a Guinean trade union leader influenced by French communists. A two-month strike in 1953 ensured that a progressive Labour Code enacted by the National Assembly over settler objections was at least partially implemented in Guinea. When in the same year Sékou Touré was elected to the Guinean Assembly as RDA member for a rural constituency, the French were obliged to recognize that his collaboration might become a necessary condition for their control of this colony.

External pressures also ensured that the French could not stand still. Besides the American insistence on containing communism by timely concessions to nationalism, the General Assembly of the United Nations was still attempting to extend its competence under Chapter XI of the Charter. And although its interventions in colonies were only rhetorical, in the Trust territories of Togo and Cameroun the United Nations offered Africans practical means of influencing French policy.

The first Africans to appreciate this were the Ewe, an enterprising people with networks of kinship and commerce across three colonial boundaries, whose sense of national identity had been sharpened by experience of colonial partition. There were at least 174,000 Ewe in French Togo, 137,000 in British Togoland, 376,000 in the Gold Coast proper, as well as cognate peoples in Dahomey. From 1946 many Ewe petitions began to reach the UN; objectives varied, but initially the strongest demand was for a self-governing, united, Eweland under temporary British tutelage. The Trusteeship Council, half of which was nominated by colonial powers, was tending to become an 'areopagus of retired Governors-General',[51] and responded cautiously; by 1951 the Ewe were therefore re-directing their petitions towards the Fourth Committee of the Assembly, with its growing anti-colonial majority. But the content of petitions also began to change, reflecting divisions among Ewe leaders; more now demanded unification of the two Trust territories, non-Ewe peoples included. But as Nkrumah's CPP gained support in Togoland, demands for integration with independent Ghana became even stronger, and attractive to anti-colonialists at the UN. To prevent such sentiments spreading among their own subjects, the rulers of French Togo had to concede reforms which, if honestly implemented, would lead to some form of controlled self-government for this small territory.

Meanwhile the possibility of attacking French colonialism through the United Nations had also been perceived by Ruben Um Nyobé, a shrewd and dedicated patriot influenced by Marxism, who as leader of the *Union des Populations du Cameroun* (UPC) since 1948 was a Vice-President of the RDA. Despite fierce administrative harassment the UPC refused to follow Houphouet by moderating its radical nationalism after 1950, but continued to build support among those Camerounian peoples most directly affected by development projects. The leaders' primary aim was to secure complete independence from France; but to broaden its appeals to the General Assembly it also embraced demands already raised in the British Trust territory for reunification of the former German Kamerun. By 1952 Um Nyobé was securing an international audience for challenges to colonialism which could not be reconciled so easily as those of Houphouet.

NOTES AND REFERENCES

1. *Empire* (Journal of the Fabian Colonial Bureau) 10 May 1948, p. 1
2. Colonial No 231 Report of the Commission of Enquiry into Disturbances in the Gold Coast, 1948, p. 24
3. *Ibid.* p. 26
4. The Coussey Committee proposals are in Colonial No 248 Gold Coast: Report to His Excellency the Governor by the Committee on Constitutional Reform, 1949. The Committee's preference, by one vote, for a two-chamber legislature was not endorsed by the Colonial Secretary, and consequential changes were made in the electoral structure. Otherwise the main departure from the Coussey proposals is described below
5. CO 537/3033 Minute by Cohen (copy) 17 June 1948

6. PREM 8/924 Creech Jones to Attlee, 4 Oct., Norman Brook to Attlee, 12 Oct. 1949
7. Colonial No 250 Gold Coast: Statement by His Majesty's Government on Constitutional Reform, 14 Oct. 1949, p. 9. cf CAB 129/36 Pt 2, CP (49) 199, Memo by Creech Jones, 8 Oct. 1949: CAB 128/16, CM 58(49)3, 13 Oct. 1949
8. L. B. Namier, *Monarchy and the Party System* (Oxford, 1952)
9. R. Saloway, 'The new Gold Coast' *International Affairs* XXXI 1955, pp. 470–1; K. Nkrumah, *Autobiography* (Edinburgh, 1957) pp. 115–17
10. Co 96/827/31648, Arden-Clarke to Cohen, Pte, 28 Jan. 1950
11. R. Rathbone, 'The Government of the Gold Coast after the Second World War', AF.AFF 67 1968. For the 1951 election, D. Austin, *Politics in Ghana* (1970) Ch. 3
12. FCB Box 81 File 2. ff. 83–88 Hyde-Clarke to Nicholson, 17 Nov. 1953
13. C. L. R. James, *Nkrumah and the Gold Coast Revolution*, (1977) pp. 156–7
14. CAB 129/61 C(53)154, Memo by Lyttelton, 'Constitutional Developments in the Gold Coast and Nigeria', 13 May 1953: CAB 129/62 C(53)244, Memo by Lyttelton, 4 Sept. 1953
15. CAB 129/66 C(54)62, Memo by Lyttelton 18 Feb. 1954. For the Braimah case, Austin, *Politics in Ghana* pp. 164–7
16. CAB 129/71 C(54)306, Memo by Lennox-Boyd, 1 Oct. 1954.
17. R. Rathbone, 'Businessmen in Politics: Party Struggle in Ghana, 1949–57', *Journal of Development Studies* 9 1973 pp. 391–401
18. CAB 128/30 Pt 1 Cabinet Minute 20 (6) 6 March 1956: Pt 2 Cabinet Minute 64 (2) 11 Sept. 1956. CAB 129/83 CP(56)204 Memo by Lennox-Boyd, 29 Aug. 1956
19. Sargent to Howe, 18 Feb. 1949, quoted Louis, *Middle East* p. 702
20. CAB 129/61 C(53)154 Memo by Lyttelton, 13 May 1954
21. CO 583/277/30658, Richards to Hill, Secret, 9 Aug. 1946, encl. Report on NCNC
22. CO 583/287/30453/3, Minute by Webber, 21 May 1948
23. CO 583/287/30453/4, Foot to Cohen, Conf. 30 July 1948
24. Speech by Foot, 11 March 1949, quoted K. Ezera, *Constitutional Developments in Nigeria* (Cambridge, 1960) p. 106
25. Colonial No. 256. Report of the Commission of Enquiry into the Disorders in the Eastern Provinces of Nigeria, November 1949. (1950)
26. CO 537/7166, Macpherson to Cohen, 15 May 1951: cf. Ezera, pp. 120–1
27. CAB 128/26 Pt 1 Cabinet Minute 27 May 1953 (6)
28. CAB 128/26 Pt 2 Cabinet Minute 18 Aug. 1953 (5) refers to a Memo by Lyttelton C(53)235 of 17 Aug. which will not be available in the PRO until 2004. For a revealing sketch of the conferences by the chairman, *The Memoirs of Lord Chandos* (1962) pp. 408–17
29. P.P. 1947–8 XI Cmd 7433. The Colonial Empire, 1947–1948
30. Brook to Attlee, 17 July 1950, quoted Morgan V, p. 47
31. CO 967/42, Cabinet Commonwealth Affairs Committee: Memo by Creech Jones, 8 Dec. 1948; minute by Attlee 15 Feb. 1949. cf. Morgan V, pp. 32–50
32. CAB 129/71 C(54)307, Commonwealth Membership: Memo by Swinton, 30 Sept. 1954; report by Norman Brook's Committee 21 June 1954. CAB

128/27 Pt II, Cabinet Minute 7 Dec. 1954 (83) Morgan V, pp. 50–66
33. For an illuminating example see Max Gluckman, 'Mau Mau Secret Rituals' *Manchester Guardian Weekly* 25 March 1954, and the reply by Sir Philip Mitchell on 20 May
34. P.P. 1959–60 X Cmnd 1030. F. D. Corfield, Historical Survey of the Origins and Growth of Mau Mau
35. HEA, Vol. III, pp. 132–3
36. J. R. T. Wood, *The Welensky Papers* (Durban, 1983) pp. 118–20
37. A. D. Roberts, 'Notes towards a Financial History of Copper Mining in Northern Rhodesia', *Canadian Journal of African Studies* 16 1982, pp. 347–59. I am grateful to Dr Roberts for drawing my attention to these links
38. *The Memoirs of Lord Chandos* (1962) p. 392
39. J-C Berthélemy, 'L'économie de l'Afrique occidentale française et du Togo, 1946–1960', RFHOM LXVII No. 248–9 1980, p. 301
40. L. S. Senghor (ed), *Anthologie de la nouvelle poésie Nègre et Malgache de langue française,* Préfacee de 'Orphée Noire' de Jean-Paul Sartre. (Paris, 1948) pp. xii, 57–61
41. FO 371/73076, Poynton to Crosthwaite 22 March 1948, encl. Le Roy to Cohen, 9 March, and MFA Note 27 Feb.: Minutes by Blanch and others
42. M. Crowder, 'Independence as a Goal in French West African Politics, 1944–60', W. H. Lewis (ed) *French-Speaking Africa* (NY 1965) pp. 26–7
43. CO 537/3545, Laurentie to Cohen, 30 Oct. 1948
44. FO 371/73038, Creasy to CO, 19 Oct. 1948
45. FO 371/73718, Note by CSO, Accra of discussion with Lefevre, 28 July 1948; DAMAS, p. 212
46. ANSOM AP 2255/6, Rapport Ruffel-Demery, 29 Ap. 1950: Note by Béchard
47. ANSOM AP 2255/6, Rapport Ruffel-Demery: DAMAS, *passim*
48. Note sur la situation au Viet-Nam, 30 Apr. 1950, in W. B. Cohen (ed.) *Robert Delavignette on the French Empire: Selected Writings* (Chicago, 1977) pp. 115–16
49. FRUS, 1950, V pp. 1558–68, Memo of Conversations, 25 Sept. 1950
50. Kenneth Robinson, 'Colonialism French-Style, 1945–55: A Backward Glance', JICH XII 1984 pp. 24–30
51. Laurentie to Labonne, 13 May 1948, quoted Marc Michel, 'Le Togo dans les relations internationales au lendemain de la guerre: prodrome de la décolonisation ou petite 'mésentente cordiale'? (1945–51), *Les chemins* p. 101

CHAPTER SEVEN

Recalculations in the 1950s

AN EXPANDING COMMONWEALTH?

The adjustments in relationships between Britain, France, and their African subjects described in the last chapter took place in a world where the formation of colonial policy was constrained by economic weakness and by acute political anxieties. If the Labour Government's despatch of troops to Korea in 1950 reflected their recognition of the primacy in foreign policy of the American alliance, Soviet communism did seem to present direct threats to colonial empire. In Malaya, where a State of Emergency was declared in June 1948, the [predominantly Chinese] Malayan Communist Party undoubtedly did so; the evidence is less clear for Bevin's warning to Attlee later that year that 'sooner or later the Russians will make a major drive against our positions in Africa'.[1] Although improvements in police and security services led to more realistic assessments, and public paranoia never matched that of MacCarthyite America, fear of communism continued to inhibit relations with colonial nationalisms. When, in British Guiana in 1953, that fear was focused on an area of direct interest to the USA, it led the Colonial Office to suspend moves to transfer power to elected leaders and to impose a more acceptable candidate.

In general, however, Churchill's government followed its predecessor's colonial policy as well as its acceptance of the Cold War alliance with the United States. Despite the presence of unreconstructed imperialists in the Conservative party (and some old-fashioned attitudes in Downing Street) there was now widespread consensus about the need to change empire into Commonwealth, and about the essential contribution of the Commonwealth to Britain's claim to remain a Great Power. If there had been hesitation in the CRO of 1947 about the admission of India and Pakistan to the magic circle, Ministers emphasized that the goal of African advancement was self-government *within the Commonwealth*, those unresolved doubts about how Commonwealth structures might be changed by enlargement notwithstanding. Even though African members might, like India, hesitate to accept any formal alignment in the Cold War, Commonwealth links might help to ensure their general benevolence.

In the early 1950s an expanding and strengthened Commonwealth seemed equally essential to Britain's economic recovery. The African colonies, like Malaya, remained essential contributors to the currency reserves of the Sterling Area, still far from secure during the Conservatives' first year of office. Despite Britain's own straitened circumstances, the commitment to Commonwealth development continued; the Labour government had increased allocations for CD&W, and the Colombo Plan of 1950 for Commonwealth economic co-operation in southern Asia reflected hopes that political co-operation with independent governments might be assisted by relatively modest disbursements of economic assistance and scientific expertise.[2] At a Commonwealth Economic Conference in December 1952 the Conservative government pursued a similar approach. While accepting an obligation to move towards eventual convertibility of sterling and freedom of international trade, Ministers of the Sterling Commonwealth agreed that central control of dollar purchases was still necessary. Gold Coast and Nigerian Ministers seeking greater freedom to invest their own reserves and establish their own Central Banks were encouraged to see the advantages of a longer-term developmental alliance; the Conference agreed that only common policies to ensure 'an adequate and stable external balance' would permit the London market to generate the capital needed for development.[3]

During the mid-1950s the economic and political constraints on Commonwealth governments began to relax. The post-Korean boom relieved the immediate pressure on sterling, and there was progress towards freer international trade. After the death of Stalin in May 1953 and the Korean armistice in July the tensions of the Cold War also became slightly less frenetic; and independent governments felt rather less pressure to choose sides. The final triumph of Mao Tse-tung and the Chinese People's Republic in 1949 provided a potential source of inspiration and support which many found more attractive than the USSR, and after the Geneva Conference of 1954 completed

France's eviction from Indo-China, China began to present herself as potential leader for a 'Third World' of peoples whose common experiences were of poverty, colonial rule, and racial oppression. Chou En-Lai took a leading part at the Bandung Conference of April 1955, attended by eighteen Asian and six African states; and although other participants declared that membership of this Third World need not preclude co-operation or military alliance with the West, it became more clear that new members of the Commonwealth might have rival claims on their political allegiance. Nkrumah, while sincerely anxious to play a role within that body, would clearly put Pan-African loyalties first. Such developments began to affect British attitudes. If many people regarded the prospective diversity within the Commonwealth as natural, and indeed capable of widening the area open to British influence, those who thought in terms of immediate national interests were less happy. Closer economic and political relations with Europe, formerly rejected by both parties as unnecessary for a great imperial power, began to seem an attractive alternative.

THE SHRINKING OF THE SAHARA

French governments had been moving towards closer integration with Europe ever since the Schuman Plan of 1950. But they saw the tightening of economic and political links with their African dependencies as a complement rather than an alternative to this, a dowry which would help safeguard French interests in the projected marriage with the former German enemy. This scenario was most immediately threatened by the spread of Arab nationalism in the Maghreb. French policies in North Africa had always been distinct from those in *Afrique noire*, formulated and executed by different ministries, and enforced by a more formidable military and police presence: colonial historiography followed colonial policy in emphasizing the historic division created by the Sahara desert. But in reality the Sahara had often served as a link as well as a barrier, providing routes for the transmission of commodities and ideas; and this would again be its role in the 1950s.

France's professed intention to guide her North African Protectorates towards internal autonomy within the French Union at first made somewhat better progress in Tunisia than in Morocco. In 1949 Habib Bourguiba, who before the war had regrouped the younger nationalists in the Neo-Destour party, returned from Cairo, and some of his colleagues joined a power-sharing cabinet. Many French politicians (mainly Socialists, but possibly including de Gaulle himself) had identified this cultured lawyer as a frustrated francophile who would be disposed to align a self-governing Tunisia with France's international interests. But after the 1951 elections the Socialists no longer participated in French governments, and Gaullist politicians, more closely in touch with North African settlers than with their silent hero, used their improved political leverage to obstruct conciliatory policies. When some Neo-Destour leaders were interned, others returned to Cairo to seek Pan-Arab support, and yet others prepared for armed resistance. In Morocco conflict became almost continually sharper after Mohamed V's Tangier speech of 1947; as Resident-General Juin worked with Berber potentates like el-Glaoui, the powerful Pasha of Marrakesh, to protect French capitalist and settler interests against both the Sultan and the Istiqlal. As Tunisian and Moroccan spokesmen tried to secure American support and to censure French policy at the UN, outraged French patriots tended to close ranks in the colonial cause. A climax was reached in August 1953 when French troops and Berber tribesmen marched into the Sultan's palace at Fez, declared Mohamed deposed, and deported him to Madagascar.

But some French politicians were counting the cost of such confrontations. Pierre Mendès-France, who became Prime Minister in June 1954, abandoned the Radical Party's traditional role as protector of settler interests. After displaying his readiness to take unpopular decisions by negotiating French disengagement from Indo-China, Mendès-France realized that France's authority in North Africa was also in peril. On a lightning visit to Tunis in July 1954 he freely conceded the principle of complete internal autonomy, re-assuring his reluctant companion Marshal Juin by announcing that full independence was not in question. Many *colons* doubted this, and feared that French politicians were planning a similar retreat in Morocco, where more strongly entrenched interests were at stake. These fears were increased in June 1955 when another left-wing Radical, Edgar Fauré, appointed Gilbert Grandval, a tough-minded but realistic Gaullist, as Resident-General; within two months settler pressure in Morocco and Paris had frustrated Grandval's attempt to initiate an orderly transfer of responsibility to moderate Moroccan nationalists.

But these settler pressures were now quickly out-weighed by a great increase in Muslim militancy, in country and town, throughout the

Maghreb. In November 1954 an armed revolt had begun in Algeria; on 20 August 1955, the second anniversary of the Sultan's deportation, there were violent and often horrific attacks on French communities in many parts of Morocco. French politicians, under pressure from Americans worried about their own military bases in Morocco, finally decided to concentrate on retaining control of Algeria and to accept the return of Mohamed V on the most favourable terms available. To the disgust of many senior administrators and army officers, Ministers abandoned one draft expedient after another for entrenching elements of formal control in either Morocco or Tunisia. In March 1956, when elections had restored a Socialist-led government to office, France accepted the full independence of both these countries. General Franco, whose discreet encouragement of Moroccan nationalists had expedited the French retreat, quickly followed suit by renouncing Spain's protectorate over northern Morocco (though not her old garrison colonies of Ceuta and Melilla). By their belated change of heart, combined with continued willingness to offer economic and technical assistance, the French hoped to preserve a substantial influence in both countries (including access to the Bizerta naval base) and to concentrate on the increasingly serious Algerian war.

Once the inadequate, or frankly fraudulent, nature of France's postwar reforms became apparent, Algerians like Ferhat Abbas, who might have been prepared to accept assimilationist solutions sincerely offered, were overshadowed by younger leaders, resolved to seek independence by revolutionary means. In impoverished regions of Kabylia and the Aurès mountains men with wartime experience of clandestine operations slowly re-grouped their military organisation; their leaders joined with old followers of the PPA and other exiled politicians in a National Liberation Front (FLN) which on 1 November 1954 launched co-ordinated attacks on a number of centres of French power. During the next two years the FLN leadership promoted a dialectic of terror, raising political passions by acts of violence (directed as often against Muslim collaborators as against Frenchmen) which were calculated to produce violent reactions. When in August 1955 123 French and Muslim residents of the Constantine region were murdered with particular atrocity, military reprisals killed many times that number: as this sequence was repeated elsewhere, local insurrections escalated into revolutionary war, and Algerians not initially involved – followers of Messali, communists, even the eminently moderate Ferhat Abbas – were induced, by reason or by violence, to accept the leadership of the FLN.

French governments which intended to combine military repression with genuine packages of social and political reforms were likewise driven into counter-terrorism by the fury of a million settlers, fearful for their lives and their property. Although the 1955 elections improved the position of the Socialists, Mollet's new government was driven off the course of conciliation by angry manifestations by the settlers of Algiers. Under a Socialist Resident Minister, Robert Lacoste, the army's strength was raised to half a million, including raw French conscripts and Senegalese mercenaries as well as frustrated veterans of the Indo-China war. Reluctantly the Fourth Republic found more and more of its resources diverted to defend the coalition of large and small farmers, substantial capitalists and *petits bourgeois* who claimed to have made Algeria French. At the same time its commitment was strengthened by hopes of developing the mineral resources of the Sahara, which some began to see as a prospective Alaska. In 1951 French technocrats had proposed forming a new Saharan territory, detached from both North and Black African colonies and controlled directly from Paris; the one solid achievement of the Algerian Assembly on which Muslims and *colons* had united was to maintain the country's boundaries by rejecting this plan.[4] Loss of Algeria would mean loss of the desert regions from which oil and gas began to flow in 1958: also of the most convenient test-site for the nuclear weapons already in secret development.

But France's interest in the Sahara did not stop at the Algerian boundary; as the revolutionary war extended into the desert their West African colonies could be directly involved. Indeed they were already affected by Algerian attempts to internationalize the war by appeals to Islamic unity, and to Third World solidarity. Cairo-based agents of the FLN secured strong verbal support from Nasser and other Arab leaders; if in arms and *matériel* it was less impressive, cross-border aid would surely increase as Tunisia and Morocco joined Libya in independence. Algerians had been admitted as observers to the Bandung Conference, which endorsed their right to 'self-determination and independence'; later in 1955, to great French embarrassment, the UN Assembly voted to discuss Algeria. It followed that France would make great efforts to avoid further conflicts in her African empire; and further, that it would be greatly advantageous to break the anti-colonial phalanx by retaining the loyal collaboration of authentic leaders in Black Africa.

But in one territory France failed to avoid armed confrontation. Roland Pré, appointed by Mendès-France to govern Cameroun, was a high-principled man whose commitment to genuine social reforms went along with determination to control the influence of the UPC, outlawed in his mind by its successful challenges to colonial authority as well as by its communist affiliations. In May 1955, a time of economic difficulty, Pré's authoritarian measures led to demonstrations and riots in Duala, Yaoundé and elsewhere, followed by proscription of the UPC. The party regrouped clandestinely and in December 1956 launched armed rebellion in Sanaga Maritime province, apparently with some reluctance; until 1960 at least the French were committed to a serious military campaign. But since they realized that it was not only UPC militants who were discontented the government found it necessary to win support, at the UN as well as inside Cameroun, by conceding more responsibility to a coalition of more moderate nationalists. And having thus launched Cameroun as well as Togo down the road to self-government, the Fourth Republic could hardly close that road to its own 'overseas territories', the support of whose elected Deputies it was increasingly anxious to retain.

That support was needed internationally, for attempts to justify the Algerian war. It was needed in parliament, where the majorities of successive governments were often measured in single figures. But it was also becoming increasingly essential within the colonies themselves, where, as Laurentie had feared, pressures for independence continued to grow, not least because of France's educational policies. Because new universities developed more slowly than in British Africa, students came in their hundreds on scholarships to France, where they tended to mix in radical company. Many were indeed affected, as hoped, by French cultural radiance, but politically the strongest radiation came from the Left. As most students simultaneously discovered that French society was more racist than its ideologues admitted, these future leaders of African society tended to adopt radical attitudes, sustained by intensified racial pride.

Something comparable was happening within the emergent labour movement. As in Britain, officials had understood that controlled trade union development could be *un moyen d'embrigader les masses*,[5] but guidance had been provided by the metropolitan labour federations rather than by individual trade unionists appointed as Labour Advisers. This threatened to implant in Africa the historic divisions of the French working class. The Socialist *Force Ouvrière* was least effective in this role; the *Confédération Française des Travailleurs Croyants* (supported by the French Catholic Church as part of a programme of constructive decolonization which sometimes anticipated that of the state) had considerable success in certain colonies; but at first the strongest influence was the Communist-affiliated *Confédération Générale du Travail*, which in 1948 claimed 61 per cent of the 72,000 trade unionists in AOF.[6] Independent-minded Africans, however, came to resent the paternal attitudes and assimilationist assumptions which even the most progressive Frenchmen often combined with an imperfect understanding of African conditions and needs; and in the 1950s resentment of attempts to impose 'external wills' on the emergent working class were increased by the cold war between rival trade union internationals, WFTU and ICFTU. In January 1957 Sékou Touré led the more militant unions into a new *Union Générale des Travailleurs d'Afrique Noire* (UGTAN), emphasizing that this was not merely a new syndicalist tactic but part of 'the rising struggle against colonialism, for national independence and economic development'.[7]

While such evidence of radicalization reminded French Ministers of the need to provide African Deputies with visible rewards for their collaboration, the political form of their response was being shaped in the Trust territories. As British Togoland prepared for a plebiscite in May 1956, which would lead to its incorporation in independent Ghana, France had to offer her subjects in Togo some genuine measure of self-government, un-French though that concept had once appeared. In 1955 the officially-favoured *Parti Togolais du Progrès* secured a majority in the Territory Assembly and a share in a new 'Council of Government'; next year Togo became an autonomous republic within the French Union. Although Frenchmen may still have hoped that the realities of power would not correspond completely with constitutional forms, this made it difficult to deny comparable status to larger and richer colonies. In 1955 an MRP Overseas Minister, P. H. Teitgen, prepared a scheme of decolonization which, as refined by his Socialist successor Gaston Defferre, had wide political implications. Recognizing that French parliamentarians could find little time or interest for detailed scrutiny of African legislation, Defferre resorted to the constitutionally dubious expedient of a *loi-cadre* or Enabling Act, authorizing sweeping reforms by Presidential Decree. The measures thus introduced roughly followed the pattern of dyarchy adopted by Arden-Clarke and Nkrumah in 1951. In each Black African colony a Territorial Assembly, elected by universal suffrage and with greatly extended powers, provided the basis for an executive Council of Government, still under the Governor's presidency but with the local

African majority leaders as Vice-Presidents, and in an increasingly strong position.

One immediate consequence was to weaken the quasi-federal centres of government at Dakar and Brazzaville, where so much power had hitherto been concentrated. The Governors-General became High Commissioners of the French Republic – essentially co-ordinators, though still very powerful ones, without their former control over allocation of federal financial resources. No provision was made for the 'Grand Councils' to evolve as federal legislatures, nor for any federal executive. Some critics believed this was a divisive manoeuvre to split the empire into weak successor states, but if some Frenchmen may have reasoned thus, others believed it would be easier to retain influence over large federated units, such as the British were struggling to establish in Central Africa and Nigeria, in Malaysia and the Caribbean. The balance of this argument was tipped by relationships among the Africans themselves. Before the 1956 elections the favoured partner of French governments had been a group of independent overseas Deputies led by Senghor, a vigilant critic of 'balkanisation'; but then the reformed RDA raised its representation to nine, and Houphouet became a Vice-Premier in the governments of Mollet and his successors. The Ivory Coast, the success story of capitalist development, was already subsidizing the budgets of 'deficit colonies' in AOF; in a federal state it would have been committed to do so on an increasing scale.* In AEF Gabon, relatively affluent from existing exports of hardwoods and with large mineral resources under survey, was in a comparable position; like Houphouet, Leon Mba put the interests of constituents before ideals of unity.

From 1956 onwards then, the activities of political militants in the African Overseas Territories were focused within the local arenas defined by the *loi-cadre*. The centralizing tradition of French colonial policy, which had often served as a brake on constitutional development, now became an accelerator, as aspiring politicians competed electorally for the offices and resources now made available

---

*Analysis of the federal budget for 1956 shows both Ivory Coast and Senegal as net contributors, through redistributed customs revenue, to the budgets of the six other territories. [J. R. de Benois. *La Balkanisation de l'Afrique Occidentale française* (Dakar, 1979) p. 161]. But all territories contributed substantially to federal expenditure on central institutions and salaries, which was largely concentrated around Dakar. Two recent studies suggest that both Dahomey and Niger may have contributed more to the federal budget than they received back from it. [P. Manning, *Slavery, Colonialism and Economic Growth in Dahomey, 1640–1960* (Cambridge, 1982) pp. 247 ff.; F. Fuglestad, *A History of Niger* (Cambridge, 1983) p. 171.

to them in territorial capitals. This was far from the approach to decolonization envisaged in 1944; but it served to cover France's rear during the increasingly fierce conflict in Algeria.

THE SUEZ WATERSHED

After 1954 the growing anger in France about the support which the Algerian revolt appeared to be receiving from Egypt was increasingly echoed in Britain. Ironically, the overthrow of Farouk and the subsequent rise to power of Colonel Gamel Abdel Nasser had initially been welcomed by Anthony Eden, who as Foreign Secretary and deputy Prime Minister in Churchill's government often disagreed with his leader about methods of maintaining British hegemony in the Middle East, and about wider international priorities. For Churchill the essential foundation of British policy remained the special relationship with the United States, on which he had staked so much during the war; Eden was inclined to resent, sometimes petulantly, America's increasing dominance within the Atlantic alliance. Churchill, while reluctantly accepting that his dreams of a revitalized British Empire had gone out of date, shared the doubts of many conservatives about accepting new Commonwealth members as leading actors on the international stage; Eden prided himself on his good relationship with Nehru and, not yet prepared to identify Britain with the movement towards European unity, saw a world role as patron of developing nations inside and outside the Common-wealth. Eden, like all his predecessors, believed a strong military presence in the Middle East was essential to protect oil supplies and sustain an imperial world strategy; but, like Bevin, he hoped to do this in collaboration with friendly Arab governments.

Nasser's evident popular support made it easier to conclude, in October 1954, the new Anglo-Egyptian Treaty which had eluded Bevin. The new regime waived its claim to sovereignty over the Sudan, confident that the principle of self-determination would work in Egypt's favour; Eden, hoping that Nasser might prove the reforming leader the Arab world was waiting for, persuaded Churchill, after anguished murmurings, to accept the risk of conditional withdrawal from the Suez base. British forces moved out to Cyrenaica (where King Idris remained co-operative) and to Cyprus. Although the Treaty provided for their return to Suez in certain emergencies, Eden's hope and expectation was that Nasser would co-operate with the western allies in regional defence; Nasser for his part, urgently aware of the economic plight of Egypt's rising population, hoped for Anglo-American support for his projected Aswan High Dam. But the logic of Middle Eastern politics, sometimes helped along by Nasser's volatile personality, was pushing him in contradictory directions. Apart from his strong verbal support for nationalists in French North Africa, Nasser's deep hostility to the state of Israel extended to those pro-British Arab leaders who seemed willing to compromise with her; and his 'positive neutrality' in the Cold War did not preclude arms purchases from the Soviet bloc. A period of deteriorating relations with Britain, France, and the USA culminated in his triumphal nationalization of the Suez Canal Company on 26 July 1956.

Though this act threatened free international passage of the Canal only indirectly, it was clearly intended as a gesture of defiance to the former imperial masters of the Middle East; the affront to prestige brought out their latent racialism and frustrated anger. Eden, now Prime Minister, had hitherto suppressed such feelings like a gentleman, but he reacted to the nationalization as an act of aggression reminiscent of Mussolini. For the French Socialist Mollet it simply heightened the fury roused by Cairo Radio's support of the FLN. When the American government took a calmer view and worked for compromise, Eden and Mollet entered into an elaborate conspiracy with Israel, with the barely concealed purpose of overthrowing Nasser and replacing him by 'a congenial Egyptian government'.[8] Their furtively designed attack on Egypt at the end of October 1956 was an atavistic reversion to methods which, in the prevailing balance of economic and military power in the world, were beyond the resources of either Britain or France.

The international reactions which aborted the attempt to re-occupy Suez revealed the fragile foundations of Eden's world policy. Condemned by the UN Assembly with only Australia and New Zealand in reluctant support, the operation dealt a heavy, though not fatal, blow to British aspirations to exercise moral influence in the world as leader of a multi-racial Commonwealth. Her influence in Arab states was further shaken – not least in Libya, where it was made clear that Britain's new bases could not be used against Egypt. America's evident hostility was more violently echoed by the USSR, happy to divert attention from its own intervention in Hungary; though real Soviet-American co-operation was never a possibility, this was a reminder that not all international issues need be subordinated to the Cold War. But the effective pressure came from the United States, who forcefully persuaded Harold Macmillan (Chancellor of the Exchequer, but originally a strong advocate of the operation) that American willingness to sustain the sterling area as a basis for British power was conditional upon satisfactory international behaviour. Although the French (with more at stake in Algeria, and less to lose in the Arab world) were inclined to press on, both governments had been reminded of the political and economic constraints on any attempt to play independent roles in the world. When in January 1957 Macmillan took over the premiership from the humiliated Eden he understood that some drastic reappraisal of British priorities was necessary.

MACMILLAN'S REASSESSMENTS

After the Suez debacle Macmillan's prior aim was to re-establish the special relationship with the United States on terms which would leave Britain the greatest practicable scope for independent initiative and political influence. The Defence Review of 1957 defined the material limits of military independence: Britain proceeded towards the production of the thermonuclear weapons tested that year, and pending development of the British-built Skybolt missile the V-bomber force was maintained for their delivery. To meet the heavy costs of this independent deterrent without over-taxing an apprehensive electorate, substantial economies were proposed, in Europe and beyond: conscription would end by 1962 and all military commitments be taken over by smaller but highly professional armed forces. But although this implied selective reduction of Britain's imperial role, there was no intention to abandon it: her forces would not only remain in the eastern Mediterranean but retain a capacity to intervene 'East of Suez' – in Malaysia, in the oilfields of Iran and southern Arabia, even offering gestures of support to India in her boundary dispute with China.[9] The Indian Ocean remained an area of high imperial importance; this implied both a military presence in East Africa and close co-operation in regional defence with the entrenched Afrikaner regime in the Union. Consequent on an exchange of letters of June 1955 Britain transferred control of the Simonstown naval base in 1957 with guarantees for continued use in peace and war, and South Africa accepted specific responsibilities for maritime defence. In 1958 she was granted certain military facilities in the three High Commission Territories.[10]

   Gradual re-appraisal of economic priorities also seemed necessary. Since 1952 the most acute pressures on the pound had eased, and in December 1958 sterling was made fully convertible. It now became less vital to control the colonies' hard currency earnings; in fact, as new governments acquired more control over economic policy they began to run dollar deficits, and the fate of sterling came to depend on Middle Eastern oil-producers outside the Commonwealth. But though Britain's economic recovery was reflected in visibly improving standards of domestic consumption, from which Macmillan was to derive electoral benefit, profound doubts were being expressed about the future. Many economists suggested that this would depend on the application of advanced technology in competition with other advanced industrial countries; some went on to conclude that investment in this direction could best be promoted by joining wholeheartedly in the movement towards economic unity in western Europe. But there was no consensus yet. Timid insularity apart, many people distrusted the agricultural protectionism which seemed to have inspired the 1957 Treaty of Rome, not least because it seemed to threaten patterns of trade which had grown up in the old imperial framework, and the new Commonwealth strategy of investment in Asian and African development.

   This view depended more on political loyalties than on economic appraisal; in 1956 Macmillan, as Chancellor, had attempted to cut expenditure on colonial development. Although the savings finally imposed were minor, the exercise had raised doubts about the speed and extent of the improvement likely to be produced by such subsidies and about the continuing willingness of Britain's consumer society to contribute to such an indeterminate commitment. And although existing companies like Unilever had begun to restructure their overseas operations, it seemed unlikely that private British investors would supply new capital on the scale required; there were already signs that they were being deterred by prospects of early independence and that American interests were more eager to step in (as Texaco had just done in Trinidad). One of Macmillan's early acts as Prime Minister was to order a cost-benefit analysis of colonial policy: a survey of the progress of individual colonies towards independence, accompanied by

> something like a profit and loss account for each of our colonial
> possessions, so that we may be better able to gauge whether, from the
> financial and economic point of view, we are likely to gain or lose by its
> departure.

The assessed advantages of the African colonies to the UK seems hardly overwhelming. Although together they still showed a modest favourable balance of trade outside the Sterling Area, East Africa had a substantial overall deficit (partly due to the cost of fighting Mau Mau); and their combined commercial importance to Britain was still less than that of the Union of South Africa.[11] In July 1957 a White Paper made clear that colonies should not expect continued development assistance from the British Treasury after independence but should look to private investment; that much of this would have to come from outside the Sterling Area; and that even in colonial dependencies British aid, increasingly in the form of skilled manpower and expertise, would depend on 'the successful development of the United Kingdom's own economy'.[12]

While this sober assessment did not preclude attempts to use British leadership of an expanding Commonwealth as a means of enhancing her position within the Atlantic alliance, it hardly provided inspiring encouragement. The conclusion voiced by the Cabinet Secretary was that there was no reason to change existing policies of encouraging gradual constitutional progress towards self-government within the Commonwealth; if Britain's economic and strategic interests would not, in general, be served by trying to prolong control over colonies seeking independence, neither should future relationships be prejudiced by hasty withdrawals. In Britain's straitened circumstances maintaining colonial rule could rarely be considered a good investment; but co-operation with former colonies within an enlarged Commonwealth could still offer opportunities to enhance her influence in the world.[13]

British Conservatives were still uncertain how to respond to those opportunities. Although Oliver Stanley had maintained his wartime bipartisan approach when Labour was in office, old imperialists who equated Conservatism with defence of the British Empire felt that responsibilities were being prematurely abandoned in West Africa; and in East and Central Africa many were prepared to go beyond Lyttelton or Lennox-Boyd in supporting the British settlers. When bi-partisanship began to break down after 1951, Conservative back-benchers rallied to support the government; but some of them still suspected Ministers of being too ready to compromise old imperial interests in order to appease rebellious subjects in Africa, woolly internationalists in Hampstead, or hard-faced men in the USA. After the Suez fiasco eight MPs who believed the government had abandoned imperial interests too readily resigned the party whip, and in 1957 they acquired a powerful patron when Lord Salisbury resigned from the government over Cyprus. Their unease about what was happening to the Commonwealth was more widely shared; neither old imperialists nor Young Conservatives looking towards Europe from their suburban strongholds could feel much enthusiasm for an unstructured association which had let 'the old Country' down at Suez.

Within the Labour Party, on the other hand, the change in the Commonwealth from the unwritten alliance which had supported Britain in two world wars to a free association of states with divergent interests but some common traditions did arouse enthusiasm. Bodies like the Africa Bureau and the Movement for Colonial Freedom which emphasized the moral primacy of racial justice regarded the new Commonwealth almost proprietorially, and were delighted by the enthusiasm which some Asian and African leaders appeared to show for it. Nkrumah, who in 1959 was sworn of the Privy Council while visiting the Queen at Balmoral, became specially enthusiastic. Yet this very development made the possibility of united Commonwealth policies still more remote, for in any conflict between Commonwealth and Pan-African loyalties there was no question which way Nkrumah would turn. In 1958 he had convened two international conferences in Accra – of eight independent African governments in April, of radical nationalists from throughout the continent in December; their denunciations of colonial imperialism (most fervently uncompromising in the second case) had consequences in the colonies of Britain and her European allies which increased Conservative disquiet.

While the future orientation of British world policy remained uncertain, Macmillan still hoped to regulate the pace of decolonization in the different regions of Africa. Lyttelton's successor, Alan Lennox-Boyd, shared the old Conservative faith in Imperial mission. While accepting, in face of doubts by officials in Whitehall as well as Africa, the political necessity of accelerating the demission of political responsibility (except in colonies of special strategic interest), he was still concerned to retain Imperial control over the process. In West Africa it now seemed wisest to complete the transition as rapidly as possible. It had already been accepted that Sierra Leone's modest resource base need not debar it from eventual independence in the Commonwealth; but violent manifestations against the new Ministers, in both Freetown and the Northern Province, raised doubts about the popularity of the ruling Sierra Leone Peoples' Party, and during the pre-Suez period the Colonial Office had been disposed to moderate the pace of constitutional change. But now progress continued unchecked, and despite a notable lack of urgency on the part of Prime Minister Sir Milton Margai, the transfer of power was eventually completed in April 1961.

In the more volatile conditions of Nigeria the Colonial Office continued its attempts to forestall the emergence of populist nationalism by devolving power to a federal government within which northern conservatives would exercise a controlling influence. Although of less central importance than Malaysia or the Middle East, this huge country would clearly be a centre of continuing British interest; it offered promising possibilities for increased trade and investment, geologists were revealing the extent of its petroleum resources, and, though military planners no longer talked of a Lagos-Nairobi trunk road, aviation routes through Lagos and Kano were of both military and civilian significance. Lyttelton's 1954 constitution had given Nigerian politicians every incentive to co-operate in a speedy transition to internal self-government in the three unequal Regions; Lennox-Boyd was clearly anxious to complete the transfer of power at Federal level as speedily and amicably as the complexities of inter-ethnic relations allowed.

During May and June 1957 a new constitutional conference in London began to face the problem of how the 'primary nations' of Nigeria – numbering over two hundred, large and small, if language is taken as the criterion of nationality – might organize their co-existence in an independent state. NCNC representatives hoped to restructure the federal authority by creating new regional governments; by recognizing additional ethnic identities they would reduce the leverage enjoyed by the rulers of the huge Northern Region, and enhance their own electoral prospects. Similar reasoning made the NPC strongly oppose restructuring; and as chairman Lennox-Boyd discreetly ensured that their view prevailed. With the principle of regional self-government already conceded the Colonial Office was anxious to complete the transfer of power as quickly as possible, rather than, as earlier in Ghana, to delay it by further tests of African opinion. Critics suggest that officials favoured the existing tripartite structure as offering opportunities to influence Nigerian policy through Northern surrogates; a simpler explanation is that they just could not face the difficulties of a thorough reform. Besides the delay, confusion and expense which administrators always expect to attend the alteration of existing structures, there was the certainty of resistance from the Hausa-Fulani oligarchy and their many British admirers. Calculating that no Southern politician would willingly incur responsibility for delaying the golden moment of independence, 'Lennox-Boyd like a clever general drew the line of battle and baited the Nigerian delegates into accepting battle on his own grounds'.[14]

His battle-plan was to redefine the problem of restructuring the Nigerian state as one of reassuring 'minorities' – a concept derived from theories of the modern European nation-state, with shallow roots in African historical experience.[15] With the agreement of the conference four distinguished British public servants were appointed as Commissioners with a curious assignment: To ascertain facts about the fears of minorities in any part of Nigeria and to propose means of allaying those fears whether well or ill founded. Fortunately for their good conscience the Commissioners identified no fears which could not be allayed by minor constitutional adjustments (including a Bill of Rights, a device derided by Lyttelton only five years before), supported by their confidence 'that Nigeria means to follow the road of liberal democracy and parliamentary government'.[16] Thus reassured Macmillan's government was able in 1960 to transfer power to an unnatural coalition of NPC and NCNC, which was initially willing to grant its former rulers limited military facilities under an Anglo-Nigerian Defence Pact.

In eastern Africa, the decolonization time-table in one peripheral territory was internationally determined. Italy's Trusteeship over her former colony of Somalia was due to terminate in 1960; throughout the 1950s preparation was made by educational expansion, the training and promotion of Somali officials, the holding of elections to representative councils. Somali national enthusiasm spread to the neighbouring British Protectorate, where Britain had feared that political reform might increase Egyptian influence; in 1954 it was heightened when Britain, against the instinct of many officials, transferred Somali grazing-lands in the Haud back to Ethiopia. Lennox-Boyd, swallowing old doubts about 'viability', tardily accelerated British preparations for decolonization to match Italy's; in July 1960 the two territories united in the Republic of Somalia (which continued to receive budgetary subsidies from both Italy and Britain). But Somali irredentism had further claims to pursue: in northern Kenya, in Jibuti (which remained a French *territoire d'Outre-mer* until 1977), and above all in the Somali districts of southern Ethiopia. Unable to support these, Britain gained less credit than Bevin had once hoped by patronizing Somali unity; but at least she avoided the international embarrassment of trying to hold a 'deficit colony' of marginal strategic significance.

In the rest of East Africa Lennox-Boyd seemed prepared to maintain a much longer presence. In Kenya the army had, by this time, contained the military threat of Mau Mau sufficiently to be able to transfer operational responsibility to the police, although continuing guerrilla warfare prolonged the State of Emergency until November 1959. It was still assumed that political decolonization would have to wait on economic transformation throughout the region. A Royal Commission appointed in 1953 on Sir Philip Mitchell's initiative examined relationships between land and population with the essentially long-term aim 'to achieve an improved standard of living'; the clearest message of its complex and detailed report was the need to encourage secure tenure of land by African farmers prepared to increase production for the market, and to end the restrictive reservation of land for exclusive European use.[17] Meanwhile the Kenya Government had already published more specific proposals to encourage African capitalist farming; the author, Roger Swynnerton, prepared much of their own evidence to the Commission. Swynnerton's plan gave priority to land purchased by Kikuyu; justifiable on a purely economic assessment, this was also politically expedient, and the British government provided five of the seven million pounds required for the first phase. Governor Baring could thus leave Kenya in 1959 hoping that prosperous African farmers, allied with the African entrepreneurs whom he had encouraged to move into retail trade and other businesses, would appreciate the advantages of gradual constitutional change designed to promote inter-racial confidence and co-operation.

But this was likely to be a long process; and prospects of an ultimate transfer of power were also blurred by a new imperial role envisaged for Kenya by architects of the East-of-Suez defence policy. To avoid political complications of over-flying, which would arise if strategic reserves were concentrated in the UK, bomber forces and highly trained air-transportable troops were to be dispersed around the Indian Ocean; in 1957 Duncan Sandys, now Defence Minister, decided to base part of this reserve in Kenya. By 1961 £7,500,000 had been invested in barracks and airfields. These measures were apparently taken without any discussion of their political implications;[18] but they appeared to indicate a long-term imperial commitment, highly encouraging to those old Empire Loyalists who failed to understand that Mau Mau had destroyed the credibility of East African settlers as possible heirs to colonial government.

Lennox-Boyd, like Lyttelton before him, continued to define his political objective as the creation of a multi-racial society. But multiracialism in Kenya now implied progressive dilution of settler privilege, guaranteed minority status for Asians, and a rapid increase in African responsibilities. Ministerial office was now open to Africans elected largely by beneficiaries of the new development policies. In retrospect it seems that the chief error in this strategy was its failure to appreciate that authentic African spokesmen could collaborate in multiracial power-sharing only if assured it would shortly give way to African majority rule. Baring and Lennox-Boyd, who had their own unrealistic images of ideal African leaders, were slow to appreciate the political importance of men like Tom Mboya, the young secretary of the trade union federation, whose skills in organization and negotiation made him a popular spokesman for growing urban populations denied normal political activity during the Emergency. Mboya was essentially a moderate and pragmatic politician, linked to the West through ICFTU; but as Nkrumah's star rose African politicians could only display their moderation *after* securing a real transfer of power. As soon as Mboya and seven colleagues were elected to the Legislative Council in 1957 on the restricted franchise approved by Lyttelton, Lennox-Boyd was under pressure to increase their number; in November he conceded parity of African and European representation in a new constitution marked by complex political arithmetic.

The time available for experiments in institutionalized multiracialism in East Africa was clearly shortening. In January 1959 Lennox-Boyd held discussions with four East African governors at Chequers, and for the first time tentatively indicated target dates for independence. Tanganyika was to come first, about 1970; Kenya and Uganda (where the outstanding problem concerned Buganda, not the settlers) might follow around 1975.[19] Lennox-Boyd hoped this would allow time for 'a middle-of-the-road group of non-sectional opinion' to emerge,[20] and the more forward-looking settlers led by Michael Blundell responded by forming the New Kenya Group, which to the horror of many of their fellows advocated 'the progressive extension of democracy'. But liberal settlers and African nationalists alike were to be surprised by the speed at which that extension actually took place.

In the Central African Federation, speedy progress towards independence was expected and desired by the white leaders of the United Federal Party, not by Africans. In June 1956 Huggins (now Lord Malvern) asked Eden's Ministers to pre-empt a possible Labour government by advancing the constitutional review scheduled for 1960 and granting the Federation independence in the Commonwealth at the same time as Ghana. Although Lennox-Boyd was 'a firm and indeed a passionate believer in the Federation',[21] he and the Commonwealth Secretary, Lord Home, rejected this presumptuous claim, warning Malvern that even Conservatives would require better evidence of African consent.[22] Yet when in November 1957 Welensky, now Federal Prime Minister, proposed complex constitutional changes which granted Africans only rigorously circumscribed voting rights, the British Cabinet over-rode objections from the African Affairs Board, which four years earlier it had lauded as the guarantor of genuine partnership. Macmillan would clearly be glad to shed responsibility for Central Africa as quickly as might prove decent. But decency was threatened as it became clear that the pressures of settler politics were increasing, not allaying, African fears. After Garfield Todd, the mildly reformist Prime Minister of Southern Rhodesia, was overthrown by the United Federal party in February 1958 it became increasingly clear that white voters in the Federation would not approve any result of the 1960 constitutional review acceptable to the UN or the Commonwealth, or to the Africans directly affected.

Meanwhile Lennox-Boyd was persisting with carefully calculated constitutional reforms in Northern Rhodesia and Nyasaland, designed to give restricted African electorates a minority interest in the formulation of policy. But such measures could not satisfy Africans aware of what was happening in Accra on the one hand, in Salisbury on the other. In the middle of 1958 Dr Hastings Banda, resident in Ghana since 1953, returned to Nyasaland, where young nationalists had prepared a hero's welcome, and assumed leadership of Congress's vehement campaign against Federation. In Northern Rhodesia, where Nkumbula's acceptance of the new territorial constitution suggested willingness to compromise over the terms of 'partnership', militants left the ANC to found a Zambian African National Congress (ZANC) under the more inspiring, non-violent, leadership of Kenneth Kaunda. After December 1958, when both Banda and Kaunda refreshed their spirits by attending the All-African Peoples' Congress in Accra, social and political tensions increased rapidly in both their countries. The crisis came in Nyasaland. Governor Armitage, worried by the ANC's success in articulating the deep popular mistrust of Federation and linking it to peasant resistance to enforced agricultural improvement, perceived 'a plot to destroy property and to murder many people both Africans and Europeans'[23] which frightened whites feared might extend throughout the Federation. On 26 February 1959 an emergency was declared in Southern Rhodesia (where a reconstituted ANC had become active); Federal troops (including white Rhodesian units) were sent into Nyasaland, provoking new confrontations and more than fifty deaths. On 3 March Armitage declared a State of Emergency, detaining Banda and other Congress leaders. ZANC, which had declared a boycott of the Northern Rhodesian elections, was banned nine days before the poll, and Kaunda and some colleagues were also arrested.

These repressive actions, intended to sustain the Federation, in fact undermined its credibility. A Commission of Inquiry under the distinguished Judge Lord Devlin failed to substantiate Armitage's fears; its searching Report, published in July, testified that Nyasa opposition to Federation was both deep and widespread, and implicitly criticized official over-reactions which had temporarily turned Nyasaland into 'a police state'. This severe verdict by their own Commissioners, following directly on revelations about atrocities committed on Mau Mau suspects in Hola Camp under the authority of the Kenya government, shook the confidence of Macmillan's government in the Federation's capacity to move towards genuine racial partnership, and in the adequacy of their own plans for eastern Africa. The Prime Minister, whose own doubts about transferring power to white settlers dated at least from 1942, began to recognize a need for still more drastic changes of African policy.

THE RESURRECTION OF DE GAULLE

The Fourth Republic's moral investment in the Suez operation had been greater than that of the British, Eden excepted. Those who wrongly assumed that the overthrow of Nasser might cut the life-support of the Algerian resistance felt betrayed, by Britain as well as by the USA, and even less disposed to compromise with the FLN. After Suez General Massu's parachute troops defeated a campaign of terrorist bombing in Algiers city by unscrupulous use of torture and counter-terror; protests from Frenchmen who still believed in the rights of man were largely neutralized by continuing revulsion against the equal cruelties of the rebels. But the methods by which the army attempted to enforce a military solution also attracted increasing criticism abroad – especially in the United States, where Eisenhower and Dulles had hitherto succeeded in containing Afro-Asian attacks on their French ally in the UN. In July 1957 Senator J. F. Kennedy, an aspiring Democratic President, demanded recognition of 'the independent personality of Algeria'; and in February 1958, when French aircraft supervising FLN movements across the border savagely bombed the Tunisian village of Sakhiet, Eisenhower, with British support, began to work actively for peace negotiations.

Although military commanders who believed they were winning the war still regarded compromise with the FLN as unthinkable, consciousness of the international embarrassment and financial cost of colonial empire – and of the human price being paid by a conscript army – had begun to change established attitudes and assumptions within France. At a popular level this emerged during 1956 in some widely-discussed articles in *Paris-Match* by the journalist Raymond Cartier. But *cartierisme* was only the public face of a deeper re-appraisal. The analysis of Jacques Marseille suggests that the 1950s saw the ascendency in the French state of modernizing technocrats whose calculations had convinced them that attempts to maintain the privileged structures of colonial rule were no longer cost-effective.[24] France needed to transfer resources into technologically-based industries able to compete in the world of multinational capitalism; too much concern for old colonial interests (as Dutch experience over Indonesia seemed to show) could only impede that process. Public and private investment, it was now being recognized, could be more profitably directed towards transferring the simpler and more labour-intensive forms of industrial production to overseas countries with sympathetic governments than towards protecting relatively high-cost colonial producers of raw materials. Some military officers seem to have been conducting their own re-appraisals along parallel lines: colonial wars were wasting the energies and lives of able officers, and draining resources which could be used to re-establish France as a serious nuclear power.

An early effect of such changing attitudes was a lessening of commitment to uphold colonial authority in Black Africa. As the *loi-cadre* took effect, power passed smoothly to those whom local elections designated as Vice-Presidents of the various territorial governments. A radical who knew his own mind, as Sékou Touré did, could now with French acquiescence demolish the structures of colonial chieftaincy and establish his own section of the RDA as effective controller of local government in Guinea. But it was still politically impossible to apply the new economic and military logic to Algeria. Too many French electors believed their interests were at stake (now including petro-chemical companies as well as older capitalist concerns, and the numerous families with kin among the *colons*), and the army, even more than the politicians, had too much moral capital at stake. No government of the Fourth Republic commanded enough authority to impose a settlement on military commanders who felt encouraged by their victories during 1957, frustrated by their international and domestic critics, and heartened by the way the *colons* looked to them for salvation. On 13 May 1958, during a prolonged Ministerial crisis in Paris, a huge public demonstration in Algiers proclaimed a Committee of Public Safety, and the shrewdly ambitious General Salan added his support to the many diverse groups who were demanding the return to power of General de Gaulle. On 1 June the danger of a military coup directed from Algiers against Paris was averted only by a constitutional transfer of plenary powers to the General, summoned from his retirement to become last Prime Minister of the Fourth Republic. In Algiers three days later, presented to a vast crowd including Muslims as well as settlers, de Gaulle declared resoundingly '*Je vous ai compris*'. But he did not yet reveal the nature of his understanding, nor how it would affect his exercise of the 'national legitimacy' which he claimed to have resumed.

What is now clear is that de Gaulle's Algerian policy would be governed by his primary goal of re-establishing France as a world power. By completing the modernization of the economy (on foundations already laid by the despised Fourth Republic), strengthening the constitutional powers of the Presidency against factious parliamentarians, and re-equipping the armed forces with the technology of the nuclear age, de Gaulle intended to make France (in partnership with West Germany) leader of a *Europe des patries* which could aspire to eventual parity with the super-powers. Any reconstruction of the ailing French Union would have to contribute to this guiding purpose. Though in one speech he raised a half-hearted cheer for *Algérie française*, de Gaulle had little sympathy for a moribund colonialism which demanded, besides economic privileges and subsidies, the military protection of a conscript army, tied down and demoralized by the seemingly endless savageries of guerrilla war. At first he hoped to retain control of France's nuclear test-sites in the Sahara, and of the oil and gas-fields which were about to come into production; but even here he would eventually be willing to sacrifice much in order to eliminate the Algerian drain on French resources. His tactical aim was to negotiate the best available deal for French interests with some stable authority that could command the allegiance of the whole Algerian population; gradually he realized that such an authority could only be the FLN, and that the terms would have to include that unequivocal recognition of independence over which negotiations with the Viet Minh had collapsed in 1946. The obligations of empire, de Gaulle declared in April 1961, were now prejudicing national revival: 'decolonization is our interest, and consequently our policy'.[25] To promote that interest he was prepared to engage in devious political manoeuvres such as he affectd to despise, and ultimately to abandon the loyal supporters of French Algeria, including many Muslims who had continued to take assimilationist rhetoric seriously.

To prepare his admirers for psychological shock, de Gaulle made a series of cryptic pronouncements, moving with studied ambiguity from 'self-determination' (September 1959) to 'an Algerian Algeria' (November 1960) and, as he prepared to negotiate with the FLN, 'a sovereign Algeria' (April 1961). Each phrase alarmed defenders of *Algérie française* to the point of revolt. In January 1960 neo-fascist militias raised barricades in central Algiers and fired on the gendarmerie; only a remarkable televised display of Presidential authority prevented the army joining this revolt. In December some officers did join civilian plots to assassinate de Gaulle during an Algerian tour, provoking renewed violence from Muslims in the capital who were assumed to have been 'pacified' in 1957. By April 1961 many senior officers were afraid that, as in Indo-China, their hard-fought gains were about to be abandoned and their Algerian allies betrayed by cowardly politicians; but the respected generals who tried to seize power in Algiers failed to win unanimous support among the officers, and the conscript soldiers rallied to de Gaulle. Those who could not follow the President's harsh logic were left with no other option than mindless terrorism.

While the French nation became more bitterly divided the FLN succeeded in evoking, not by any means the unanimous support of Algerian Muslims, but a growing consciousness of purpose among participants in the struggle. Among the disciplined *moujahiddin* of Colonel Boumedienne a revolutionary ideology evolved, grounded in Islam but eclectically appropriating political and economic doctrines judged relevant in nation-building. Though never capable of defeating the French army in battle, the liberation army had by 1958 secured too broad a base of popular support to be itself defeated. Because de Gaulle, increasingly impatient to end a war so damaging to France's international standing and domestic regeneration, knew he could find no other *interlocuteurs valables*, in negotiations at

Evian in March 1962 he made concessions previously judged unacceptable. Algeria's independence was accepted as a prior condition for the military cease-fire, with self-determination reduced to the form of a ratifying plebiscite. Instead of permanent guarantees for minorities, the rights of French citizens were protected for a transitional period of three years, after which they could opt for Algerian citizenship. Existing levels of French economic and technical assistance were guaranteed for the same three-year period, which was also that allowed for the withdrawal of French armed forces; but France could retain a lease of the Mers-el-Kebir base for fifteen years, as well as certain airfields and other facilities. Most important, France recognized the territorial integrity of Algeria, thus renouncing not only suggested partitions which would have retained European control over favoured coastal areas but any possibility of detaching the Sahara. For the petro-chemical industry de Gaulle could secure only promises that a Franco-Algerian Commission would give preference to French companies in granting future concessions. He instructed his negotiator that,

> We must concede these details rather than reject an agreement; for there is no comparison between the primary interest, which consists of reaching an agreement, and the secondary interest, which consists of holding a little longer certain things which in any case we do not reckon to hold for ever.[26]

For the first time in Africa the independence settlement corresponded more closely with the immediate aims of the successor government than with those of the decolonizers.

Many of the terms agreed at Evian did not last even as long as intended: Mers-el-Kebir, for example, was evacuated in 1968. The legal status of agreements negotiated with the FLN rather than with the Provisional Government was itself questionable; but the real force for amendment was the sheer momentum of events. Provisions for the future status of French residents were overtaken by the frantically hurried exodus of most of them, to the accompaniment of more destructive violence by their *Organisation de l'Armée Secrète*. On the Algerian side peace released suppressed conflicts among the FLN leaders, which vastly complicated their task of creating (rather than, like earlier succession states, inheriting) the institutions of a sovereign state. All the same, the long-term effects were beneficial to both sides. The Algerian republic, sustained more by its own mineral resources than by continued French assistance, made notable if chequered progress with its aim of creating a modern Islamic culture which would be 'national, revolutionary and scientific'; while the Fifth French Republic, released from its Algerian Nessus shirt to enjoy unprecedented prosperity, began to assume that leadership in Europe which de Gaulle claimed as its historic destiny.

In dealing with Black Africa de Gaulle found it easier to identify stable authorities with whom to negotiate new relationships. Initially at least these could only be the Vice-Presidents already designated in each Overseas Territory under the terms of the *loi-cadre*. The Fifth Republic's constitution was designed to commit elected African leaders to membership of a new federal Community, whose President, chosen by an overwhelmingly French electoral College, would retain jurisdiction over foreign policy, defence, currency, and large areas of economic and financial policy. Any Overseas Territory rejecting this option in the constitutional referendum, de Gaulle made it clear, would be deemed to have voted not only for immediate independence but for an immediate cessation of French assistance and co-operation. The freedom which Africans were being offered in their own countries would thus be limited by continuing dependence on France; but as de Gaulle argued during a hectic election tour of Madagascar, AEF, Ivory Coast, Guinea and Senegal, this reflected the realities of the modern world. Full independence, in an age of *ensembles organisés*, could only be illusory and ineffective.[27]

Most of the African leaders to whom de Gaulle proposed this qualified form of decolonization recognized the force of his argument. Student radicals of the 1950s saw the case for continued French assistance when they returned to official posts whose emoluments, under a second *loi Guèye* of 1950, had been assimilated to those payable in France. For the French, though now preparing to pass some of the costs of development assistance and commodity price support to their partners in the EEC, were more willing than the British to commit substantial resources to maintain special relationships with African colonies after they had attained self-government. And the strong personal respect which de Gaulle had enjoyed in Africa since 1940 made the inequalities inherent in such co-operation easier to bear. Commentators observed a powerful human chemistry, a 'carnal bond' which besides inspiring Batéké tribesmen to create a long-nosed military cult-figure called Ngol could reduce tough party bosses to sentimental sycophancy. The trans-cultural charisma which de Gaulle restored to the tarnished figure of Marianne made it less difficult for African patriots to justify continued deference to the former colonizer.

Yet they were also under heavy emotional pressure to demand nothing less than sovereign independence. Under the lengthening shadow of the Algerian war the Pan-African messages coming out of Accra met stronger responses among French-speaking Africans. Orators in all parties used the words 'independence' and 'unity' more frequently, emphatically, and effectively. The sense of revolutionary solidarity among colonized peoples, voiced by the Martiniquan psychiatrist Frantz Fanon in *Les Damnés de la Terre* (1961), could no more be prevented from spreading south of the Sahara than could the radio-activity generated by French nuclear tests in southern Algeria in February 1960. Even though French Ministers (anxious to demonstrate African acceptance of the Algerian war, to retain the loyalty of African mercenaries fighting there, and to avoid further military diversions like Cameroun) continually raised the political rewards on offer to loyal collaborators, many Africans felt a psychological need to make gestures of defiance.

Sékou Touré had before 1950 already established the PDG, his section of the RDA, in control of the internal government of Guinea. Confident of his strength, he instinctively rejected de Gaulle's challenge to choose between independence and a still nebulous French Community; the human chemistry between these two men produced an explosive reaction. In the referendum conducted under French auspices on 28 September 1958 95 per cent of Guinean voters followed Touré's leadership and voted against the new Community constitution. In most other colonies the voters, likewise following their elected leaders, voted in favour by comparable margins. The exception was Niger, most remote and undeveloped of the West African colonies, where another trade unionist Minister, Djibo Bakary, followed Touré in calling for rejection. But his leadership was already being challenged by his chiefly allies as well as by RDA opponents, who were strong in western areas of the country; French administrators, worried about Niger's uranium resources and about possible communist influence on the Algerian border, had no difficulty in turning the vote against him. When only 24 per cent voted No, on a low poll, Djibo Bakary resigned, later taking refuge abroad. Meanwhile de Gaulle petulantly withdrew all French assistance from the government of Guinea, hoping to demonstrate the dire consequences of Sékou Touré's proud option for 'freedom in poverty'. Soviet support, to which Touré initially turned, did prove unsatisfactory and inadequate; but Americans, sympathetic Frenchmen, and fellow-Africans proved willing to help fill the gaps which de Gaulle had torn in the state fabric. The new republic survived, and

by surviving encouraged the cause of independence elsewhere.

After reluctantly rejecting independence, some African leaders
hoped to restore some of the unity jeopardized by the disappearance of
the two quasi-federal Governments-General. Senghor, fearing that
Imperial Dakar would sink like Vienna to the status of a provincial
capital, took the initiative in creating 'a Negro-African nation of the
West' under the historic name of Mali.[28] This seemed ominous to
Houphouet (who, retaining high Ministerial office in Paris, became
de Gaulle's closest African collaborator); he intended to reserve most
of the revenue derived from the Ivory Coast's booming economy for
use within his own national constituency. In face of Houphouet's
evident displeasure Senghor's Mali was reduced to two of the former
colonies, Senegal and Soudan, and within eighteen months their
needs and interests proved incompatible.

But as hopes of unity collapsed through such divergences,
independence proved attainable with de Gaulle's blessing after all. By
the end of 1960 the seven remaining West African territories and the
four of Equatorial Africa – together with Madagascar, where a
coalition government under Philibert Tsirinana became the
beneficiary of the new constitution – had secured recognition of what
de Gaulle preferred to call their 'international sovereignty'. It was
clear that since the Community could never become a genuine
federation of equals, political pressures would continue to run
towards independence: having secured initial oaths of allegiance
through his referendum, de Gaulle now saw less purpose in enforcing
formal legal constraints – and much virtue in sponsoring African
members of the UNO who could be induced to support French policy
in Algeria. There had been happy precedents earlier in 1960, when
both Cameroun and Togo became independent without ill effects for
France; in 1961 indeed Cameroun brought new peoples and territory
into the residual Community when the southern part of the British
Trust territory gave a 70 per cent vote in a UN plebiscite in favour of
reunion with Cameroun.

This rush to independence meant that the Community as
originally conceived was still-born; relationships between France and
her former colonies would resemble those within the Commonwealth
rather than the institutional model set out in the constitution. But de
Gaulle's essential purposes were still maintained through the office
of Secretary-General, working under close Presidential supervision.
'For the General', the first holder declared, 'there was one
fundamental aim: the maintenance of the bonds which History had

created between the African states and France'.[29] Those who shared these purposes continued to talk of a renovated or contractual Community, surviving like the smile of the Cheshire Cat. Some sort of domesticated animal had clearly survived. Its skeleton could be traced through a growing network of bilateral treaties and inter-state associations; its vital functions were sustained through the budget of the French Ministry of Co-operation, ensconced in the offices in the Rue Oudinot which had been the heart of the colonial empire. The radiance of French civilization and influence in the world continued to be promoted by generous distributions of French francs, a constant supply of eager *co-opérants*, and a number of military agreements which left mobile intervention forces firmly based in many of France's former colonies. Even if France had not completed her decolonization in quite the manner which de Gaulle intended, the compacts on which she based her new political relationships were in most cases to prove mutually advantageous and durable.

THE SUDDEN DEATH OF BELGIAN AFRICA

Until the later 1950s only the British and French were seriously preparing to liquidate and replace their colonial governments in Africa. Because Belgium cherished no aspirations to Great Power status she experienced less international pressure to accelerate political reform in her huge Congo colony; and though Ruanda-Urundi received periodic UN visitations these two land-locked kingdoms were never high on the Trusteeship Council's agenda. Nor was there much interest within Belgium. Leopold II's desire to give his country a colonial vocation had made limited impact upon politicians and the public; (it was largely foreigners who forced the liquidation of his infamous Congo Free State). The material interests of Belgian capitalism and the spiritual concerns of the Catholic Church both harmonized with the practices of colonial administrators; the European population, which postwar immigration raised to over 100,000, was discouraged from seeking settler self-government on the Rhodesian model. There were arguments in Brussels over some aspects of policy, but white people in the Congo remained serenely confident in the benevolence and durability of Belgian rule. Those who exercised authority, whether governmental, economic or spiritual, broadly agreed that all the postwar situation demanded was the gradual enlargement of African responsibilities and rights within local communities (though perforce that process might have to be somewhat more rapid in the Trust territories).

Belgian rule, foreigners observed, was relatively intensive; in relation to population there were more white officials, more para-military forces, more agricultural officers enforcing more drastic programmes of compulsory cultivation, than elsewhere in tropical Africa. The justificatory rhetoric emphasized the paternal spirit of Belgian rule; and Africans whose traditional sources of temporal and spiritual authority had been suddenly overthrown do sometimes seem to have felt a need for the tutelage of new father figures. But in the postwar world paternal roles became more difficult everywhere, and especially in colonies where even the kindest Europeans had to work within racially discriminatory institutions and conventions. The Belgians found adolescence particularly difficult to handle. Though they announced their intention to create a Congolese middle–class who would eventually attain full citizenship in some form of Belgo-Congolese community, the 'Cards of Civic Merit' which were supposed to mark the first stage were issued so grudgingly as to become themselves a source of grievance. Moreover the middle class envisaged was one of clerks, artisans and traders rather than professional men or substantial capitalists. Although primary education, provided almost wholly by Christian missionaries, compared well in quantity and quality with other colonies, it was closely geared to the practical needs of a colonial society. The Universities of Lovanium (Catholic) and Elizabethville (lay) were established only in 1954 and 1956 respectively; by independence there were in total sixteen Congolese graduates.

Africanization was taken more seriously by the missionary churches. The first modern Congolese priest was ordained in 1917, the first Bishop consecrated in 1956; by 1960 there were some six hundred Roman Catholic priests and about five hundred formally ordained Protestant ministers, in addition to many pastors in unauthorized independent churches. Missionary evangelism had been strikingly successful; of some sixteen million Africans under Belgian rule in 1950 about three and a half million were professed Catholics, and almost half as many Protestants.[30] But the most powerful agents of future Christian expansion were to be the disciples of Simon Kimbangu, the outlawed prophet who died in 1951 after thirty years in a colonial gaol. Few Belgians appreciated the latent strength of such smouldering rebellions against paternalist constraints.

The first moves towards more rapid change originated outside the Congo. In 1954 a Liberal-Socialist coalition government was formed in Brussels, without the *Parti Social Chrétien* which had dominated postwar politics. Its attempts to favour lay education at the expense of missionary schools made Congolese policy a subject of contention in Belgium; and as missionaries rallied their converts in support, contention spread to the Congolese themselves. In this context a suggestion by a Belgian academic, A. J. van Bilsen, that the Congo needed a plan for 'emancipation' within thirty years, aroused unusual attention. By 1958 Léo Petillon, a former Governor-General serving briefly as Minister, recognized the need for some political initiative by appointing a committee; this recommended an elaborate pyramid of representative Councils, with complex systems of indirect election to neutralize the hazards of manhood suffrage. Ten years earlier Creech Jones might have admired this exercise in constitution-mongering; but Congolese who would then have been satisfied with recognition and representation were now beginning to demand control.

A broadening political consciousness among the educated minority had become evident since 1956. In that year a Manifesto in the Catholic journal *Conscience Africaine*, hailing van Bilsen's suggestion of emancipation in thirty years, demanded participation in its planning; and a young postal worker called Patrice Lumumba prepared an eloquent, though deferential, appeal to Belgians to make more sincere efforts to secure 'the collaboration of the Congolese elite'.[31] In Ruanda a Trusteeship Council visitation in 1957 inspired new demands, on behalf of the submerged Hutu majority as well as the Tutsi oligarchy. Among the Bakongo political excitement was created by the implementation of the *loi-cadre* in AEF, and by the visit to Brazzaville in August 1958 of de Gaulle, whose wartime prestige remained strong on both banks of the Congo; a cultural association known as ABAKO turned itself into a political party which quickly established ascendency when local elections were instituted in Leopoldville. As in Congo-Brazzaville, where the cult of André Matswa was providing political resources for Abbé Fulbert Youlou and the RDA, ethnic solidarity among the Bakongo was fortified by the spirits of colonial martyrs. From beyond the grave, Kimbangu provided the ABAKO leader, Joseph Kasavubu, with a charisma lacking in his own personality; leaders of Kimbanguist congregations acquired sudden political authority, and some believed that the prophet himself was returning to guide the hands of Kasavubu.[32]

Once such *évolués* had founded political movements, these became affected by a dual process of political radicalization. The leaders became increasingly inspired by the ideology and rhetoric of populist nationalism; Lumumba, now leader of the *Mouvement National Congolais*, returned from the All-African Peoples' Conference in Accra in December 1958 ardently preaching Pan-African solidarity in the struggle against imperialism. At the same time the political consciousness of city-dwellers was carried back into their rural areas of origin – a process unwittingly expedited by Belgian administrators who deported troublesome agitators out of town. Loyalty to the 'primary nation' now began to complicate the ideologues' simple vision of unity within colonial boundaries. Those who founded the *Parti Solidaire Africain* (PSA) in Leopoldville in February 1959, while sympathetic to the general aims of ABAKO, were also anxious to prevent Bakongo candidates dominating provincial elections at the expense of persons native to Kwilu and Kwango districts. This growing 'politicization of ethnicity' increased the pressure on aspiring Congolese leaders as well as on the Belgians.

So no sooner had the Belgians unveiled their political initiative than their power of initiative was decisively challenged. On 4 January 1959 the banning of an ABAKO meeting in Leopoldville triggered widespread riots in a city where growing African unemployment was increasing racial tension. Control of the African townships was temporarily lost; the official total of 49 dead was certainly an underestimate. King Baudouin and his Ministers reacted quickly by linking their announcement of constitutional reform with promises of independence to follow. The Belgian public's indifference to Africa was suddenly shaken by the nightmare of an Algerian-type war. Moreover, though capitalism in the Congo was still basically healthy, its spectacular postwar growth had slowed since the mid-50s, and the growing charges of development expenditure had pushed the budget into deficit. Like their European partners, Belgians began to appreciate that colonies could become more of a burden than an asset to the metropolis. Clergy who understood that the future of the Congolese church could only be secured by African Christians were already disengaging from their close involvement with the colonial state; the great corporations too now began to consider how their investments might be safeguarded under African rule. Belgian support for colonial empire evaporated quickly as African hostility, sustained by widespread international sympathy, became seriously apparent.

After January 1959 Belgian Ministers telescoped fifteen years' hectic experience of West African decolonization into eighteen months, culminating in their acceptance of 30 June 1960 as Independence Day. But they miscalculated the consequences. Any Congolese government, they assumed, would remain heavily dependent on Belgium for advice and assistance: for investment capital and budgetary subsidies, for civil servants and technical experts, for officers of the *Force Publique*, which would still retain decisive control over Congolese society. Moreover, the very proliferation of political parties, competing to present the most convincing programme for independence with the support of particular ethnic groups, seemed to give the Belgians a strong voice in selecting their own successors. Since the nationalist euphoria was not yet focused on any single leadership, discreet external patronage might prove decisive. Ten regionally-based parties, and other smaller groups, divided the 137 seats in the national elections of May 1960; although Lumumba, whose MNC won 33 of these, emerged as head of a coalition government, his demagoguery might be partially checked by the Presidency of Kasavubu, the more phlegmatic and introverted ABAKO leader.

But if Belgium retained some influence in Leopoldville, she was rapidly losing it at local levels. While outside observers scrutinized the rhetoric of party leaders, deeper political movements were taking place. Rural areas as well as towns were reacting against the control exercised by Belgian administrators and agricultural supervisors, and the spread of radical sentiments was facilitated by the basic literacy which Christian missionaries had diffused so widely. When ABAKO began election propaganda in rural areas in 1959 the PSA responded by selling their own membership cards in Kwilu and Kwango districts, and found their countrymen prepared for more fundamental rejections of colonialism than they had expected. As news of the Loepoldville riots spread, resentment that had formerly been suppressed or channelled into Kimbanguist 'sectarianism' was manifested in innumerable minor acts of localized violence, civil disobedience, or dumb insolence.[33] As the authority of the colonial state was rejected, administrators had to turn to local party leaders for help in collecting taxes and maintaining a semblance of ordered government.

Since party organizers had to build on foundations of ethnic loyalty, this period of nationalist euphoria tended, paradoxically, to accentuate divisions among Congolese. In southern Katanga these were made more serious by external intervention. Moïse Tshombe, a prosperous businessman and leader of the CONAKAT party, was anxious not only to preserve the dominance in Katanga of the Lunda and Yeke peoples over Luba immigrants, but to prevent the resources of its huge and profitable mining industry being expropriated in Leopoldville by a centralized regime. In this he was naturally applauded by the mighty *Union Minière du Haut Katanga* and other capitalist and settler interests, which provided considerable moral and material support to CONAKAT as a form of insurance for their investments. As early as March 1960 what was called 'an unofficial Katangese delegation' visited Welensky to discuss possible new relationships with the Central African Federation;[34] and as Belgium seemed likely to accept demands for a centralized government, Tshombe and his allies became increasingly alarmed. When on Independence Day Lumumba answered a homily from King Baudouin by fiercely denouncing Belgian rule in the name of populist nationalism, they prepared to defend their interests.

Lumumba's speech also raised the expectations of soldiers in the *Force Publique*. Five days after independence they mutinied against Belgian officers who had failed to recognize that the moral basis of colonial discipline had disappeared. Public order broke down in many areas; Belgian troops re-emerged from the large bases they had retained under the independence settlement but seemed unwilling to act under Lumumba's direction. Belgian civil servants, settlers and technicians began to leave the country in thousands. On 11 July 1960 Tshombe, with evident approval from foreign residents, declared that Katanga had seceded as a separate state. South Kasai, where the diamond corporation *Forminière* was powerful, followed suit on 8 August. This loss of its most negotiable resources threatened to strangle the Congo's independence at birth.

Facing the double danger of a disintegrating state and a revival of Belgian control, Lumumba appealed for support to fellow African leaders, to the United Nations, to the United States, and to the Soviet Union. Both the latter powers were already watching the Congo, the USA apprehensive about established economic and strategic interests, the USSR sensing opportunities to extend its still tenuous influence in Africa by patronizing the Pan-African cause. Hitherto the Americans, by judiciously distinguishing their African policies from those of their European allies, by growing disbursements of economic and educational assistance, and by covert intelligence activity, had been fairly successful in securing the goodwill of new governments in Africa and had respected their policies of non-alignment. But the sudden appearance of a power vacuum in a country with such resources of strategic minerals threatened for the first time to make tropical Africa a theatre of the Cold War. Gradual movements towards Russo-American detente had been reversed by the collapse of an international 'Summit' in May 1960: on 4 August Harold Macmillan gloomily observed that the international situation 'has a terrible similarity to 1914. Now Congo may play the role of Serbia'.[35] The best hope of avoiding that danger was that the United Nations might provide forces and technical advisers who could act in a genuinely neutral role; by preparing conditions in which the Congolese could recover control of their own government, Secretary-General Hammarskjold hoped that UNO would in effect take over that terminal imperial role of preparing decolonization which Belgium had handled so badly. In the end he largely succeeded, but at the cost of his own life, and of bitter international controversies which would inhibit his successors from taking any such bold initiative.

UN intervention might have been less hazardous if the government in Leopoldville, whose authority it was supposed to uphold, had been united in its own aims. But the precarious unity of Lumumba's coalition could not withstand the strain of the mutiny and the secessions, still less the surreptitious intrigues and interventions of frantic foreigners. On 5 September 1960 Lumumba, regarded by some Westerners as a potential Soviet client and by others as a menace to their property, was dismissed by President Kasavubu; three months later he was captured by hostile Congolese while trying to join followers who had formed an alternative government in Stanleyville, taken to Katanga, and assassinated. For almost a year there was no effective central government (though local life seems to have continued in some areas without too much turmoil). It is difficult to distinguish the part played in these violent events by antagonisms among Congolese from the more or less covert interventions of foreigners; but evidence disclosed in the United States makes it clear that, under both Eisenhower and Kennedy administrations, the Central Intelligence Agency was an increasingly unscrupulous and active participant.[36]

By August 1961 the United Nations, with American support, had reconstituted a Congolese army and promoted a new national government of pro-Western sympathy; but Tshombe's regime, confidently installed in Katanga, remained a focus of foreign intrigue. Though officially recognized by no foreign government, and continually pressed by UN representatives to renounce secession, Tshombe continued until January 1963 to collect revenues from *Union Minière* with which to pay a mercenary army and its Belgian regular officers. As an apparently reliable protector of foreign investment against communist penetration he received support in various forms from interests in Belgium, France, Britain, South Africa and the Central African Federation. Soviet-American rivalry was focused on Leopoldville, but as pro-Western elements gained the upper hand there the Russians became more interested in provincial revolts. China also perceived her first good opportunity to try to apply the thoughts of Chairman Mao to Africa, providing material as well as ideological support to a rebellion of rural radicals in southern Kwilu, led by the former PSA leader Pierre Mulele. Revolt spread to Lumumba's home districts round Stanleyville, and was suppressed only after an American airlift of Belgian parachutists in November 1964. Not till a year later, when the army finally took power under General Joseph [Sésé Séko] Mobutu, did the Congo achieve a still somewhat precarious stability, in conditions more satisfactory to *Union Minière* and the Americans than to followers of the martyred Lumumba.

Meanwhile Ruanda-Urundi, where the pace of constitutional reform had been overtaken by events in the Congo, also became independent in July 1962: but, despite efforts by the Trusteeship Council to maintain its unity, as two separate states, and with much bloodshed. Here the acceleration of political activity sharpened ethnic antagonisms in an exceptionally dangerous way, especially in the northern kingdom of Ruanda. While the Tutsi ruling oligarchy prepared to benefit from reforms proposed by a UN visitation in 1957 the submerged Hutu majority not only formed its own political party, PARMEHUTU, with some Belgian encouragement, but began to attack Tutsi chiefs. In January 1961, when Belgium was fully occupied in the Congo, PARMEHUTU proclaimed the Republic of Rwanda, and drove 130,000 Tutsi into exile; the independence settlement essentially ratified this coup. Burundi became independent at the same time under its Tutsi monarchy, which had been less oppressive than its neighbour; politics here initially crystallized around two rival ruling clans, and the conflict between Hutu and Tutsi did not reach its bloody climax until 1972.

At first sight, the precipitous decolonization of Belgian Africa represented a triumph of radical Pan-Africanism: henceforth the termination of colonial rule seemed to be generally acknowledged as the first duty of any tutelary power, rather than a boon to be conceded when the trustees judged their preparations to be complete. Rulers now felt some obligation to justify any extensions of their rule by demonstrating special circumstances before the Special Committee on Decolonization established by the UN General Assembly in November 1961, which took over the running from the more moderate Trusteeship Council. Refusal to recognize this change in international climate, Portugal would soon discover, carried serious diplomatic penalties.

But the Congo crisis also showed clearly that the withdrawal of imperial authority could actually increase foreign intervention. Africa was now a Cold War battlefield. Since Stalin's death the Soviet Union had again become willing to offer support to bourgeois nationalist movements, as part of 'the anti-imperialist national-liberation revolutions' of the age.[37] Although she had not yet shown much skill in dealing with potential African allies, even those as potentially sympathetic as Sékou Touré, her initiatives had stimulated that American interest which became so evident during the Congo crisis. After the inauguration of President J. F. Kennedy in January 1961 the State Department, the Agency for International Development, and the CIA all became more active in Africa, as American rhetorical commitments to African freedom became more resounding. The new mood was encouraged by growing evidence that Black Americans were more seriously interested in Pan-African causes than had been expected; most Americans first learned that strong Black Muslim movements existed in their cities through protests about the murder of Lumumba outside UN headquarters in New York. Spear-headed by the Peace Corps and the CIA, Kennedy's New Frontier began to advance into uncharted African territory.

NOTES AND REFERENCES

1. FO 371/71660 Problems connected with defence against Communist infiltration in the Colonies: Bevin to Attlee, 6 Nov. 1948
2. cf. Louis. *British Empire in the Middle East* pp. 609–13, quoting Memo by P. J. Stent, 21 Nov. 1949
3. Y. Bangura, *Britain and Commonwealth Africa* (Manchester 1983) pp. 30–4
4. Tayeb Chenntouf, 'L'assemblée algérienne et l'application des réformes prévues par le statut du 20 septembre 1947', *Les chemins* pp. 371–5
5. L. Merat, *Fictions et Réalitiés coloniales* (Paris, 1946) p. 108
6. R. Pasquier, 'La formation des cadres syndicalistes africains: l'exemple de la CFTC', *Les chemins* p. 517

7. Sékou Touré, *General Congress of the U.G.T.A.N.* (Paris, 1959) p. 18
8. R. Rhodes James, *Anthony Eden* (1986) pp. 469, 484–5
9. P.P. 1956–7 XXIII Cmnd 124. Defence: Outline of Future Policy
10. P.P. 1955–6 XLV Cmd 9520. Exchange of Letters on Defence Matters between the Governments of the United Kingdom and the Union of South Africa, June 1955. J. D. B. Miller, *Survey of Commonwealth Affairs: Problems of Expansion and Attrition 1953–69* (1974) p. 130
11. Morgan V, pp. 88–100, esp. Macmillan to Salisbury, 28 Jan. 1957, pp. 96–7
12. P.P. 1956–7 XXVI Cmnd 237 The United Kingdom's Role in Commonwealth Development; Morgan III, pp. 13–17
13. Report by Norman Brook on Future Constitutional Development in the Colonies, 6 Sept. 1957, quoted Morgan V, pp. 100–2
14. K. W. J. Post & G. D. Jenkins, *The Price of Liberty* (Cambridge, 1973) p. 392, quoting the acute observations of a participant, Dr Chike Obi
15. I develop this point in 'From Strangers to Minorities in West Africa', *Transactions, Royal Historical Society* 5th series, 31, 1981, pp. 95–113
16. P.P. 1957–8 IX Cmnd 505 Nigeria: Report of the Commission appointed to enquire into the fears of Minorities and the means of allaying them, pp. iii, 89: cf *The Memoirs of Lord Chandos* pp. 410–11
17. P.P. 1955–6 XIII Cmd 9475 East Africa Royal Commission, 1953–1955: Report, June 1955
18. P. Darby, *British Defence Policy East of Suez, 1947–1968* (1973) pp. 84–5, 123–5, 185–8, 203–8
19. C. Douglas-Home, *Evelyn Baring: The Last Proconsul* (1978) pp. 283–4
20. Lennox-Boyd, 22 April 1959: Hansard, Commons, 5th series, 604: 562
21. Lord Boyd, 15 March 1978: K-G p. 2
22. J. R. T. Wood, *The Welensky Papers* (Durban, 1983) pp. 460, 476–80
23. P.P. 1958–9 XXV Cmnd 814 Report of the Nyasaland Commission of Inquiry p. 87
24. J. Marseille, *Empire colonial et capitalisme francais* Ch. XV
25. Press Conference, 11 April 1961; *Marchés Tropicaux et Mediterranéens* No. 805, 15 Apr. 1961
26. de Gaulle to Joxe, 18 Feb. 1962, quoted A. Horne, *A Savage War of Peace* (1977) p. 514. For text of the agreements and commentary by the head of the Provisional Government, Benyoucef Ben Khedda, *Les accords d'Evian* (Alger, 1986)
27. Speech by de Gaulle at Dakar, 26 Aug. 1958: C. de Gaulle, *Discours et Messages* Vol. III *Avec le Renouveau* (Paris, 1970) pp. 38–9
28. L'Sédar Senghor, *Congrès Constitutif du PFA: Rapport sur la doctrine et le Programme du Parti* (Paris, 1959) p. 87
29. Raymond Jamot, 19 Oct. 1979, in *La Politique Africaine du Général de Gaulle* (Paris, 1981) p. 124 This symposium throws much light on the new period of Franco-African relations, as do many of the papers in M-J & F.
30. Adrian Hastings. *A History of African Christianity* (Cambridge, 1979), pp. 43–4
31. P. Lumumba, *Congo, My Country* (1962) p. 7. This is the English edition of a book published in French in 1961, but originally written in 1956.
32. M. Simba, *Le Messianisme congolais* (Paris, 1972) pp. 132–3

33. H. F. Weiss, *Political Protest in the Congo* (Princeton, 1967), Part III
34. J. T. Wood. *The Welensky Papers* p. 769
35. H. Macmillan, *Pointing the Way* (1972) pp. 264-5
36. S. Weissman, 'CIA Covert Action in Zaire and Angola: Patterns and Consequences', *Political Science Quarterly* 94, 1979, pp. 263-86; cf. R. D. Mahoney, Jr, *JFK: Ordeal in Africa* (NY 1983)
37. I. Potekhin, *African Problems* (Moscow, 1964) pp. 43-4

CHAPTER EIGHT
The End of the Affair

THE CONVERSION OF THE CONSERVATIVES

Even before the Congo crisis focused international attention on tropical Africa, Harold Macmillan was realizing that his attempt to maintain a privileged relationship with the United States at the head of the Atlantic alliance could be jeopardized if Britain remained too closely identified with the residues of her colonial empire in eastern and southern Africa. Besides damaging British relations with new Commonwealth members and with the UN, colonial commitments might also prejudice any application for membership of the EEC, within which de Gaulle was clearly planning to redefine Euro-African relationships for the post-colonial age. As the pressure on Britain's financial and military resources continued to tighten, Africa seemed a region where many commitments could safely be contracted.

For a Conservative leader, imperial contraction was a delicate political operation. Since the Suez debacle the old imperialist elements in the party had begun to re-group. One of the eight MPs who had then resigned the Whip was Julian Amery, son of the former Colonial Secretary and also Macmillan's son-in-law; on returning to the party he served as Lennox-Boyd's Under-Secretary at the Colonial Office, among other Ministerial appointments. The Joint East and Central African Board which represented business and settler interests in that region had links with the Conservative Party,[1] and some MPs were closely involved with such companies as Tanganyika Concessions, strong supporters of Tshombe's secession in Katanga. Others placed high value on loyalties to 'kith and kin' in Central Africa, but still more so in Kenya, where, the Prime Minister noted, 'settlement has been aristocratic and upper middle-class (much more than Rhodesia) and has strong links with the City and the Clubs.'[2]

Lord Salisbury remained a prestigious and powerful patron of all these groups.

In the General Election of October 1959 African policy for the first time became a party issue, if a minor one. While Party manifestoes naturally placed overwhelming emphasis on domestic issues, the Labour Party declared that 'the future of Africa is poised as perilously as that of India in 1945'; attacking Macmillan's rejection of the Devlin Report, it reiterated the Party's commitment, since 1956, to self-determination on the basis of 'one man, one vote'. The Conservatives spoke only of ending racial discrimination in multi-racial countries and of protecting rights of minorities – which were hardly those at issue in Central Africa. Sixty per cent of Labour candidates, but only four per cent of Conservatives, mentioned Central Africa in their personal manifestoes; almost a third of Labour candidates but no Conservatives referred to the Hola Camp atrocity. Both parties referred to African issues in television broadcasts. In Scotland many churchmen, alerted by persons whom the Prime Minister regarded as 'dangerous and subtle agitators'[3], criticized the government's discharge of its trusteeship for African rights in the Federation; this possibly played a minor part in its loss of four Scottish seats, with a contrary swing to Labour of 1.4 per cent.[4]

Though generally reassuring, these results may have reinforced Macmillan's belief that a change of course was needed. Lennox-Boyd, whose strong commitment to Federation was reassuring to imperialists, had already decided to retire from politics to business; to replace him at the Colonial Office Macmillan appointed his former Minister of Labour, Iain Macleod. Macleod's dedication to politics, allied to a capacity for coolly ruthless calculation which appealed to all sections of the Conservative Party, had already marked him, at 46, as a likely future leader. But not all had yet perceived the moral passion which this Yorkshire-born Highlander could bring to issues affecting the liberty of nations and individuals; Macleod had been deeply shocked to discover that the government in which he served had tried, however unwittingly, to dissemble its responsibility for the brutal atrocities of Hola Camp. Sensitive both to the moral challenge of African nationalism and to the political perils of resisting it, Macleod concluded, as he later put it, that the dangers of over-rapid decolonization were less than those of moving too slowly. 'Terrible bloodshed in Africa'[5] would also bring terrible problems, domestic and international, for the government. His sense of urgency increased when in early 1960 de Gaulle finally agreed to independence for his Black African colonies, and the Belgians announced their intention to follow.

Macleod's mission was thus to provide genuine moral conviction in justification of that speedy disengagement from imperial responsibilities which had become politically necessary. The reassuring formula of 'multiracialism' still had comprehensive appeal; but Lennox-Boyd's attempts to apply it had assumed the ascendency of enlightened white leaders willing to admit to governmental responsibilities African representatives who would share their values and recognize their interests. Macleod doubted whether privileged settler communities would spontaneously select such leaders within the limited time available unless the British government applied pressure to move them more rapidly. His general tactic was thus to insist on substantial extensions of the African franchise within complex constitutional structures which, while delaying the advent of democratic equality, would oblige politicians to seek support outside their own racial constituencies and to adjust their programmes accordingly. This was to prove more successful in East Africa than in Rhodesia.

Many among the generation of African leaders who had come to maturity since the war were well disposed towards *this* form of multiracialism. Some had been deeply impressed by the friendly and egalitarian spirit in which many units of the second colonial invasion tried to enlist Africans in the work of nation-building. Trade union and co-operative advisers, teachers in schools and universities, many younger officers in the administrative and technical services, had without deliberate intent built a capital of goodwill which, until squandered by the indifference of later British governments, was a priceless asset to statesmen seeking to terminate colonial rule and prepare for continuing co-operation. The practical help and moral support offered from within the UK by many politicians, university teachers, clergy and journalists worked in the same direction. Macleod was perhaps the last leading British Minister fully to appreciate the practical value of this moral asset. But he knew that the condition of continuing racial collaboration in eastern Africa was clear endorsement of the right to early majority rule. Julius Nyerere, after 1958 the most effective democratic leader in Africa, increasingly set a pace which Macleod had to struggle to maintain.

Unfortunately, since the British government had no power to apply Macleod's tactic of delaying the impact of democratic franchises by elaborate constitutional checks to Southern Rhodesia, it offered no solution to the pending problems of Central Africa. Welensky's supporters continued bull-headedly to regard the existing Federation as a great political achievement which the British government was morally committed to uphold; they expected the scheduled Review Conference, after noting the record of material advancement in all communities, to approve a full transfer of power to a predominantly white electorate. If, as Welensky claimed, Federation had been definitively enacted in 1953, the increasingly strong opposition voiced by Kaunda, Banda and their British supporters was not merely misguided but treasonable. But Lennox-Boyd, as well as Macleod, accepted that the Colonial Office had prior obligations to promote substantial constitutional reforms in Northern Rhodesia and Nyasaland; and Macleod perceived, more clearly than Lennox-Boyd, that African leaders elected after such reforms were almost certain to reject Federation on any terms which Southern Rhodesian whites could accept.

The terms of reference and membership of the Advisory Commission which Macmillan was to appoint in preparation for the Review Conference were therefore crucially important. Welensky insisted that the option of recommending dissolution of the Federation or the secession of any member should be excluded; before the British election it was agreed that the Commission should advise on 'the constitutional programme and framework best suited to the achievement of the objects contained in the Constitution of 1953'.[6] This apparent endorsement of Welensky's view that the Commission should take political acceptability of the Federation as given, and simply suggest adjustments to its constitutional structure, had the consequential effect that the Labour Party debarred itself from participating. The twenty-six Commissioners eventually appointed after tense negotiation between London and Salisbury – eight whites from Central Africa, five non-Congress Africans, two retired governors, the brother of the Australian Premier, a Canadian historian, some cross-bench British notables and a core of Conservatives led by Lord Monckton – seemed inherently unlikely to be carried away by nationalist rhetoric. Yet their very respectability would make it more difficult to reject their considered verdict. As Macmillan noted publicly, if they found they could not work effectively within their terms of reference they would hardly hesitate to say so; and most of the British members accepted appointment on the commonsense assumption that the possibility of secession could not be excluded.

The future of Federation clearly held the key to broader questions: how far a Commonwealth changed by the entry of numerous rather weak African states might be expected to provide practical support for British world policies, and how such a body could be reconciled with

Britain's close relations with a South Africa devoted to an ever more rigorous enforcement of apartheid. Despite his continuing movement towards Europe, Macmillan could see great diplomatic advantages in remaining at the centre of an inter-continental group of governments, whose divergence of political outlook was in practice often mollified by their common language of discourse. Commonwealth relations were coming to be characterized by inclusiveness rather than close identity of interest; but could the forthcoming conference of Prime Ministers successfully include both Nkrumah and Verwoerd?

With such issues in mind the Prime Minister began an extensive African tour in January 1960. In Accra Macmillan was received with typical Ghanaian hospitality, though a speech referring to the wind of change in Africa attracted little external attention. In Central Africa he noted a widespread 'sense of uncertainty', which the studied ambiguity of his own pronouncements did little to dispel: hard decisions would have to await Monckton's report. Macmillan was still hoping that Macleod's more liberal approach might reconcile African leaders to remaining in the Federation on terms which would not drive Southern Rhodesian whites to secede themselves. The climax came in South Africa, where there was no lack of publicity for the speech to Parliament on 3 February in which Macmillan exhorted members to consider how the wind of change represented by African national consciousness would necessarily affect their relations with older Commonwealth members.

But Verwoerd was little moved by Macmillan's eloquence; and before the Prime Ministers assembled race relations in South Africa were further and irreparably damaged. On 21 March 1960 sixty-seven unarmed African demonstrators were killed by police at Sharpeville in the Transvaal, and world-wide anger made it yet more difficult for Macmillan to 'steer the Commonwealth through this crisis'.[7] South Africa still had some strong supporters, including some older Commonwealth leaders like Menzies as well as Conservative MPs; Britain's economic interests and prospects in the Union were more important than in any part of tropical Africa; and South Africa was playing an essential role in regional defence. But in May 1960 any definite rupture was avoided. Nkrumah, at his first Commonwealth conference, proved less insistent than the Malayan Premier in criticizing South African internal policies, and any discussion of South Africa's continued membership was deferred pending a referendum on her new Republican constitution.

But during the next ten months there was climatic change in the international atmosphere of African policy. The United Nations Assembly, following its admission of sixteen new African member states, adopted an uncompromising Declaration on the Granting of Independence to Colonial Countries and Peoples [Resolution 1514 (xv)]. The Congo crisis focused the attention of the Security Council on the effects which African independence might have on the relations of the great powers. And the election of J. F. Kennedy to the American Presidency brought the United States into more active sponsorship of speedy decolonization.

Kennedy had long judged such sponsorship to be both morally correct and politically shrewd. Since publicly supporting Algerian nationalism in July 1957 he had given much prominence to African questions in his campaign speeches. Besides catching the idealism of young white voters, his rhetoric helped capture the growing political consciousness of Afro-Americans for the Democratic Party. Once installed in January 1961, Kennedy made clear that he would actively pursue a policy of 'Africa for the Africans' – or at least, for such Africans as showed no attachment to Soviet communism. Conscious that Khruschev's more flexible approach to co-operation with African governments of the national bourgeoisie was liable to increase Soviet influence, Kennedy responded by active if sometimes heavy-footed searches for rival regimes to sponsor. While the idealism of the New Frontier was put to constructive use by the creation of the Peace Corps, which had three thousand volunteers in Africa by 1965, instruments of policy inherited from Eisenhower were used more intensively. Governments vulnerable to Russian blandishments, like Sékou Touré's, were offered competitive packages of economic assistance; after much puzzling over the ideological leanings of Kwame Nkrumah, American finance was provided for his ambitious Volta River project. American policy, formulated by persons of varied outlook and executed by diverse government agencies, was often incoherent and contradictory; despite the rhetoric, economic interests and Cold War contingencies tended to dominate policy towards South Africa, the Portuguese empire and the Congo crisis, and the CIA was prone to disburse subsidies and sponsor assassinations with little regard to policy direction.[8] Nevertheless, Kennedy's intention to identify the USA with a rising tide of African nationalism was clearly signalled to his British ally.

In a world where so much public discussion focused on the ethics of race relations, Macmillan's hopes of plastering over the contradictions in the Commonwealth were frustrated. On 5 October 1960 white South Africans voted for a Republic; precedent required her reapplication for Commonwealth membership, which Macmillan ruled must be considered by a new conference in March. Opposition began to grow. The Canadian Prime Minister, Diefenbaker, became convinced that 'to give unqualified consent to South Africa's application would be to condone the policies of apartheid'. Abubakr Tafawa Balewa, at his first conference, was aware of deep feelings in all Nigerian parties. On the eve of the meeting Julius Nyerere declared that Tanganyika, now scheduled for early independence, could not join any association including a racialist South Africa. Such lectures on racial morality merely stiffened Verwoerd in rejecting Macmillan's attempts at compromise; he refused to remain in the Commonwealth on terms which would expose him to further attack at later meetings or to accept the full accreditation of African ambassadors. On 15 March 1961 he announced the withdrawal of South Africa's application for continued membership.

These dramatic events, coupled with the unfolding of Macleod's policies for eastern Africa, suggested that the Anglo-African Commonwealth might be about to become a central plank of Britain's world policy. But appearances proved deceptive. Britain's close economic, military and Intelligence relations with South Africa continued. Still more significant was the announcement three months later that the British government was applying for full membership of the EEC. For those political leaders who now believed that Britain's future lay in closer relations with Europe were coming to regard many of her colonial links as economic and political liabilities.

Had the decision for Europe been made earlier, they need not have been so. The Six, under French leadership, were already negotiating new relationships with former African colonies on an inter-continental basis, to be initially defined in a Convention of Association (a new use for that versatile French word) signed at Yaoundé on 20 July 1963. From this there would subsequently develop a complex system of reciprocal trading preferences, price-support arrangements, and co-ordinated aid programmes through which new African states could secure, within the constraints of the international capitalist economy, a privileged relationship with the European Community. Early participation in such a Eurafrican structure might have facilitated Britain's honourable exit from some of her African commitments (though at the price of difficulties with other Commonwealth members); Yaoundé represented a modern form of the sort of Eurafrican relationship projected (as an alternative to partition) at the Berlin Conference of 1884-85, and later briefly envisaged by Llewellyn Smith in 1918, and by Neville Chamberlain in 1938.[9] But negotiating entry into this new Eurafrican association from outside was to raise difficulties, with foundation members reluctant to share their privileges more widely and with anglophone Africans suspicious of neo-colonialism. Britain's long hesitation between Europe and the Empire-Commonwealth was to prejudice her relationships with both during the last hurried phase of her decolonization.

THE LIQUIDATION OF BRITISH EAST AFRICA

In East Africa Kenya clearly provided the crucial test for Macleod's hopes of moving rapidly from institutionalized multiracialism to African majority rule. Baring and Lennox-Boyd had been preparing for an extended terminal period of reform under British control: as Macleod took office the Emergency was formally terminated and the legal barriers to African land tenure within the Highlands removed. Plans, inspired by the Royal Commission, for encouraging African capitalists in town and country were well under way. The new constitution, which established parity of African and European representation while envisaging a gradual extension of common electoral rolls, was expected to encourage the moderate policies of racial co-operation favoured by Michael Blundell's New Kenya Party (which Macleod's settler brother supported). But Lennox-Boyd had underestimated the pace at which African nationalists and their supporters, inside and outside Kenya, would demand progress towards majority rule.

As Lennox-Boyd expected, the fourteen Africans elected under his constitution were initially disunited about the shape and speed of future reforms. Divisions between articulate radicals like the Luo entrepreneur Oginga Odinga and more moderate representatives of less developed areas like Ronald Ngala and Daniel Arap Moi reflected differing ethnic or regional interests as well as ideological disagreements: by discreetly exploiting these colonial officials might obtain considerable opportunities for initiative. But they faced a subtle politician in Tom Mboya, whose achievements for trade unionists provided him with an authentically national following, and, through the ICFTU, with cosmopolitan contacts inside and outside Africa. In 1958 Mboya joined with Nyerere in founding the Pan-African Freedom Movement for East and Central Africa

(PAFMECA), which would become the most effective embodiment of regional Pan-Africanism; and at Accra in December he was on Nkrumah's initiative elected chairman of the momentous All-African Peoples' Conference. During 1959 the conflicts in the Central African Federation had repercussions in Kenya which assisted Mboya, Odinga, and other Luo and Kikuyu radicals to achieve temporary ascendency among the African legislators. When Macleod convened a constitutional conference at Lancaster House in January 1960 the African delegates were agreed in demanding early independence ('Uhuru'), and the release of a man whose imprisonment assumed huge significance for nationalists and settlers alike: Jomo Kenyatta, accused since 1952 of responsibility for Mau Mau.

Macleod was not ready to make such an emotionally-charged gesture, nor the Conservative Party to accept it; but, after some shadow-boxing, he was able to secure African acceptance of a complex new constitution, under which Africans, elected on a greatly extended common roll, could expect to secure 33 of the 65 elective seats. For the first time the Colonial Office formally acknowledged that Kenya was 'an African country'; Africans patient and skilful enough to work within temporary constitutional constraints without forfeiting popular confidence could now hope to inherit power in a foreseeable future. As an earnest of this, Britain began to provide funds to purchase land in the White Highlands for redistribution to African farmers, thus simultaneously responding to a major Kikuyu grievance and allowing settlers unwilling to contemplate the new order to negotiate withdrawal on comfortable terms.

By conceding the principles of majority rule and land reform Macleod retained some capacity to influence their implementation: for African unity remained precarious. When those most eager for early independence (chiefly Luo and Kikuyu) formed the Kenya African National Union (KANU), Ngala led the more cautious spokesmen of other peoples into the Kenya African Democratic Union (KADU). In its electoral campaign KANU emphasized its nationalist purity by refusing to envisage office before Kenyatta's release: support for this martyred prophet of Uhuru was made a touchstone of authentic radicalism, although nobody was able to ascertain the current opinions of Kenyatta himself. Meanwhile more fundamental debates were taking place within the KANU leadership. While Odinga wished to promise wide redistribution of land to the landless, Mboya, who had observed with alarm the consequences of Lumumba's attempts to break with foreign capitalists, wished to promote capitalist development by encouraging substantial African farmers to repurchase the land which would be made available. The saliency of the Kenyatta issue enabled economic liberals like Mboya to make ground without losing their nationalist credentials.[10]

In the 1961 election KANU polled twice the vote of KADU; but the deadlock over Kenyatta's release meant that it was Ngala, supported by Blundell's New Kenya Party, Asian representatives, and the remaining official placemen, who formed an interim government. Far-sighted Europeans now understood that there would be little advantage in prolonging British rule; their best hope now was to try to govern 'by example, influence and persuasion.'[11] In August 1961 the KADU coalition defused one politically explosive issue by securing the release of Kenyatta; as a further safeguard against a monopoly of power by a populist coalition of Luo and Kikuyu, a new Lancaster House Conference, chaired by Reginald Maudling in January 1962, agreed on substantial devolution to Regional Assemblies. In April the two parties formed a coalition to complete the transition to independence, with Kenyatta as Minister for Constitutional Affairs and Economic Planning. Contrary to rumour, detention had neither weakened his abilities nor embittered his attitudes; at the election of 1963 his authority ensured a large majority for KANU, with its moderates in the ascendent. The former *bête noire* of the settlers, whom in 1960 a British governor had called a 'leader to darkness and death' became the Prime Minister who led Kenya to self-government in June 1963, and in December to independence.

For some time this was generally welcomed as a triumphant decolonization of what had always been thought a problem colony. Politically, liberal reformers did have some cause for worry. The decentralization secured by KADU was rapidly reversed; KANU entrenched itself as the dominant and eventually the single party, though providing real opportunities for intra-party debate and selection. If Kikuyus were ascendent in Nairobi, other peoples – including Europeans, though less evidently Asians, willing to identify themselves with the new Kenya – retained access to power. In economic policy Kenyatta, while wearing the fashionable cloak of 'African Socialism', adopted most of the prevailing orthodoxies of capitalist development theory. The greater part of the 'million acres' of land eventually purchased under settlement schemes financed by the British Treasury and the World Bank was resold to well-to-do African entrepreneurs, who in effect became shareholders in the new regime. Landless squatters and labourers, former 'freedom fighters' emerging from the forests, and the growing numbers of urban poor were left to seek their personal Uhuru in the open market.

Setting Kenya on the path to early majority rule was the crucial step in Macleod's strategy of rapid disengagement from East Africa. Tanganyika presented fewer difficulties: Julius Nyerere's success in establishing TANU as a focus for the aspirations of all the country's peoples was confirmed by success in winning all the African seats in the two-stage elections of 1958-59. The patriotic euphoria aroused throughout Africa by Ghanaian independence created a stronger impulse than Trusteeship Council debates had ever generated. Governor Sir Richard Turnbull, an experienced colonial adminis-trator, quickly recognized that government could not be carried on without TANU's collaboration; Europeans and Asians elected to the legislature with the party's support confirmed that this was a party committed to inter-racial co-operation under majority rule. Soon after taking office Macleod agreed that responsible government should follow further, more democratic, elections in September 1960; after the inevitable TANU victory Nyerere formed a government and, at a constitutional conference in Dar-es-Salaam, negotiated the final steps to independence in December 1961. His own integrity, eloquence, and concern to marry the values of democratic socialism with those of African community life immediately made Nyerere an influential figure among African leaders, and in the Commonwealth. Europeans whose hopes of seeing their own democratic ideas fulfilled by Nkrumah or Sékou Touré were beginning to wane also reinvested much emotional capital in Nyerere's version of African Socialism.

In Uganda, whose future as 'primarily an African state' had been accepted since 1953, decolonization was delayed partly by concern about effects in neighbouring colonies, but also by pressure from Buganda to retain, if not a completely separate existence, at least its historically privileged status. When in 1959 a constitutional Committee recommended direct democratic elections to the Ugandan legislature the traditionalist Baganda bureaucracy, supported by many farmers, traders and aspiring politicians, refused to co-operate; cultural loyalties apart, such people saw more benefit in maintaining the separate identity of their primary nation than in following the trend towards independence within colonial boundaries. Nevertheless Macleod announced in February 1960 that elections, followed by a constitutional conference, would be held next year. For the first time, political contenders had either to seek party support on a nationwide basis or to entrench themselves in defence of sectional interests. The cause of populist nationalism, intermittently voiced by earlier groupings, was taken up by a new Uganda People's Congress (UPC) led by Milton Obote, a Lango from the north. Baganda traditionalists responded by refusing to co-operate in decolonizing the central government; the Lukiko, or Buganda Parliament, made an abortive declaration of independence, and only 3 per cent of the Baganda electorate turned out to vote in the election of March 1961. The abstentions allowed the Democratic Party of Benedicto Kiwanuka to make a clean sweep within that kingdom; this was essentially a Roman Catholic party, inspired by resentment of Protestant ascendency in Buganda but with support in other parts of the country. Consequently the UPC, while winning a clear majority of votes cast nationally, secured only thirty-five seats against the DP's forty-three.

Macleod now made it clear that Baganda particularism would not be allowed to obstruct the transfer of power, and the Kabaka's ministers reluctantly agreed to attend the planned conference in September 1961, hoping to negotiate some sort of federal compromise rather than the unitary state favoured by the UPC. When Kiwanuka tried to gain credit in Buganda by procrastinating, Macleod applied pressure by advancing the date of independence. By-passing Kiwanuka, the Buganda Court party agreed to accept a federal constitution with entrenched rights for Buganda, whose MPs were to be indirectly elected through the Lukiko; they formed a new party, the Kabaka Yekka, which in alliance with the UPC won the election of April 1962. In October this unstable coalition led Uganda to independence, and the Kabaka later became first President of the Republic. By forcing the pace of political change Macleod had preserved the unity of Uganda at the cost of intensifying internal conflicts (not only in Buganda). But it was no longer Britain's responsibility to deal with these.

There remained Zanzibar. As constitutional reform proceeded during the later 1950s, parties formed along more or less racial lines. The Zanzibar National Party, formed in 1956 under mainly Arab leadership, also commanded support in some African quarters, notably the trade unions. Some of its leaders were influenced by the anti-colonial nationalism of the Middle East, others by Marxism. In 1960 Macleod's decision to expedite a transfer of power coincided with the death of the aged and respected Sultan Khalifa. Although the ZNP with its African allies retained a precarious majority in the successive elections which followed, many people became apprehensive about what policies it might follow under an independent Arab Sultanate. As Independence Day (10 December 1963) approached the ZNP lost the vital support of the trade union movement and its Marxist leader Abdul Rahman Mohamed ('Babu').

One month afterwards the Sultan was overthrown by a revolutionary coup in the name of socialism and the under-privileged African majority. But Nyerere was as worried as the British by the prospect of volatile revolutionaries controlling these strategic islands, and later in 1964 he negotiated the union of Zanzibar with Tanganyika in the new state of Tanzania. The revolutionaries retained control of internal policies, but their foreign relations and influence on the mainland came under the controlling authority of TANU's more pragmatic brand of socialists. This remained the only effective step towards that federal union of East Africa which both British and African leaders had once hoped to promote.

Given the residual Empire Loyalism of British Conservatives, Macleod's expeditious liquidation of the East African empire was a considerable political achievement. Although back-bench apprehension about the speed of change (in Northern Rhodesia more than in East Africa) had led Macmillan to move Macleod from the Colonial Office in October 1961, Maudling, his more emollient successor, did not reduce the pace. Most East African settlers eventually understood that Mau Mau had destroyed such hold as they had on the colonial state, and those who could not face the prospect of life under African rule withdrew more or less grudgingly with their compensation money. When the Zanzibar revolution was followed by mutinies in the armies of Tanganyika, Kenya and Uganda there was international concern about the region's stability, and British troops returned briefly by invitation; but the Indian Ocean was not yet an area of great Soviet activity and it was clear that the British government, though still planning to retain military facilities in Kenya, had no intention of re-establishing direct control.

Central Africa continued to raise more difficult problems. With its more substantial settler population and its mineral resources, it lay closer to the old Imperial heart of the Conservative Party; and one of its component states was already beyond Whitehall control, in both law and practical reality. But failure to apply Britain's new principle of African majority rule would raise profound difficulties within the multi-racial Commonwealth.

THE END OF THE CENTRAL AFRICAN FEDERATION

The Nyasaland emergency had not only ensured that Monckton's review of the Federal constitution could not be the simple technical exercise which Welensky desired; it restored the initiative in British policy-making to the Colonial Office, the department responsible for public order in the protectorates, as against those Ministers who still cherished Federation as part of a grand Imperial design. Besides the moral indictment of British trusteeship implicit in Devlin's report, the material cost of existing policy had increased. The disorders of the 1950s had already meant increasing the Nyasaland police force, which in the inter-war years numbered around 500, to 130 officers and 2200 men; in 1959 Governor Armitage approved further increases of 100 officers and 1000 men.[12] In the longer run it now appeared that the Federation might require some support from British military forces, for which the post-Suez defence policy made no provision. Macleod could thus argue that any long-term British commitment to suppress African nationalism was politically as well as morally unacceptable, and that negotiations with Congress leaders represented the only realistic course. In March 1960 the new Chief Secretary and future Governor of Nyasaland, Glyn Jones, had talks with Banda in prison; Macleod then visited Central Africa, over-ruled Armitage as well as Welensky, ordered Banda's release in time to testify before Monckton, and on 1 April personally gave him some indication of his plans for an early constitutional conference. Clearly any such conference would raise the issue of whether an African majority in Nyasaland would be allowed to secede from the Federation. Some Rhodesian whites, always sceptical of the country's value and aware of the possible costs of control, were now prepared to let it go; but as Welensky realized, any admission of a right of secession would be taken up in Northern Rhodesia. The militant nationalists of ZANC had now regrouped as the United National Independence Party (UNIP), which after Kaunda's release in January 1960 became a highly organized mass party, gaining support among trade unionists who had previously been kept somewhat aloof from politics. Kaunda was personally deeply committed to non-violent methods, but increasingly there were manifestations of the violence latent within Northern Rhodesian society.

The Monckton Commission, which assembled at Victoria Falls on 15 February, spent three months in the Federation taking evidence, and could hardly have escaped the clear evidence of African alienation in the two northern territories. As was inevitable with so large and heterogeneous a Commission, the Report presented to Macmillan on 7 September 1960 was a complicated document; only eight of the twenty-five members signed without entering one or more Notes of Reservation, and two Africans submitted a Minority Report.

The majority asserted their belief in the economic advantages of Federation (though still without enquiring too, closely into their distribution), but could not avoid registering the 'widespread, sincere and ... long-standing' hostility of northern Africans. Their crucial conclusion was that 'Federation cannot, in our view, be maintained in its present form' – although this was immediately followed by the comment that 'to break it up at this crucial moment in the history of Africa would be an admission that there is no hope of survival for any multi-racial society on the African continent'. After recommending far-reaching constitutional and legislative changes at both federal and territorial levels the Commissioners (white Rhodesians included) were obliged to acknowledge that the British Government retained the right to consider requests for secession, and should announce its willingness to do so.[13]

In fact the survival of Federation had already been prejudiced by the conference on the Nyasaland constitution which, as Macleod had promised Banda, took place in London in July 1960. Banda and his colleagues (now re-grouped as the Malawi Congress Party) proved willing to compromise over details of African representation and franchise; nevertheless the constitution which emerged provided for an African majority, elected on such conditions that it was extremely unlikely to consent to continued incorporation in the Federation. African hostility was everywhere becoming so manifestly strong as to out-weigh the economic advantages emphasized (though not closely analysed) by Monckton. Perceptive businessmen like Sir Ronald Prain of the Rhodesian Selection Trust and Sir Jock Campbell of Bookers were already reinsuring their future in the protectorates by approaches to African leaders, and in October Macleod announced a new review of the Northern Rhodesian constitution. Meanwhile riots in the Salisbury townships showed that Africans in Southern Rhodesia too were beginning to reject the Federal regime.

In December 1960 the Federal review conference assembled in London, bringing for Welensky and many of his colleagues their first personal contact with Banda and Kaunda. Formal presentations of position produced only confrontations and walk-outs, and the conference soon adjourned to allow separate conferences to open on the constitutions of Southern and Northern Rhodesia. Sir Edgar Whitehead, the Southern Rhodesian Premier, who had introduced draconian legislation to control the new African militancy, was nevertheless planning reforms which he hoped might enable him to negotiate full independence from Britain. In February 1961 a complex new constitution was agreed which substituted a

Declaration of Rights for most of the British government's residual rights to intervene in internal affairs, but in return extended somewhat the hitherto negligible importance of the African electorate. Continuing this attempt to persuade middle-class Africans to collaborate with the more liberal settler-politicians, Whitehead outlawed a number of relatively minor, though highly offensive, discriminatory practices; and, more significantly, prepared to attack the major grievance by repealing the Land Apportionment Act. But for the rest of 1961, attention within the Federation focused on the crucial question of the distribution of power in Northern Rhodesia.

In January 1961 the leading settler politicians walked out of the Northern Rhodesian constitutional conference. Since there were clearly irreconcilable conflicts about the opportunities which could safely be offered to African nationalists, Macleod prepared to publish his own proposals. Like the more far-sighted European residents, he had now identified Kaunda's UNIP as offering the best hope of future peace and progress, and was determined that the new constitution, however hedged by complicated electoral arithmetic and delaying mechanisms, should register the ultimate primacy of African voters. Since this would mean the end of Federation in any form acceptable to Rhodesian whites, Macleod's proposals were bitterly resisted by Welensky, who complained with increasing bitterness that British Ministers were retreating from earlier promises whose implications they had failed to foresee. In response to reports of Federal mobilization and a possible declaration of independence the Ministry of Defence prepared airborne forces in Kenya for possible intervention; but there were doubts about the willingness of some officers to act against the settler regime.

For a time it seemed that Macleod was moving too fast. The Conservative imperialists, stimulated by an extra-Parliamentary 'ginger group' called the Monday Club which had become alarmed by the pace of change in Kenya, were heavily lobbied by Welensky and his allies; in February 1961 over ninety Conservative back-benchers whose residual empire loyalism had been disturbed by Macleod signed an 'Early Day motion' cautioning against early majority rule. The Commonwealth Secretary, Duncan Sandys, was already anxious to moderate the pace of change, and Macmillan's support of Macleod began to waver. All concerned could in any case see the advantage of avoiding confrontation until the Southern Rhodesian electorate endorsed their new constitution in July, and so negotiations about the complicated but vital details of political arithmetic in Northern Rhodesia continued through 1961. Macleod's February White Paper was revised in June, in hope of appeasing Welensky and his supporters; and on 10 October Macleod himself was promoted to duties on the home front. But this did not alter the constitutional responsibilities of the Colonial Office, nor the determination of its staff to discharge them in the African interest. In February 1962 Maudling introduced more changes, apparently minor but with the predictable effect of giving decisive electoral advantages to the best-organized African party.

The promised review of the Federal constitution, postponed by this series of constitutional changes and elections in the territories, now seemed a lost cause. On 9 March Macmillan persuaded the Home Secretary, R. A. Butler, to accept responsibility for all Central African affairs during what would clearly be a terminal phase. Recognizing that, after the Northern Rhodesian elections, Banda's demand to secede was likely to be followed by one from Kaunda, Butler first attempted to discover whether these leaders would allow the ghost of Federation to walk in the form of some looser economic association; but increasingly he had to fall back towards a negotiated dissolution on terms which would least disrupt existing administrative structures and economic relationships. Nyasaland's right of secession was virtually accepted in May, and confirmed in December 1962; by that time the Northern Rhodesian elections had resulted in a Nationalist majority, though divided between representatives of UNIP and of Harry Nkumbula's ANC. Despite attempts by the Federalists to win over the latter party, Kaunda and Nkumbula formed a coalition which in March 1963 demanded and received the right of secession. Since the Southern Rhodesian electorate had by then rejected Whitehead in favour of white politicians more interested in securing independence for themselves, the inter-governmental conference at Victoria Falls in June had only to negotiate the details of Federal dissolution.

The decolonization of Malawi and Zambia thus took place on the now normative basis of African majority rule; those who dreamed of some multiracial alternative had over-estimated the potential liberalism of white settlers. Nostalgic supporters of the Federation, even if they admit its failure to create a political and social context for real inter-racial partnership, emphasize that it did encourage investment and an overall growth in GDP estimated at 54 per cent; but the benefits of this were unevenly distributed. Nyasaland, while benefiting from the redistribution of Federal revenues, remained a seriously underdeveloped colony, still dependent on exporting labourers to the Union and the Rhodesias and on continuing budgetary support from the UK. Banda soon realized that in the Malawi he had inherited many expectations would remain unfulfilled, and the new government had to maintain its authority by methods even more rigorous than those of the colonial 'police state'. Kaunda's Zambia inherited rich mineral resources, at a time when world copper prices were again rising; but during the Federal period its contribution to the other two territories had been of the order of £77,000,000. An autonomous Northern Rhodesian government would certainly have grown more rapidly, and would have chosen different investment priorities – generating power in the Kafue basin rather than at Kariba, for example. These two countries had matured politically through the experience of resisting Federation. But Zambia had lost economically, and Malawi's gains are highly debatable.[14] The undoubted gainer from Federation was Southern Rhodesia, whether measured by net government outlays, incoming investment, or European immigration. Among the many assets which passed into her possession were the University College and the switches controlling the Kariba power-station. Most decisively, the 1963 settlement left the bulk of the Federation's considerable military forces under the control of a Southern Rhodesian government which, reflecting the racial complacency of immigrant electors, had just rejected the mild reformism of Edgar Whitehead in favour of the Rhodesia Front, led by Winston Field.

AFRICA FOR THE AFRICANS?

When on 25 May 1963 representatives of thirty-two African governments signed an agreement in Addis Ababa to establish an Organization of African Unity (OAU), the Pan-African ideal, recently most effectively championed by Kwame Nkrumah, was realized in a qualified form. The leading principles defined in Article III of the OAU Charter were the sovereign equality of all member states; non-interference in internal affairs; and 'respect for the sovereignty and territorial integrity of each state, and for its inalienable right to independent existence'. The beneficiaries of decolonization thereby Africanized the European partition; pre-occupation with consolidating their individual power-bases was already taking precedence over attempts to create more effective regional centres of economic or political power. Article II of the Charter proclaimed among the purposes of the OAU 'to eradicate all forms of colonialism from Africa'; and in the General Assembly of the United Nations and the Special Committee on Decolonization it established in 1961 the African group could exercise influence by virtue of numbers unrelated to the strength of individual states. But their capacity to secure effective support from the five Powers who held the right of veto in the Security Council remained to be tested.

Over much of the continent it would not be necessary; remnants of empire were becoming embarrassing burdens. Macmillan's determination to transfer power in Nyasaland and Northern Rhodesia to governments responsible to African electorates demonstrated, no less clearly than de Gaulle's negotiations at Evian, that decolonization had become the normal policy of European democracies. The certainty that both the United States and the Soviet Union would wish to conciliate the anti-colonialism of the OAU and their allies in the United Nations confirmed their own recalculations based on colonial costs and benefits. As Duncan Sandys, perhaps the last true imperialist to hold office in Britain, had sadly told Welensky, the British people had 'lost their will to govern', at least by the use of force. There were still some important exceptions, for Britain and others. But when in July 1963 the OAU established a Co-ordinating Committee for the Liberation of Africa, it acknowledged that Britain, France and Spain had already recognized the right of colonial self-determination, even if diplomatic pressure might be required to expedite its implementation.[15]

Spain was a recent convert. Franco, who had made his reputation in Morocco, had hoped during the war to take over France's Protectorate over the Sultan and make that country the base for an expanded African empire; but since 1945 he had confined his imperial role to discreet patronage of Arab nationalists in the empire of others. Moroccan independence left him with no alternative to withdrawal from the Spanish zones in the north and south of that country (though not from Ceuta, Melilla, and other remnants of an older Spanish imperialism); and in the 1960s he came to realize that by endorsing the rhetoric of anti-colonialism he might secure African support for Spain's claim to Gibraltar. Abandoning the fiction that Rio Muni and Fernando Po were Spanish provinces, he agreed in 1963 to referenda, followed by union and substantial autonomy; and in October 1968 the artificial state of Equatorial Guinea received a form of independence, for which it had been most inadequately prepared, under a bloodthirsty dictator, Macias Nguema. In 1969 an historical anomaly was removed by the cession to Morocco of the small enclave of Ifni; but for the time being Spain retained her vast desert territory in the Sahara, which contained few inhabitants but rich resources of phosphates and other minerals. In the early 1970s nationalism began to inspire the Sahraouis also; observing the effect of prolonged colonial war on his Portuguese neighbours the aged Franco withdrew in 1976, leaving the Sahara to become an apple of discord between Morocco, Mauritania and a determined and courageous Sahraoui resistance movement.

With the crucial exception of Rhodesia, Britain's demission of responsibility was virtually completed in 1963, to general relief in the political world. Through the 1960s euphoria for the cause of African independence declined in all the countries of the Atlantic alliance, as the weaknesses of the post-colonial order became more clear. The disorders in the Congo and the violence in Rwanda were reproduced elsewhere. Constitutional governments followed and outdid their colonial predecessors in authorizing the detention of persons judged dangerous to their own security, and in over-riding the judiciary in order to maintain the authority of the state; inequalities among Africans widened as the new rulers increased their emoluments by the old expedient of taxing the farmers, or by less regular methods; ethnic conflicts which had been muted in the cause of nation-building were revived and intensified by modern electoral politics. A military coup which killed President Olympio of Togo in January 1963 proved to be the first of many. As the favourable economic climate of the 1950s changed, hopes of rapid development faded (though prophecies of doom and disaster began only with the famines and inflation of the 1970s). There were still substantial numbers of articulate people, notably those who had worked in Africa during the terminal phase of liberal imperialism or more recently as volunteers, who recognised continuing British responsibilities; these were influential in the Labour and Liberal parties, and were represented within the governmental machine in the Ministry of Overseas Development, established by Harold Wilson in 1964. But old paternalists felt that the Colonial Office, its major trusteeships terminated, was being 'chuck[ed like] a rotten carcase on the rubbish heap so that the vultures can peck its decaying flesh'.[16] In 1964 it was absorbed by the Commonwealth Relations Office, which was itself taken over, along with the Overseas Development Ministry, by the Foreign Office in 1970. These mergers signalled an intention to deal with former African colonies on the same basis as other foreign states, except in so far as they managed to establish special relationships within the Commonwealth, which each of them joined on independence. With the appointment of a Secretary-General in 1965 it did seem possible that the Commonwealth would establish a new role for itself in international relations; but almost immediately that body was placed under prolonged strain by the dispute over British responsibilities in Rhodesia.

About Britain's remaining African colonies, however, there was little dispute. The Gambia, with its quarter-million inhabitants, had once seemed the *reductio ad absurdum* of any policy of general colonial independence; during the 1950s its leaders showed interest in schemes for constitutional integration into the United Kingdom, such as were being discussed for Malta. The Colonial Office recoiled from such un-British expedients, and on 18 February 1965 The Gambia became an independent state. There had been much talk of a possible federation with Senegal, but the merits of this solution were (until an internal crisis in The Gambia in 1981) out-weighed by conflicts of outlook and interest. In fact The Gambia proved a more 'viable' international entity than many larger states, perhaps because its very size exempted it from trying to maintain such costly symbols of international sovereignty as an army or a lavish foreign service. (At one time it was reported to maintain the only profitable airline in Black Africa, by the simple method of operating no large aircraft of its own.)

International acclamation of the principle of independence even for small and economically weak colonies also enabled the British government to shed their embarrassing responsibility for the three High Commission Territories of southern Africa. Missionary education had produced an articulate leadership here, and as apartheid was more rigidly enforced within the Union resistance to incorporation hardened (notably in Basutoland, where a Congress Party was formed in 1952); even British politicians sympathetic to South Africa realized that transfer without consent would be politically unacceptable. Constitutional reforms were introduced, but only under the 1960s wind of change did full independence for these vulnerable communities seem a possible option. In 1962 an all-party Constitutional Commission recommended independence for the Basuto; Seretse Khama emerged as national leader under a new Bechuanaland constitution; and in 1966 Parliamentary legislation established the independent states of Lesotho and Botswana, despite deep misgivings expressed on all sides of the House.[17] Swaziland, where the old King Sobhuza II had been slower to accept representative institutions, followed in 1968. Pretoria now resigned itself to substituting economic hegemony for political control. All three states remained heavily dependent on the Republic, not only for their foreign commerce but for the employment of a growing labour force; up to half of all Basuto males were usually absent as migrant workers. The economic aid which Britain provided, as conscience money for former neglect, could not alter this dependence. From 1959, Verwoerd, recognizing that economic dominance might be an effective substitute for political control, had begun to parody British decolonization policy by establishing nominally 'independent' governments in the Union's internal labour reserves; the truly independent states, even if less easy to control politically, might he hoped be obliged to occupy comparable positions within South Africa's regional strategy.

Pressure to decolonize was not confined to the African mainland. The OAU, prompted by Madagascar, declared its interest in 'all the islands surrounding Africa'; this of course included the former plantation colony of Mauritius, although its population was of predominantly Asian origin. As independence became an issue the British government took the precaution of detaching the outlying dependency of the Chagos Islands, in order to permit the construction of an American strategic air base on Diego Garcia. In Mauritius itself the French-speaking elite looked forward to majority rule with apprehension; nevertheless the Labour government granted self-government in 1965, and independence three years later. Prime Minister Ramgoolam's adherence to the OAU was followed by that of the 66,000 people of the Seychelles islands when they became independent in 1976. With outstanding exceptions (Hong Kong, Gibraltar, the Falklands) colonies had become acute embarrassments, which most British politicians were eager to discard with small concern about the future of their inhabitants.

The Fifth Republic's renunciation of an imperial role in Africa, strikingly demonstrated in 1960, and again at Evian, was a little less total and unconditional. Decolonization, as de Gaulle proclaimed in 1961, had become France's policy because it was now her interest; but she retained other interests in Africa which he and his successors pursued rather more consistently and effectively than the British. As already noted, the collapse of the institutional Community was followed by sustained efforts to maintain 'the bonds which History had created between the African States and France'. Because French expectations about the performance of independent regimes had always been less than those of the British technicians of decolonization, there was less disillusionment when new leaders moved towards single-party government, or were overthrown by military coups: fewer inhibitions about committing French forces to sustain rulers like President Bongo of Gabon or (until 1979) the self-proclaimed Emperor Bokassa of Central Africa. While the expenses of aid and commercial preference were diffused among France's partners in the EEC, the franc zone was preserved, and substantial credits disbursed through the Ministry of Co-operation (which, like the British ODM, fought a usually losing battle to operate independently of the Ministry of Foreign Affairs and the very active Presidency). Military forces were maintained in countries of special importance to France's political and economic strategies (notably Senegal, Ivory Coast, Gabon and, until 1973, Madagascar), and interventions took place in other francophone territories (including the former Belgian Congo, now Zaire). Considerable resources were also invested in promoting the teaching and use of the French language throughout the world; at a time when British governments seemed to be losing interest in the African Commonwealth, successive French Presidents exerted themselves to create some francophone equivalent.

Although de Gaulle's decolonization earned France credibility and respect within the OAU, France moved less rapidly than Britain to liquidate the remnants of her formal empire. In particular, to a more notable degree than Britain she reacted to the growth of Soviet-American rivalry in the Indian Ocean by maintaining an independent military presence, based on the island of Réunion. Like Mauritius, this was originally a plantation colony, with no surviving aboriginal population; there was a substantial presence of French settlers and business interests, and Michel Debré, one of de Gaulle's closest colleagues, represented the island in the Parliaments of the Fifth Republic. In 1946 Réunion, unlike the African Overseas Territories, had been set on a genuinely assimilationist route to decolonization as a *département*, subject to French law and represented in the French Parliament like those in the metropolis; its people paid the same taxes as Frenchmen and enjoyed the same increasing level of social security benefits and public services. Most Réunionnais were content with this status, which was accepted by the UN and, with occasional murmurs of concern, by the OAU. The Comoro Islands in the Mozambique Channel, with a largely Muslim population of varied origin, aroused more controversy. In 1974 a referendum favoured independence; but when this was proclaimed next year the largest island, Mayotte, where French interests were largely concentrated, opted to remain French, with the somewhat indeterminate status of *collectivité territoriale*, and in 1976 a mercenary coup installed a more pro-French regime in the main islands. France also retained a strategic footing in the Red Sea in the small colony of Jibuti until 1977, when she conceded independence under pressures from within and without. But with its peoples, the Afars and Issas, divided by the war between their respective kinsmen in Ethiopia and Somalia, France was able to justify retaining a strong strategic presence.[18]

However, none of these residual traces of French imperialism ever provoked strong attacks from the anti-colonial coalition. The main efforts of the OAU's Liberation Committee were concentrated on entrenched colonial regimes, mainly in southern Africa, whose rulers showed no inclination to transfer power voluntarily: the Portuguese colonies, the self-governing settler regime in Rhodesia, and, underwriting them all, the powerful Republic of South Africa, with its own Namibian dependency. Colonial rule here would not be eliminated without struggles whose implications extended beyond the control of the OAU and involved relations between the super-powers.

Where decolonization took place by negotiated agreement, one benefit to the former rulers was a period of amicable relations with the successor regimes which would at least defer any intrusion by hostile powers. But where colonial rule ended in rupture greater possibilities clearly existed for Communist states to improve their own international position by patronizing liberation movements. Rivalry among the powers for influence over the succession states of Indo-China was a dominant theme of international relations during the 1950s and 60s; and one of the fears which drove Anthony Eden into the Suez folly of 1956 was that Nasser's Egypt might become a surrogate of Soviet Russia. Such fears, greatly exaggerated when applied to the Middle East, long proved groundless in Black Africa; even the opening with which de Gaulle presented the Soviet Union in Guinea in 1958 was so maladroitly handled that within three years the Russian Ambassador was asked to leave. Until the mid-1950s Russians' defective understanding of African conditions, and their lack of facilities to observe them, had been compounded by Stalinist doctrinal rigidities; and although experience and study thereafter produced more flexible approaches to bourgeois nationalists like Nkrumah, leading to some development of diplomatic and commercial relations, these rarely became close and sustained. But in 1960 Lumumba's appeal to Moscow, and the subsequent internationalization of the Congo problem, provided the Soviet Union with a legitimate entry into African politics, causing some Western leaders to fear that the Red Army might make an appearance among the mines of Katanga wearing the blue bonnets of the United Nations. This danger at least had been averted; but the growth of armed resistance in the Portuguese colonies created a new danger, of an alliance between the Soviet Union and those peoples who were unable to secure independence by negotiation.

Africans who despaired of achieving freedom and prosperity within the capitalist world now had an alternative source of ideological and material support in Communist China. At the Bandung Conference of 1955 Chou En-Lai, as Foreign Minister, had argued that shared experience of colonialism, exploitation and racial contempt made China a natural leader for non-aligned nations of the 'Third World'; although the main thrust of his diplomacy was naturally concentrated in Asia, Chou cultivated close relations with Egypt and the Algerian FLN, and in 1965 embarked on a tour of capitals in tropical Africa. This was not wholly successful. While the thoughts of Chairman Mao, and his experience in leading revolutionary transformations in a peasant society, did seem to have more to offer Africans than Russian Communism, the Chinese too made many blunders and backed many losers. Most African rulers distrusted revolutionary rhetoric, but were ready to seek practical benefits. Some, such as advice on rice cultivation, were clearly advantageous (though Taiwan was competing in this particular field); the most spectacular was the financial and technical assistance provided for a railway between Tanzania and Zambia. This large project, first proposed in 1965, was begun in 1970 and fully completed in 1976 (when the Rhodesian crisis which had provoked it was on the way to resolution). The relevance of Maoist ideology to the problems of African peasantries also proved somewhat less than expected, except when the peasants were engaged in revolutionary war; the guerrilla armies of FRELIMO in Mozambique were to become perhaps the principal beneficiary of Chinese advice.

Such activities by communist states in Africa, despite the modesty of their successes, progressively affected the policies of the USA. Bright hopes, encouraged by Kennedy's electoral rhetoric, that America would now pursue a vigorous regional policy to promote political emancipation and economic development were gradually tarnished. Promotion of 'Africa for the Africans', besides opening new opportunities for American businessmen, continued to correspond to the traditional ideals both of East Coast liberals, and of Black American militants and Civil Rights activists who were looking to free Africa for inspiration in their own struggles. But the initial enthusiasm of Secretary Mennen Williams was quickly tempered by interests and government agencies for whom Africa was simply one secondary front in the global confrontation with the USSR. It was not only in the Congo that the exclusion of Soviet influence took priority over support for leaders elected by Africans. While the American Ambassador was offering Nkrumah conditional support in grand development plans for the Volta valley, the CIA was in close touch with Ghanaians plotting his overthrow. In Angola, Kennedy felt obliged to withdraw the financial and diplomatic support he had originally offered to the rebellion of Holden Roberto in face of threats from Salazar to withdraw Portugal from the NATO alliance and to deny the United States use of the vital bases in the Azores. Conflicts in Indo-China and in Latin America increasingly took priority in America's global strategy. Although American spokesmen continued to express disapproval of racial regimes in southern Africa, American investments in those countries continued to grow, and the members of OAU realized that they could expect little more than moral support for attempts to complete the liberation of the continent.

Soon after the installation of President Nixon in 1969 Henry Kissinger instigated a cool reappraisal of American interests in southern Africa on behalf of the National Security Council. Little moved by sympathy for the predicaments of African leaders, Kissinger regarded American interests on the continent as secondary, and divided between areas of black and white rule. Though American trade and investment in Black Africa was greater than in the white-ruled countries, the latter were especially important in relation to strategic minerals (including uranium from Namibia, chrome from Rhodesia), to the world gold supply, to strategic bases which might be needed in the Indian Ocean, and to space-tracking facilities in the Republic. His general conclusion was that the United States should edge discreetly away from any general support for African nationalism, aim to reduce conflicts between the two groups, and encourage Prime Minister Vorster in his apparent willingness to pursue a regional policy of détente with South Africa's less radical neighbours.[19] Behind this appreciation lay liberal hopes that economic development in South Africa would require the recruitment of a skilled African labour force and the development of an African consumer market, and consequently a gradual erosion of apartheid. Kissinger also speculated on the possibility of limited liberalization in the Portuguese empire under Salazar's successor, Caetano. Though this memorandum avoided great optimism about either possibility, it made clear that, beyond maintaining the UN

211

arms embargo against South Africa and most of the mandatory sanctions against Rhodesia, the Nixon administration would apply no strong pressure to complete the decolonization of the continent. Given the ineffectiveness of the OAU in face of the entrenched colonial regimes, it seemed that their subjects would have to rely on their own efforts for liberation. The decolonization process, in the sense in which the term has been used here, had come to a temporary halt.

THE FORCED DECOLONIZATION OF PORTUGUESE AFRICA

This book has so far given little attention to relationships between Portugal and her African dependencies, on the ground that until the revolution of 1974, brought about in large part by the armed resistance of Africans, the Portuguese government was making no preparations to terminate its colonial control. Until recently the historiography of Angola, Mozambique and Guiné-Bissao has focused on the initiatives of the liberation movements, emphasizing not only their military courage but their political campaigns to restructure African societies through their revolutionary struggles. Only recently have British historians given much attention to the ways in which political and economic developments in postwar Portugal affected relations with the colonies. The picture which is emerging seems rather more complex than has been widely assumed.[20]

Certainly, the 'corporative and unitary Republic' of Salazar never intended to promote independence in countries which in 1951 were formally declared to be overseas provinces. Salazar resisted pressure to begin transfer of power to African hands, whether originating from moderate reform groups led by African *assimilados*, from the OAU or from his American allies. (Goa, it is true, was lost in 1961 to an Indian invasion condoned by the UN; but none of Portugal's African neighbours had armies of that calibre.) But if Portugal refused to copy political trends in other imperial states, her economic development was showing signs of following theirs, though at a distance. As industrialization promoted by Salazar took effect during the 1950s and 60s her economy began to develop towards Europe. More markets were found and more investment was sought there: emigrants increasingly preferred unskilled employment in France (or Brazil) to seeking uncertain fortunes in Africa. Portugal's membership of the European Free Trade Area formed in 1960 was a sign of that re-orientation from empire towards Europe which the Dutch, French and British had to varying degrees already begun.

Nevertheless neither government nor capitalists were prepared to relinquish political control over the colonies. Perhaps the primary obstacles were political, or psychological; since colonies provided evidence that this small weak state had once been a power in the world, Portuguese politicians had long sought to maintain patriotic credibility by defending them. But Angola and Mozambique, at least, had economic value too. They supplied raw materials to Portuguese industry (if not always on the most advantageous terms available), and offered preferential markets; until 1966 over 40 per cent of Angola's imports and a third of Mozambique's were provided by Portugal. Large Portuguese multinational enterprises which were now emerging, such as the *Companhia Uniao Fabril*, took advantage of preferential legislation to invest in industry and mining in Africa, particularly in Angola. During the 1940s and 50s deficits in the Portuguese balance of payments were made up by surpluses earned by the overseas territories (as had been the case, over a shorter period, in the sterling area). And, despite the pull of more developed regions, emigration to the colonies was successfully promoted by the government. The white population of Angola rose to about 335,000 and that of Mozambique to 200,000; these people, with their kinsmen at home, represented a considerable, though unsophisticated, colonial lobby. It has been suggested that around 1960 Salazar may have begun to consider tentative moves to transfer some power to bodies in the colonies which would represent settlers and *assimilados*. Since 1954 it had been made easier for qualified Africans who wished to do so to exercise civil rights, and conceivably there may have been thoughts of an eventual 'Brazilian solution', with self-governing states closely bound to Portugal through the economic interests and cultural formation of their ruling elites. But after 1961 Lisbon became more determined to retain control in order to attack the armed resistance movements. Social reforms, including some relaxation of the detested labour laws, continued, especially after Caetano succeeded Salazar in 1968; but these were now clearly inadequate to satisfy nationalist movements whose objectives had been formulated through direct experience of Portugal's earlier policies.

Despite the repressive power of Portuguese administrators and secret police (PIDE) political dissent had been crystallizing in all their African colonies during the 1950s. The leaders were usually men whose citizen status allowed some limited scope for action – citizens from Goa or Cape Verde, resident Portuguese, *mestiços* or *assimilados*. Some members of these elites who had been permitted an overseas education came together to envisage the possibility of co-ordinated resistance throughout the empire. Meanwhile in Africa many local communities continued to adopt their own methods of active or passive resistance. In 1961 these two levels of dissent began to converge in Angola, much stirred by events across the Congolese border. In February an African crowd, under unidentified leaders, launched repeated attacks on Luanda gaol; on 15 March there were violent and indiscriminate attacks on Portuguese in northern coffee-growing areas, led from across the border by the Union of Peoples of Angola, later to become the FNLA. The leading student of Angolan resistance calls this 'the last of the traditional revolts and the first rural uprising to have a political base'.[21] It was essentially a Bakongo movement; its leader, Holden Roberto, had at one time dreamed like Kasavubu of restoring the old Kongo kingdom, though he now professed more Pan-African aims. The immediate effect of this ill-planned rising was to provoke bloody Portuguese reprisals. But this armed initiative won Roberto support in many African states – and also in the USA, where his aims seemed less dangerous than those of a hard-pressed group of radical ideologues in Luanda known as the MPLA.

During the 1960s many competing resistance movements appeared in Portugal's African colonies, financed, armed and counselled by various patrons in Africa, and by non-Africans interested in the international balance of power. From these often confusing alignments there emerged three revolutionary parties which, by applying Marxist doctrine and experience to conditions in their own societies, eventually became successors to the Portuguese. In the small West African colony of Guiné the PAIGC was formed in 1956 by a small group of clerks and civil servants; many were from Cape Verde Islands, an unproductive archipelago under the same colonial administration, whose independence they also demanded. Insurrection on the mainland began late in 1962 under the leadership of Amilcar Cabral, a highly intelligent political strategist whose appreciation of the needs of rural Africans had been sharpened by his career as an agronomist. Despite heavy concentrations of Portuguese troops with modern armaments, the PAIGC claimed by 1969 to have secured popular confidence, and so political control, of two-thirds of the countryside. In Mozambique three exiled organizations united in

1962 in a common front called FRELIMO; two years later this launched military campaigns which speedily secured effective control of the two northern provinces. By 1968 FRELIMO had also established bases in Tete Province, site of the huge Cabora Bassa Dam project on which Salazar's development plans depended. Resistance forces in Angola remained more divided, and foreign investment in this richest of the Portuguese colonies continued to increase. While the MPLA developed the most consistent operational challenge and the most sophisticated revolutionary doctrine, it suffered from internal splits (with ideological, ethnic and personal origins) and from the external rivalry both of the FNLA, still supported from Zaire, and from 1966 of UNITA, a movement of the southern Ovimbundu people which enjoyed some support from Zambia.

Kissinger's appreciation of 1969 therefore concluded that 'The outlook for the rebellions is one of continued stalemate: the rebels cannot oust the Portuguese and the Portuguese can contain but not eliminate the rebels'.[22] In that case the outcome would depend on external factors. Under President Nixon American policy-makers became seriously worried by signs of growing Communist influence in the leading liberation movements, including specific links between the MPLA and Castro's Cuba. American economic and military co-operation with Portugal within the NATO framework was therefore discreetly increased, with the hope, as in South Africa, that economic development would eventually necessitate more generous treatment of the African labour force, and so reinforce tendencies towards a more liberal policy which some detected under Salazar's successor, Marcelo Caetano.

Such hopes were frustrated by the continuation of hostilities, and by the evolution which this brought about in the aims of the resistance movements. Leaders of PAIGC, FRELIMO, the MPLA, knew that military success would depend on the battle for 'hearts and minds' – on convincing those whose initial aim was simply to free their own local community from Portuguese intrusion of their possible future within a free, modern, people's state. Organizing production and ordered social life in areas which the guerrillas had liberated often involved confronting deeply entrenched beliefs and taboos – about the authority of elders, the power of witches, the proper duties of women. It was not a matter, as for party leaders in the decolonized empires, of gradually taking over the colonial state; the MPLA leader Agostinho Neto spoke of 'free[ing] and moderniz[ing] our people by a dual revolution – against their traditional structures which can no longer serve them, and against colonial rule'.[23] By 1974 all three movements had achieved remarkable progress in this heroic enterprise: so remarkable, indeed, as to conceal from contemporary admirers weaknesses in their position which have subsequently become more evident. Since the revolutionary consciousness of local communities could only be raised from within their traditional culture and by people who spoke their language, this process of nation-building might have the paradoxical effect of reviving the ethnic identity of 'primary nations', somewhat as electioneering did elsewhere; divisions such as were evident in Angola would later surface in the other colonies. The guerrillas could not drive out Portugal's well-equipped modern armies; but by 1973 the PAIGC controlled most of Guiné; FRELIMO was the dominant force in Tete province and was beginning to operate in south Mozambique; and the MPLA could claim to be the broadest-based of Angola's three resistance movements.

Though unable to complete their own liberation, the guerrillas produced conditions for the liberation of Portugal itself. The maintenance of large conscript armies – up to 40,000 men in Guiné, over 60,000 each in Angola and Mozambique – placed increasing strains on Portuguese society and its economy. Between 1960 and 1971 military expenditure rose from 4.55 to 8.3 per cent of GNP, and to 45.9 per cent of government expenditure. A total of 7674 dead in fourteen years of colonial war, only half of these in action, was not an intolerable casualty rate; but the conditions in which these campaigns dragged inconclusively on were demoralizing to the conscripts, and frustrating to their commanders.[24] On 25 April 1974 a conspiracy of middle-ranking officers seized key points in Lisbon and installed a military junta under General Spinola, who had recently returned from the command in Guiné complaining that the army was being frustrated by the lack of any progressive political design for the empire. Spinola's own political aims were vaguely defined; he seems to have hoped to negotiate peace with the promise of a fairly speedy transfer of power within some continuing federal framework. But the revolution in Lisbon had destroyed the willingness of the colonial armies to continue fighting, and on 27 July Spinola announced that negotiations for an early transfer of power would open immediately, beginning with Guiné. But as revolutionary pressure increased Spinola himself resigned on 30 September, leaving the increasingly left-wing leaders of the Armed Forces Movement to negotiate the liquidation of the Portuguese empire with the African resistance leaders.

In Guiné, where Portugal's material interests were small and the resistance most united and effective, negotiations with Luiz Cabral (brother and successor of the murdered leader) were rapid, and independence was recognized before Spinola's resignation. Shortly before this FRELIMO agreed to a cease-fire in Mozambique, to be followed by a transitional government which led the country to independence in July 1975. After that government had suppressed a settler rebellion, the victorious guerrilla movement embarked on the difficult task of creating an authentically African version of Marxist socialism in a particularly hostile international environment. President Samora Machel remained determined not only to enforce sanctions against the settler regime in Rhodesia, at considerable cost to the Mozambican economy, but to intensify military, logistic and ideological aid to the guerrillas of the Popular Front. In reprisal the Rhodesians encouraged resistance from sections of the Mozambican population, such as the Makua people, who did not accept FRELIMO's authority; later the patronage of rebellion was taken over by South Africa, a country on which the Mozambican economy remained heavily dependent. July 1975 also saw the new rulers concede independence to island colonies where the terrain had obliged the nationalists to work from exile. The PAIGC, which represented Cape Verde as well as Guiné, negotiated the separate independence of those islands, and austerely undertook the difficult task of their development; the plantation islands of Sao Tomé and Principe became independent under the MLSTP, hitherto a party of exiles.

In Angola the material stakes of independence were highest, and the openings for external intrigue considerable. Spinola's strategy had been to follow the cease-fire by establishing a coalition government, with all three resistance movements represented, which would prepare for independence during a transitional period of two years; his secret aim was to avoid possible dominance by the MPLA. Since that party was suffering internal splits, and since both UNITA and FNLA controlled substantial regional power-bases, this was not an unrealistic plan; it was initially endorsed by the OAU. It was frustrated partly by the ineptitude of its external patrons. President Mobutu's patronage of UNITA and FNLA made them suspect to more radical colleagues; even more damaging to those parties were their friends in South Africa and the USA. The CIA, which had long-established links with FNLA, now regarded Jonas Savimbi as a stronger barrier against the MPLA's Marxism; by July 1974 it was supplying arms and advice to UNITA, hoping to place Savimbi in a dominant position before the planned independence date of 11

November 1975. During the months which were supposed to prepare an orderly transfer of power fighting among the claimants led to a breakdown of order and the flight of many foreigners. The MPLA, though strong in Luanda, in some eastern areas, and among the Mbundu people, lacked the degree of national support which made the PAIGC and FRELIMO the unavoidable heirs of Portugal; in the struggle for power they came to rely on sympathizers among the Portuguese revolutionaries, notably the last Governor, Admiral Rosa Coutinho, but also on military assistance from the Soviet Union and their allies, notably from the Cuban army. This military support enabled the MPLA to assume power in Luanda on 11 November, while evidence of South African and American support discredited their rivals in the continuing civil war in the eyes of other African states. As the new government consolidated its position, multi-national companies with interests in Angola's resources, notably Gulf Oil, made the best terms they could. American ineptitude had helped produce the least desirable outcome: the globalization of southern African politics by the intrusion of Soviet power.

The repercussions of the fall of the Portuguese empire for the remaining colonial dependencies of southern Africa were far-reaching. The continuing civil war in Angola would greatly impede recently initiated attempts to negotiate a decolonization of Namibia, and still does so at the time of writing. But on the other hand the triumph of FRELIMO had finally broken the deadlock in the long struggle for power in Zimbabwe.

FROM RHODESIA TO ZIMBABWE

The dissolution of the Central African Federation in 1963 had left the British government with the problem of negotiating the independence of Southern Rhodesia, which the whole of its European population believed to be overdue. Had the election of 1962 endorsed the Whitehead government's programme of reform it seems possible that Macmillan might have been preparing to risk international odium in order to dispose of an uncomfortable responsibility; as it was many whites believed that Butler had promised them independence at the same time as the northern territories as part of the dissolution process.

African opposition made this impossible. Although Nkomo and other leaders of the National Democratic Party had considered accepting the reforms offered by Whitehead in expectation that more could follow, the party eventually refused to co-operate, hoping with the help of foreign sympathizers to compel more drastic changes. Riots and other demonstrations of discontent during 1961 led Whitehead to proscribe the party in December, but it was immediately reconstituted as the Zimbabwe African Peoples Union (ZAPU). This new body began to receive sympathy and small arms from Cairo, Moscow and other sources, and was in turn outlawed in September 1962. Two months later a boycott of the elections by most of the Africans whom Whitehead had enfranchised led to his defeat by Winston Field's Rhodesian Front.

Unlike earlier political movements formed by settlers, the Rhodesian Front was a 'populist' party – expressing a form of national self-consciousness, rooted in the determination of white Rhodesians to retain standards of life which few of them could hope to achieve elsewhere in the postwar world. Like African populist parties, its supporters were liable to make extreme demands and to repudiate moderate leadership. Unlike those parties, however, the Rhodesian Front was not applauded in the outside world when it did so. Although Field had influential supporters in the UK (as well as in South Africa and elsewhere) Macmillan, and his successor Sir Alec Douglas-Home, were unwilling to incur the odium of conceding independence to a government which would not offer even token political concessions to the African majority. ZAPU's refusal to compromise had ensured that Rhodesia would not achieve independence through constitutional negotiations, but after confrontation and armed struggle.

Initially however the position of Zimbabwean nationalists did not seem strong. Their champions abroad were unable to reinforce their rhetoric by effective support inside Rhodesia; the political liability of accepting Communist support out-weighed the fire-power received. Moreover the nationalists themselves were not united. Although NDP and ZAPU had in some areas begun the process of channelling the growing force of peasant radicalism into political protest, there was discontent with Nkomo's leadership, and in August 1963 a group led by the Reverend Ndabaninghi Sithole founded the Zimbabwe African National Union (ZANU). The immediate conflict appears to have been partly political and ideological, partly personal and factional; but, ominously, most of the ZANU leaders were Shona, while Nkomo retained wide support among the Ndebele. Most important of all, the nationalists faced a determined settler regime which already controlled the security resources of an unusually strong colonial state, including the bulk of the former Federal army and its modern Air Force.

Decolonization in Africa

In April 1964 Field, judged by many supporters to have lost a golden opportunity to secure independence at the dissolution of the Federation, was ousted from the leadership of the Rhodesian Front in favour of Ian Smith, a hard-boiled former fighter-pilot determined to secure the White Rhodesian birthright. ZAPU and ZANU were banned, their leaders imprisoned or restricted, the press controlled; the British were assured that African opposition to the existing constitution had thereby been removed. But the Conservative government refused to accept Smith's assurance that African assent could be adequately expressed through an *indaba* of government-appointed chiefs, and when Labour took office in October 1964 any chance of British consent seemed still more remote. After appointing a sympathetic military commander Smith called an election at which the white voters overwhelmingly endorsed his intransigence; on 11 November 1965 he issued a unilateral declaration of Rhodesian Independence in language parodying that of 1776.

African government, and their supporters inside and outside the Commonwealth, now demanded that Britain should exercise her sovereignty by bringing this rebellion to an end; and many active Labour supporters were anxious to do so. Inside Harold Wilson's Cabinet however they were represented only by one junior member, Barbara Castle. Others, in varying degree, shared the fashionable disenchantment about the capacity of African successor regimes to provide good and just government to their subjects, or proper protection to the interests of foreigners. British military planning made no provision for this contingency, and Wilson's forceful Defence Secretary, Dennis Healey, saw clearly the dangers of mounting operations against Rhodesian resistance. The logistical difficulties of assembling superior forces were formidable; the cost would play havoc with the carefully-pruned priorities of the defence budget; senior officers who had personal links with Rhodesia could not be trusted to obey orders unconditionally; and even a successful operation would bring no resolution. No successor regime capable of taking over the government seemed available, so Britain would be committed to a protracted, costly and unrewarding period of colonial rule. Such objects might have been over-ridden by superior political priorities; (three of these four arguments might have excluded a Falklands expedition in 1982). But Healey, George Brown and other leading Ministers no longer shared the euphoria of Labour idealists about African nationalism and the multiracial Commonwealth. Some of their advisers even regretted the departure of South Africa; Simonstown was still essential to defence planning, uranium from

Namibia was needed to maintain Britain's nuclear capacity, and security services continued to co-operate in the containment of Communism in the region. And more broadly, Healey and others, having accepted the logic which took Macmillan on his belated course towards closer association with Europe, were anxious not to commit too many resources to policies where France and Germany would be reluctant to follow.[25]

The Prime Minister's attitude was less clear-cut. He not only excluded, at an early stage, any question of military intervention, but made this publicly clear; it is possible but unlikely that calculated ambiguity on this subject, backed by precautionary troop movements into Zambia, might have had deterrent effects. At the same time, whether out of personal conviction, deference to the Labour idealists, or concern about the strongly expressed views of members of the Commonwealth (as well as of the UN), Wilson steadfastly refused to consider recognizing Rhodesian independence without further concessions to the African majority, and genuine evidence of their consent. After issuing dire warnings about the consequences of a unilateral declaration of independence (UDI) Wilson staked his personal reputation by a dramatic last-minutes flight to Salisbury on 25 October. His high moral attitude however masked his ultimate impotence. When Smith went ahead, Wilson's responses were constrained by the economic difficulties besetting his government, by the lack of commitment within his Cabinet, and by his Parliamentary majority of three. With bi-partisan support, economic sanctions were ordained, endorsed and made mandatory by the UN, and implemented at some cost to the British economy (though much more to that of Zambia and other African neighbours). But it soon became clear that sanctions were not being applied by South Africa, by the Portuguese rulers of Mozambique, or by some important multinational companies. Despite repeated warnings of impending doom, Smith's illegal regime survived, took some effective internal measures to counter the impact of sanctions on foreign trade, and strengthened its control over manifestations of African resistance. Wilson, desperately anxious to relieve the pressure from domestic, Commonwealth and foreign critics, agreed to meet Smith aboard warships of the Royal Navy in 1966 and again in 1968. But the rebel regime showed no readiness to accept his new formula, adopted on insistence from Commonwealth members, of NIBMAR: No Independence Before Majority Rule.

So when Wilson's government was defeated in the election of June 1970 its Rhodesian policy seemed deadlocked. Sanctions, while inflicting real hardship upon many Rhodesians, were with South African assistance being evaded at crucial points, and successful measures within Rhodesia to substitute for lost imports were promoting economic growth. Attacks on settler farms launched from Zambian bases by both ZAPU and ZANU after UDI failed to find support among the African population, and the well-armed security forces seemed in secure control. Many of the African traders, teachers and peasant farmers, the aspiring middle classes who elsewhere in Africa led nationalist movements, had still not crossed the mountain ridge which separated patient collaboration in expectation of reform from outright resistance. Under a new Republican constitution Rhodesia was still prosperous enough to attract thousands of white immigrants.

Most Conservative leaders, though they maintained a large degree of bi-partisan support for Wilson's policies, had little heart for continued sanctions; and they were under some pressure from their own right wing. During the period in opposition sympathy for the white Rhodesians had provided a rallying point for nationalist, in some cases racialist, elements in the party; by 1971 a re-organized Monday Club claimed to have the support of thirty MPs, including not only traditional imperialists like Amery, but Ministers like Geoffrey Rippon and rising back-benchers like Norman Tebbit.[26] Edward Heath, the new Prime Minister, was determined to concentrate on negotiating British entry to the EEC; at this period he was inclined to be brusquely dismissive of Africans' priorities, as he demonstrated when in January 1971 a Commonwealth conference in Singapore objected to British arms sales to South Africa. Douglas-Home, back at the Foreign Office, hoped to be rid of an embarrassing responsibility. After preliminary soundings he visited Salisbury in November 1971 and persuaded Smith to make constitutional changes which, though of limited immediate effect, opened theoretical possibilities of African majority rule in a distant future. These, Home agreed, could provide a basis for legitimizing Rhodesian independence provided they could be shown to be 'acceptable to the people of Rhodesia as a whole', as assessed by a Commission of persons experienced in British colonial administration under a judge, Lord Pearce. But, contrary to Smith's expectation of African passivity, Pearce's judiciously discriminating enquiries revealed that Rhodesia was 'alive with political activity at the grass roots', and that African opinion generally understood and rejected the proposals.[27]

Henceforth Smith's regime was on the defensive. The appointment of the Pearce Commission stimulated a re-grouping of the suppressed nationalists; the African National Council, founded in December 1971 to contest the proposed settlement, brought former members of both ZAPU and ZANU into temporary alliance under the apparently benign leadership of Bishop Abel Muzorewa of the United Methodist Church. But a more powerful threat had been developing with the growing success of FRELIMO, after 1968, in penetrating Tete province and operating along Rhodesia's eastern borders. ZANU militants crossed the frontier freely, entered into close alliance with FRELIMO units, and gradually learned with them how the revolutionary experience of China and Cuba might be applied in identifying needs and spreading political education in rural Mashonaland. On 21 December 1972 a small ZANU force launched the first attack on a white farm for six years, so opening an increasingly effective guerrilla war. The government accused the guerrillas of securing support by 'terrorism', but there was much more to their success than intimidation. On the one hand, political militants in touch with a wider world convinced Africans who rejected Smith's 'settlement' that there could be an alternative and revolutionary future; at the same time spirit mediums and other religious authorities inspired a renewal of past relationships between human communities and their land. The latter process, it is true, could revive awareness of historic differences among the peoples of Rhodesia; for the present these were less significant than the common purpose, not yet fully reflected among political leaders.[28]

Late in the day, white Rhodesians began to appreciate the advantages of transferring political power to Africans whose material interest and cultural inclinations might be served by gradual transitions from the colonial past. In July 1973 Smith began new negotiations with Muzorewa, the most pliable leader who still commanded broad support. The danger of a bloc of revolutionary states under Marxist influence extending from Angola to Mozambique was now creating considerable alarm abroad. Since the Labour government elected in 1974, though guiltily conscious of its responsibility, lacked the power or will to effect a transfer of power, the attempt to negotiate the decolonization of Rhodesia now became an international exercise. The first initiatives were made by governments, and by multinational corporations associated with them, in two neighbouring states with complementary interests in avoiding the spread of revolutionary war: Zambia and South Africa. These two unlikely collaborators saw a common interest in a compromise settlement which would register the electoral sovereignty of the African majority while leaving control of security and of the levers of economic power in what Smith called 'civilized' control. In August 1975 Vorster achieved the greatest success for his policy of promoting regional 'détente' by meeting Kaunda at Victoria Falls, while Smith reluctantly attempted to open negotiations with Nkomo, Sithole and Muzorewa in a railway carriage above the Zambezi.

But this initiative did not advance very far; it soon seemed that stronger external pressure would be needed. Nkomo was receiving moral support, and some not very appropriate arms supplies, from the Soviet Union; ZANU, through Mozambique, appeared receptive to Chinese influence. Vorster, while worried by these developments, grew increasingly afraid that over-commitment to Smith might in the long run endanger white supremacy in the Republic itself, and in Namibia (where UN pressure began to increase in 1974, and the guerrilla armies of SWAPO might now expect increasing support across the Angolan border). Henry Kissinger, now Secretary of State, had been alarmed by the Angolan debacle, and was determined to make Smith reach agreement with African moderates before the rural population became radicalized by the experience of resistance and the ideology of their new neighbours. Samora Machel understood his intentions; comparing the guerrillas of 1976 to secondary school students, Machel added: 'When it becomes a revolutionary struggle, that is the university. Dr. Kissinger is coming to close the university before they can get there'.[29] The Rhodesian economy was now imperilled by the delayed effects of sanctions, the closure of eastern trade-routes, the flight of capital and settlers; pressure from Kissinger and Vorster, tempered by promises of future aid, compelled Smith to concede the principle of majority rule within two years. But they failed to pin him down on crucial questions concerning the exercise of power during the transitional period, and an ill-prepared constitutional conference convened by Britain in Geneva was adjourned without agreement.

Meanwhile the rulers of neighbouring African states were working to secure greater unity among the bitterly divided nationalist and guerrilla leaders. In October 1976 ZAPU and ZANU agreed to ally in a Patriotic Front; but even more significant was the rise to leadership within ZANU of Robert Mugabe, a dedicated and clear-sighted radical who secured the confidence of the guerrilla forces in Mashonaland, as well as of Machel. The success of the international decolonization exercise now turned upon whether Smith, under stronger economic pressure from the new American President Carter, would concede to moderate African leaders terms sufficiently attractive to immunize the African population against the appeal of this leadership. Proceeding independently of the Anglo-Americans, Smith made an 'internal settlement' with Muzorewa and Sithole in March 1978, establishing a form of power-sharing in preparation for the election of a new multiracial government of 'Zimbabwe-Rhodesia'. But though this new constitution seemed revolutionary to most white Rhodesians, it entrenched control of the security forces, judiciary, and civil service in firm white hands; it was accordingly rejected by the Patriotic Front, their external allies, and most importantly by the guerrillas. Muzorewa's government never exercised authority over the whole territory of 'Rhodesia-Zimbabwe'. During 1979 7729 persons were killed, including 408 members of the security forces; 95 per cent of the country was placed under martial law and the forces of the Popular Front became the effective government of many areas. The Conservative majority returned to Westminster in May 1979 contained a large number of Monday Club supporters, and Prime Minister Margaret Thatcher shared their desire to accept the new constitution, recognize the Muzorewa-Smith government as legitimate, and end sanctions. But under strong pressure from Commonwealth governments (notably Nigeria, during the oil-boom Britain's major African market) prudence prevailed, and a final constitutional conference was convened in London from September to December 1979.

Before her confrontation with Commonwealth leaders at the Lusaka conference in August, Mrs Thatcher had been anxious to ratify independence on the basis of constitutional adjustments, of a sort which had frequently been negotiated at Lancaster House. On this occasion however the assumption that the sitting government had been freely and democratically elected was challenged by the Patriotic Front, and by external parties whose attitudes could not be ignored. The new Foreign Secretary, Lord Carrington, did not share the readiness of the Tory Right to discount the Commonwealth now that it had become a means by which African states could bring pressure on Britain, and persuaded Mrs Thatcher to insist on a genuine test of African opinion (though both still hoped this might endorse the Muzorewa compromise).

The crucial arguments now concerned the way in which authority would be exercised and supervised while arrangements were being made for the military cease-fire which would have to precede the independence election. Without a degree of control which British governments had previously been reluctant to accept, the Rhodesian army might have used the process of concentrating the guerrillas in designated Assembly Points as a means of disarming the forces which had forced them to negotiate. But hard bargaining by representatives of the Patriotic Front, and realistic advice from his military advisers, led Carrington to accept the risks of resuming effective as well as legal responsibility. Lord Soames, the Governor appointed to carry out this delicate exercise, was given the support of a Commonwealth monitoring force of 1548 men, whose presence proved vitally important. After hair-raising difficulties, the cease-fire was implemented, the guerrilla armies were preserved in their Assembly Points for integration in the forces of the new state, and an election was conducted on 29 February 1980 in conditions which most of the two hundred Commonwealth and foreign observers could accept as tolerably equitable. Despite the expectations and active exertions of most white Rhodesians, of the British government, and of other foreign interests, Muzorewa was routed; Nkomo won the twenty mainly Ndebele seats; but ZANU secured a clear majority of 57 seats out of 100. In April Britain transferred the last remnants of her colonial authority to a coalition government under Robert Mugabe.[30]

It soon became clear that many of the fears which had delayed the transformation of Rhodesia into Zimbabwe had become greatly exaggerated. There was no forcible expropriation of industrious white farmers; the British and American governments provided funds to purchase for redistribution the land of those who chose to emigrate, but on conditions which precluded uncompensated land transfers in the immediate future. Africans proved by no means unprepared for the responsibilities of government; educational facilities provided during UDI, both in the University of Rhodesia and abroad, provided Zimbabwe with good administrative cadres. Although a North Korean military mission exercised a baleful but temporary influence, the new state did not become a communist client. By backing Nkomo, and that somewhat ineptly, the Soviet Union had missed an opportunity, and the western alliance had avoided the blunders which furthered communist influence in Angola. Old ethnic antagonisms, which had sometimes been re-sharpened by the way past solidarities were evoked in the cause of national liberation, did cause conflict; personal and political rivalries between ZANU and ZAPU contributed to Ndebele fears of becoming second-class Zimbabweans. But in general the problems of Zimbabwe have been no more dangerous than those of most new African states, and have been tackled more effectively. As in Algeria and Mozambique, a regime which had to achieve decolonization through armed struggle learned much from the experience.

As far as formal decolonization was concerned, there remained only the problem of Namibia. Pressure brought upon the South African government by a 'Contact Group' of western nations which Carter had established was relaxed after the election of President Ronald Reagan in November 1980, and his choice of a policy of 'constructive engagement'. Most African leaders continued to believe that their continent would not be free until the institutions of racial tyranny had been destroyed, not only in Namibia but in the Republic itself; but the military and economic strength of that state seemed impregnable for the immediate future, so long at least as the capitalist states of the Atlantic alliance acquiesced. Six years later the growing militance of the banned African National Congress, and of African trade unions, brought that acquiescence into question, and made the future of the mild reforms introduced under P. W. Botha more questionable. But there still seemed little possibility of the Republic undergoing any genuine internal decolonization.

NOTES AND REFERENCES

1. M. Kahler, *Decolonization in Britain and France* (Princeton, 1984) pp. 303–6
2. H. Macmillan, *At the End of the Day* (1973) p. 290 (Diary, 20 Jan. 1961)
3. H. Macmillan, *Pointing the Way* (1972) p. 136 (Diary, 24 May 1959)
4. D. E. Butler & R. Rose, *The British General Election of 1959* (1960), pp. 85–7, 132, 264–5, 278
5. Macleod in *The Spectator* 31 Jan. 1964; cf. D. Goldsworthy, *Colonial Issues in British Politics* (Oxford, 1971) pp. 35–6,361–72
6. P. P. 1959–60 XI Cmnd 1148 Report of the Advisory Commission on the Review of the Constitution of Rhodesia and Nyasaland, p. 6; cf. J. T. Wood, *The Welensky Papers* Ch.25
7. Macmillan to the Queen, 3 April 1960: Macmillan, *Pointing the Way*, p. 486. The text of the Cape Town speech is at pp. 473–82
8. See R. D. Mahoney, *JFK: Ordeal in Africa* (NY 1983)
9. P. Gerbet, 'La Communauté européenne et l'Afrique', *L'Afrique noire depuis la Conférence de Berlin* (CHEAM, Paris, 1985) pp. 193–209: cf. J. D. Hargreaves, *ibid* pp. 95–6; above, pp. xx & xxx
10. Cf. D. Goldsworthy, *Tom Mboya* (1982) pp. 170–3
11. Philip Rogers, 1 March 1960, quoted C. Leys, *Underdevelopment in Kenya* (1975) p. 59
12. John McCracken, 'Coercion and Control in Nyasaland: Aspects of the History of a Colonial Police Force', JAH 27, 1986, pp. 140–1
13. P. P. 1959–60, XI, Cmnd 1148. Report of the Advisory Commission on the Review of the Constitution of Rhodesia and Nyasaland, pp. 111 and Ch.16

14. A. Hazlewood (ed) *African Integration and Disintegration* (1967), pp. 185–250, 'The Economics of Federation and Dissolution in Central Africa'
15. J. Woronoff, *Organizing African Unity* (Methuen, 1970) pp. 201–8
16. Sir Hilton Poynton to Sir L. Helsby, 28 Oct. 1964, quoted Morgan, IV, pp. 24–5
17. Hansard (Commons) 5th series 732. 26 July 1966, 1581–1671
18. J. Houbert, 'France in the Indian Ocean: Decolonizing without Disengaging', *The Round Table* 298, 1986,, pp. 145–66; M. Newitt, *The Comoros Islands* (Boulder, 1984). Cf. D. Bach, 'La France en Afrique subsaharienne...' in S. Cohen & Marie-Claude Smouts, *La Politique extérieure de Valery Giscard d'Estaing* (Paris, 1985) pp. 284–310
19. National Security Council Interdepartmental Group for Africa: Study of Southern Africa, 15 Aug. 1969. Text in B. Cohen & Mohamed El-Khawas (ed) *The Kissinger Study of Southern Africa* (Nottingham, 1975)
20. The following paragraphs are a somewhat crude attempt to simplify conclusions of G. Clarence-Smith, *The Third Portuguese Empire, 1825–1975*, (Manchester, 1985); R. A. H. Robinson, *Contemporary Portugal: A History* (1979); M. Newett, *Portugal in Africa* (1981)
21. R. Pelissier. *La Colonie du Minotaure* (Orgeval, 1978) p. 706
22. *The Kissinger Study* ... p. 87
23. Quoted by B. Davidson, *In the Eye of the Storm* (1972) p. 279
24. Robinson, *Contemporary Portugal* pp. 126,184
25. B. Reed & G. Williams, *Dennis Healey and the Politics of Power* (1971) pp. 189–191; R. H. S. Crossman, *The Diaries of a Cabinet Minister* II, (1976) p. 615 (8 March 1966)
26. P. Seyd, 'Factionalism within the Conservative Party: The Monday Club', *Government and Opposition* VII 1972
27. P. P. 1971–2 VIII Cmnd 4964 Rhodesia: Report of the Commission on Rhodesian Opinion under the Chairmanship of the Right Honourable the Lord Pearce, May 1972: paras 62, 418: Cmnd 4835 Rhodesia: Proposals for a Settlement, Nov. 1971
28. T. O. Ranger, *Peasant Consciousness and Guerrilla War in Zimbabwe* (1985) esp. Ch. 5
29. Quoted in D. Martin & P. Johnson, *The Struggle for Zimbabwe* (1981) p. 236
30. J. Davidow, *A Peace in Southern Africa: The Lancaster House Conference on Rhodesia, 1979* (Boulder & London, 1984)

CHAPTER NINE
Retrospect

Many people expect a closing chapter briefly to epitomize the events that have been studied; but though this may assist reviewers and students preparing for examinations it is rarely good history. Clearly, none of the labels by which participants chose to characterize the ending of colonial rule provides more than a simplified glance at complex realities; this book has described something more than either a triumphal 'forward march of Africa' (Padmore,1954), or a 'remarkable record of liberation and nation-building' by enlightened rulers (Creech Jones, 1959).

Some later attempts to encapsulate the process are a little more subtle. It would be possible to read into this book a record of successes and failures of 'neo-colonialism': of deliberate attempts by Europeans to shed the costs of colonial control while perpetuating its advantages. Many of those who initiated colonial reform in Britain and France did have such intentions – and did not regard them as dishonourable, for according to liberal beliefs about the harmony of interests their former subjects would share in the benefits of the new relationship. 'Association' between the EEC and former colonies may not be entirely equal, but does convey some benefits on both sides; 'collaboration', as a substitute for control, need have nothing in common with the Nazi 'New Order' in wartime Europe.

But the intentions of the original decolonizers, whether 'neo-colonial' or not, do not explain the results. This book has shown how the pace of change was greatly hastened, largely under pressures generated by the changing international balance of political and economic power; the direction of change altered more or less fundamentally by the growing strength and confidence of African patriots; and the nature of the intended process thereby transformed. It was the combined force of international and African pressure which obliged Belgium, Spain and (after prolonged warfare)

Portugal to undertake belated measures of decolonization, and which will eventually compel change in the Republic of South Africa. History quickly reduces the intentions of policy-makers to size.

In France, because de Gaulle was able to recognize these forces and to some extent ride with them, the original design was not entirely lost. French governments, capitalists and scholars are still prepared to invest in developing 'the bonds which History has created between the African states and France', and sometimes receive due political, economic and intellectual rewards. Rulers in many francophone states, while anxious to make the best of their Association with the EEC, still value their privileged status in France's policies towards the 'Third World' even more highly.

But during the period of the Macmillan government the balance tipped decisively against those who wanted Britain to give comparable priority to maintaining relations with her former African colonies. After the belated and somewhat reluctant option for Europe, British governments became positively eager to liquidate possible neo-colonial assets. Relationships which might have been fruitful for all parties have been prejudiced, on the British side, by economic and political ties with South Africa, by attempts to apply short-sighted forms of cost accountancy to educational and cultural policy, and by sour hangovers of colonial empire. Masochistic anti-colonialism is often the reaction of the Left against the Imperial past: racialist attacks on immigrants the uglier right-hand profile. Even among liberal well-wishers, paternalism has given way to the ineffective avuncularism of those anxious to advise and to offer limited financial support, but without retaining responsibility.

This book has not attempted to appraise the performance of post-colonial Africa. No doubt the new rulers bear a primary responsibility for present troubles in their countries; this is what independence means. But men have to operate in conditions shaped by history; and Africa's most recent historical experience is of colonial rule. In one sense, neo-colonialism – the continuity of structures, relationships and attitudes formed in that period – is simply an unavoidable legacy of history. What is not inevitable is the use which Europeans and Africans attempt to make of that legacy.

Decolonization and Cold War: an outline chronology

Note: events in italic refer to the development of the Cold War.

1944

6 June	*Invasion of Western Europe.*
Aug.	Formation of NCNC
6 Dec.	Richards proposals for Nigerian Constitution
Dec.	Senegalese soldiers killed at Thiaroye

1945

Jan.–Feb.	Riots in Buganda
11 Feb.	*Yalta Agreement*
8 May	*V-E Day*
8 May	Sétif massacre
June–July	Nigerian Strike
July–Aug.	*Potsdam Conference*
6 Aug.	*Atomic bomb on Hiroshima*
14 Aug.	*Japan surrenders*
Sept.	USSR claim Trusteeship in Tripolitania
24 Sept.	Riots in Duala
Oct.	Pan–African Congress in Manchester

1946

Jan.	*De Gaulle resigns*
5 Mar.	*Churchill's 'Iron Curtain' speech at Fulton*
March	New Gold Coast Constitution published
April	Nkrumah attends Fabian Clacton conference

April–Dec.	Nigerian tour by NCNC leaders
11 April	*Loi Houphouet-Boigny outlaws forced labour in AOF & AEF*
May	*Draft French constitution rejected by referendum*
Oct.	*Adoption of revised French constitution*
Oct.	Bamako Congress founds RDA
Dec.	*Start of Indo-China war*

1947

Feb.	George VI tours South Africa
25 Feb.	Creech Jones Local Government despatch
March	*Truman doctrine (Greece & Turkey)*
March	Insurrection in Madagascar
April	Casablanca riots
May	*Communist Party leaves French government*
June	*Marshall Plan*
July–Aug.	*Sterling Convertibility fails*
Oct.	*Foundation of Cominform*
Oct.–Mar. 1948	Railway strike in AOF
Nov.	Nkrumah appointed Secretary of UGCC
Nov.	C.O. Governors' Conference
Dec.	*Breakdown of Four-Power Conference in London*

1948

25 Feb.	*Communist coup in Prague*
28 Feb.	Accra Riots
17 March	*Brussels Treaty (WEU)*
April	Foundation of UPC (Cameroun)
May	*Creation of Israel: first Arab war*
May	Smuts defeated by Malan in South African election
May	Egbe Ọmọ Oduduwa foundation meeting at Ife
June	*Berlin Blockade*
	Malayan Emergency
June	Watson report on Gold Coast
9 Sept.	Bourguiba returns to Tunis
Sept.	Nkrumah visits Abidjan
29 Sept.	C.O. African Conference opens in London
20 Oct.	Barbé addresses Abidjan meeting
Oct.	Péchoux Governor of Ivory Coast

1949

Jan	*Truman's 'Point Four' Programme*

April	*NATO alliance*
May	*End of Berlin blockade*
June	Nkrumah forms CPP
Aug.	*Devaluation of sterling*
	USSR test atomic bomb
Sept.	Marriage of Seretse Khama
	Riots in Buganda
Oct.	British Cabinet accepts Coussey report on Gold Coast
	Victory of Chinese People's Republic
Nov.	UN decision on Italian colonies
	Shootings at Enugu
Dec.	Establishment of NPC in Nigeria
Dec.-Jan.1950	Widespread 'disorders' in Ivory Coast

1950

Jan.	'Positive Action' in Gold Coast
Jan.	*China and USSR recognize Viet-Minh*
	Truman orders hydrogen bomb
Feb.	*British election*
May	*Schuman Plan for Iron & Steel*
	Colombo Plan
June	*Korean War*
Sept.	Pleven overtures to Houphouet

1951

Feb.	Gold Coast election: CPP in office
May	*Nationalization of Anglo-Iranian Oil Co.*
June	Macpherson constitution enacted for Nigeria
Sept.	Victoria Falls conference on Central African Federation
Sept.	*Japanese Peace Treaty*
Oct.	*British election: Churchill P.M.*
Nov.	Elections in Sierra Leone: Milton Margai in office
24 Dec.	Libya independent

1952

May	Increasing violence in Kikuyuland
July	Fall of Egyptian monarchy
20 Oct.	Mau Mau Emergency
Oct.	*British atomic bomb tested*
Nov.	*Eisenhower elected President of USA*

| Nov.–Dec. | *Commonwealth economic Conference* |
| 17 Dec. | *Security Council Resolution on Tunisia* |

1953

March	*Death of Stalin*
May	Riots in Kano
10 July	Nkrumah 'Motion of Destiny'
30 July	Nigerian Constitutional conference (London)
July	*Korean Armistice*
	USSR test H-bomb
Aug.	French deport Mohamed V from Morocco
Sept.	Central African Federation
Oct.	*Constitution of British Guiana suspended*
Nov.	Cohen deports Kabaka

1954

Jan.	Nigerian Constitutional conference in Lagos
8 May	*French defeat at Dien Bien Phu*
June	Elections in Gold Coast
July	Foundation of TANU
21 July	*Geneva agreements on Indo-China*
31 July	*Mendès-France visits Tunis*
Sept.	*Signature of SEATO*
19 Oct.	Anglo-Egyptian Treaty
Oct.	Lyttelton Constitution in Nigeria
1 Nov.	Beginning of Algerian war

1955

April	*Bombs in Cyprus*
	Bandung Conference
May	*West Germany joins NATO*
	Warsaw Pact
22–30 May	Riots in Cameroun
Aug.	Grandval resigns: violence in Morocco
Nov.	Mohamed V returns to Morocco

1956

1 Jan.	Sudan independent
26 Jan.	*Mollet government formed*
2 Feb.	Violent settler demonstrations in Algiers
Feb.	*Khruschev denounces Stalin*
29 Feb.	Deferre introduces *loi-cadre* for Black Africa

March	Morocco and Tunisia independent
June	Plebiscite in Togo
July	Elections in Gold Coast
26 July	Nasser nationalizes Suez Canal
21 Oct.	*Beginning of Hungarian rising*
30 Oct.	*Anglo-French ultimatum to Egypt*
4 Nov.	*Soviet intervention in Hungary*
5 Nov.	Suez landings
Dec.	Civil war in Cameroun

1957

6 March	Ghana independent
March	*Eisenhower meets Macmillan in Bermuda*
	Treaties of Rome establish EEC
May	*British test H-bomb*
May–June	Second London conference on Nigerian constitution
2 July	J. F. Kennedy refers to 'independent personality of Algeria'
Sept.	Second Bamako conference of RDA

1958

Feb.	Fall of Todd (S. Rhodesia)
8 Feb.	French bomb Sakhiet (Tunisia)
April	Accra conference of African states
13 May	Coup in Algiers
1 June	*De Gaulle Prime Minister*
July	*Revolution in Iraq: crises in Lebanon, Jordan*
July–Oct.	*Tension over Chinese claim to Quemoy*
21–6 Aug.	De Gaulle's African tour
Sept.	Foundation of PAIGC (Bissao)
Sept.	*Commonwealth Economic Conference: sterling fully convertible*
28 Sept.	*Referendum approves constitution of Fifth Republic*
2 Oct.	Independence of Guinea
Dec.	African Peoples' Conference in Accra

1959

Jan.	*Castro in power in Cuba*
26 Feb.	Emergency in Southern Rhodesia
3 March	Emergency in Nyasaland
July	Devlin Report
Oct.	British election: Macleod Colonial Secretary

1960

1 Jan.	Independence of Cameroun
24 Jan.	Barricades in Algiers
Jan.	Lancaster House conference on Kenyan constitution
Feb.	Macmillan in Cape Town
	Monckton Commission in Salisbury
March	Sharpeville shootings
27 April	Independence of Togo
May	*U2 incident wrecks Summit meeting*
26 June–1 July	Independence and union of two Somalilands
1 July	Independence of Belgian Congo
July	Nyasaland constitutional conference
August	Break-up of Mali federation: ten new independent African states
Sept.	Monckton report on Central African Federation
1 Oct.	Independence of Nigeria
Nov.	Independence of Mauritania
Nov.	*J. F. Kennedy elected President*
Dec.	*National Front for Liberation of South Viet-Nam formed*
Dec.	Review conference on Federation meets and adjourns

1961

Feb.	Lumumba murdered
Feb.	Riots in Luanda
	New constitution in Southern Rhodesia
	Conservative 'revolt' over Northern Rhodesia
March	South Africa leaves Commonwealth
13 March	UPA attacks in north Angola
April	Independence of Sierra Leone
20–26 April	Generals' abortive coup in Algiers
April	*Abortive US invasion of Cuba; (Bay of Pigs)*
June	*Khruschev and Kennedy meet in Vienna*
3 Aug.	*Parliament approves British approach to EEC*
13 Aug.	*Berlin Wall erected*
Oct.	Maudling succeeds Macleod as Colonial Secretary
9 Dec.	Independence of Tanganyika

1962

Feb.	Maudling decision on Northern Rhodesian constitution

19 March	Cease-fire in Algeria
June	FRELIMO formed in Dar-es-Salaam
3 July	Algerian independence
June	*Geneva agreement on Laos*
9 Oct.	Independence of Uganda
22–28 Oct.	*Cuban missile crisis*
20 Oct.	*China invades India*
Dec.	Rhodesia Front wins election in Southern Rhodesia
	UK accepts Nyasaland's right to secede
18–21 Dec.	*Macmillan and Kennedy meet at Nassau*

1963

Jan.	*De Gaulle vetoes British application to EEC*
Jan.	Military coup in Togo
29 Mar.	British government accepts dissolution of Federation
16 Sept.	*Federation of Malaysia formed*
10 Dec.	Independence of Zanzibar
12 Dec.	Independence of Kenya
31 Dec.	Dissolution of Central African Federation

Bibliographical Essay

The historiography of decolonization is, and will remain for many years, in a transitional phase. In part, this is because of the changing perceptions of historians; those who viewed the achievements of African nationalism during the 1950s with sympathy or euphoria were obliged to take more critical approaches by the misfortunes of the 1960s, still more by the economic and environmental crises which have dominated Africa during the 1970s and 80s. African-born historians tend to ask different questions from foreigners; radicals with theoretical interests do not have the same focus as old-fashioned historians like myself, applying more or less disciplined acts of memory to events in which we once felt marginally involved.

Our sources of evidence are also changing. As a general rule, public archives, the traditional nourishment of political history, are open to study after thirty years; in practice they are fuller and still easier of access in Britain than in France (and this study has not attempted to gain access to those in Belgium, Portugal or Spain). In the USA, and in some African countries, more recent documents may be available. There are substantial official publications of statistical and other material relating to economic or social development, and some extremely important reports concerning political crises. Some important collections of private papers are available, though in only a few cases do these allow us to compare political memoirs, autobiographies, and oral testimonies with fully-documented biographies. Beyond this, there is a mass of contemporary material, from academic studies to newspaper reports, which may be invaluable in recalling attitudes of past times. Some episodes have been the subject of more or less thorough historical studies, and all historians are grateful for the opportunity to stand on the shoulders of these authors; but often they have to work with slender clues in trying to answer the questions they believe to be important. I have in general confined specified references to major documents, direct quotations, and relatively unfamiliar sources; this essay describes some of the printed works which have been of most use to me, and which may help readers to pursue their own enquiries on subjects I have raised. (Place of publication is London unless otherwise stated.)

The most comprehensive introduction, not confined to Africa, is R. F. Holland, *European Decolonization, 1918-1981* (1985). Two older works are Henri Grimal, *La Décolonisation, 1919-1963* (Paris, 1963: English translation, 1978) and Rudolf von Albertini, *Decolonization: the Administration and Future of the Colonies, 1919-1960* (Köln, 1960: English translation, N.Y.1971; paperback edition, 1982). Two broader surveys of recent African history are B. Davidson, *Africa in Modern History* (1978) and Bill Freund, *The Making of Contemporary Africa* (1984).

Some of the more recent work focused on Africa is contained in the following conference reports:

A. H. M. Kirk-Greene (ed), *Africa in the Colonial Period. III The Transfer of Power: The Colonial Administrator in the Age of Decolonisation* (University of Oxford, 1979).

W. H. Morris-Jones & Georges Fischer (eds) *Decolonisation and After: The British and French Experience* (1980).

Prosser Gifford & Wm Roger Louis (ed), *The Transfer of Power in Africa: Decolonization,1940-1960* (New Haven, 1982). A further volume will appear shortly.

Les Chemins de la Décolonisation de l'empire colonial français. Colloque organisé par l'Institut d'Histoire du Temps Présent le 4 et 5 octobre 1984 sous la direction de C-R Ageron (Paris, 1986).

There is a useful survey by Michael Twaddle, 'Decolonization in Africa: A New British Historiographical Debate', in B. Jewsiewicki & D. Newbury (ed) *African Historiographies: What History for Which Africa?'* (Beverly Hills, 1986).

Works on Colonial Policy

Basic works of reference are W. M. Hailey, *An African Survey* (1938; Second edition, largely rewritten, 1956); and for an earlier conspectus R. L. Buell's quaintly-named *The Native Problem in Africa* (NY, Two vols, 1928). W. K. Hancock, *Survey of British Commonwealth Affairs* (Two volumes in three, 1937-42) is a seminal historical study. There are many valuable papers in L. H. Gann & Peter Duignan (eds), *The History and Politics of Colonialism, 1870-1960* (Four volumes, 1969-75); Vol. 5 (1973) is a useful bibliography.

Decolonization in Africa

British Policy and Politics

A stimulating interpretation is John Gallagher's posthumous *The Decline, Revival and Fall of the British Empire* (Cambridge, 1982). A more detailed study is R. D. Pearce, *The Turning Point in Africa: British Colonial Policy 1938-1948* (1982); cf. comments in AF AFF by Flint (82, 1983) and Pearce (83, 1984). A basic source is Lord Hailey's *Native Administration and Political Development* (1942: reprinted with Introduction by A. H. Kirk-Greene, Nendeln, 1979). A. Cohen, *British Policy in Changing Africa* (1959) gives the view of a man whose importance is discussed by Ronald Robinson in L. H. Gann & P. Duignan, *African Proconsuls* (NY, 1978). For the organizational structure, J. M. Lee & M. Petter, *The Colonial Office, War and Development Policy* (1982).

Fundamental source material is somewhat frustratingly presented in the five volumes of D. J. Morgan's *Official History of Colonial Development* (1980). Economic policy is discussed by S. Constantine *The Making of British Colonial Development Policy, 1914-40* (1984); E. A. Brett, *Colonialism and Underdevelopment in East Africa* (1973); Y. Bangura, *Britain and Commonwealth Africa* (Manchester 1983); Jane Bowden, 'Development and Control in British Colonial Policy, with reference to Nigeria and the Gold Coast, 1935-1948' (Ph.D thesis University of Birmingham, 1980). David Fieldhouse, besides his broad survey of *Black Africa 1945-1980* (1986) has an important study of 'The Labour Governments and the Empire-Commonwealth' in R. Ovendale (ed) *The Foreign Policy of the British Labour Governments. 1945-51* (1984).

Political background is provided by J. M. Mackenzie, *Propaganda and Empire* (Manchester, 1984) and (ed) *Imperialism and Popular Culture* (Manchester, 1986); P. S. Gupta, *Imperialism and the British Labour Movement. 1914-1964* (1975); J. M. Lee. *Colonial Development and Good Government* (Oxford, 1967); D. Goldsworthy, *Colonial Issues in British Politics, 1945-1961* (Oxford, 1971). M. Kahler, *Decolonization in Britain and France: The Domestic Consequences of International Relations* (Princeton, 1984) is a valuable comparative study.

Other Colonial Powers

X. Yacono, *Les étapes de la décolonisation française* (Paris, 3rd edn 1982) is a brief introduction. J. Suret-Canale's *Afrique Noire* is a comprehensive study by a committed scholar: only the first part of Vol. III, *De la colonisation aux indépendances, 1945-60* has appeared (Paris, 1972); there is a translation of the second volume, *French Colonialism in Tropical Africa, 1900-1945* (1971). The most important recent study is J. Marseille, *Empire colonial et capitalisme français: Histoire d'un divorce* (Paris, 1984). For political background, R. Girardet, *L'idée coloniale en France, 1871-1962* (Paris, 1972); C. R. Ageron, *France coloniale ou parti colonial?* (Paris, 1978); C. M. Andrew & A. S. Kanya-Forstner, *The Climax of French Imperial Expansion* (Stanford, 1981). D. B. Marshall has an important study of *The French Colonial Myth and Constitution-Making in the Fourth Republic* (New Haven, 1973), and E. Mortimer, *France and the Africans, 1944-60* is a most useful narrative.

J. Stengers, 'La Belgique et le Congo', in *Histoire de la Belgique contemporaine* (Brussels, 1974) is a masterly introduction: R. Anstey, *King Leopold's Legacy: The Congo under Belgian Rule 1908-60* (1966) a fuller study. A good introduction to Portuguese policy is M. Newett, *Portugal in Africa* (1981): see also G. Clarence-Smith. *The Third Portuguese Empire, 1825-1975* (Manchester, 1985).

Works focused on particular countries or regions

There is now a very extensive literature concerning African history since the war: the Bibliography in *The Cambridge History of Africa* Vol. VIII (c.1940-75), edited by Michael Crowder, (Cambridge, 1984) may be consulted. This note lists only works particularly relevant to the study of decolonization. My own *The End of Colonial Rule in West Africa: Essays in Contemporary History* (1979) develops some points briefly touched on in this volume. D. Austin, *Politics in Ghana, 1946-60* (1964); James Coleman, *Nigeria: Background to Nationalism* (Berkeley, 1958) and K. Ezera, *Constitutional Developments in Nigeria* (Cambridge, 1960) remain important. Two more recent biographical studies are K. W. J. Post & G. D. Jenkins, *The Price of Liberty: Personality & Politics in Colonial Nigeria* (Cambridge, 1973), on Adelabu; and L. Spitzer & Laray Denzer, 'I. T. A. Wallace-Johnson and the West African Youth League', IJAHS, VI, 1973, pp. 413-52, 565-601.

Ruth Schachter-Morgenthau, *Political Parties in French-Speaking West Africa* (Oxford, 1964) is another pioneer work which remains important. More recent studies of particular countries tend to be dominated by polemics related to the post-independence policies of Senghor, Houphouet, or Sékou Touré: compare P. H. Siriex, *Felix*

Houphouet-Boigny: L'homme de la paix (Paris, 1975) and J. Baulin, *La politique intérieure d'Houphouet-Boigny* (Paris, 1982), both by former associates. R. A. Joseph, *Radical Nationalism in Cameroun* (Oxford, 1977) and J. Tronchon, *L'insurrection malgache de 1947* (Paris, 1974) are solid studies. For the Maghreb, see C. A. Julien, *L'Afrique du Nord en marche* (Paris, 1952); C. R. Ageron. *Histoire de l'Algérie contemporaine*, Vol. II (1871-1954); and Alastair Horne, *A Savage War of Peace* (1977).

Vol. III of the *History of East Africa* edited by D. A. Low & Alison Smith (Oxford, 1976) is a standard work of reference. A very large volume of work on Kenya is analysed in D. F. Gordon, *Decolonization and the State in Kenya* (Boulder, 1986). W. R. Ochieng & K. K. Janmohamed (ed) *Some Perspectives on the Mau Mau Movement* (Nairobi, 1977) is a special issue of the *Kenya Historical Review*; the latest contribution is D. Throup, 'The Origin of Mau Mau', AF AFF 84, 1985. John Iliffe, *A Modern History of Tanganyika* (Cambridge, 1979) is as good on decolonization as on earlier periods. D. A. Low, *Buganda in Modern History* (1971) includes some essential work. The most comprehensive study of Congolese independence is still Crawford Young, *Politics in the Congo: Decolonization and Independence* (Princeton, 1965); H. F. Weiss, *Political Protest in the Congo* (Princeton, 1967) is also important.

Richard Gray, *The Two Nations* (1960) and P. Mason, *Year of Decision* (1960) are good contemporary studies of the Central African Federation, whose origins have been re-examined by R. Hyam in 'The Geopolitical Origins of the Central African Federation: Britain, Rhodesia and South Africa, 1948-53', HJ 30 1987. J. R. T. Wood, *The Welensky Papers* (Durban, 1983) makes some important evidence available in a rather unsatisfactory form. R. Rotberg has a good study of *The Rise of Nationalism in Central Africa* (Cambridge, Mass, 1965). Robert Blake writes *A History of Rhodesia* (1977) primarily from the settler point of view; his book may be complemented by T. O. Ranger, *Peasant Consciousness and Guerrilla War in Zimbabwe* (1985). For the war of independence, D. Martin & P. Johnson, *The Struggle for Zimbabwe* (1981).

For the history of nationalism in Angola, R. Pelissier, *La Colonie du Minotaure* (Orgeval, 1978) and J. Marcum, *The Angolan Revolution* Vol. I, 1950-62 (Cambridge Mass, 1969). Basil Davidson, *In the Eye of the Storm* (1972) draws deeply on personal experience. A. & B. Isaacman provide an introduction to *Mozambique: From Colonialism to Revolution*, and T. W. Henriksen a fuller account of *Revolution and Counter-Revolution: Mozambique's War of*

Independence, 1964-74 (Westport, 1983). M. Wilson & L. Thompson, (ed) *The Oxford History of South Africa* Vol. II (Oxford, 1971) provides a slightly bland introduction to a deeply controversial subject. T. G. Karis & G. Carter, (ed) *From Protest to Challenge. A Documentary History of African Politics in South Africa, 1882-1964* (Four Vols: Stanford, 1972-77) is an important source-book.

International contexts

Two masterly works by Wm Roger Louis treat aspects of decolonization in wide international settings: *Imperialism at Bay, 1941-1945: The United States and the Decolonization of the British Empire* (Oxford, 1977) and *The British Empire in the Middle East, 1945-51* (Oxford, 1984). V. Rothwell, *Britain and the Cold War, 1941-47* (1982) contains useful background. D. Killingray & R. Rathbone (ed) *Africa and the Second World War* (1986) includes valuable studies. P. Darby, *British Defence Policy East of Suez. 1947-1968* (1973) and J. D. B. Miller, *Survey of Commonwealth Affairs: Problems of Expansion and Attrition. 1953-1969* (1974) are authoritative studies of postwar policies. I have learned a great deal while supervising the Ph.D. thesis of C. John Kent, 'International Dimensions of British West African Policy, 1939- 1949' (University of Aberdeen, 1986). There is a broad survey of American policy in P. Duignan & L. H. Gann, *The United States and Africa: A History* (Cambridge, 1984) and a closer study of the Kennedy administration by R. D. Mahoney, *JFK: Ordeal in Africa* (NY, 1984). A symposium edited by D. G. Lavroff sets *La politique africaine du Général de Gaulle (1958-1969)* (Paris, 1980) in a wide context. C. Legum provides contemporary documentation on *Pan-Africanism* (1962) and I. Geiss's book of the same title (1974), historical background. George Padmore (ed) *Colonial and Coloured Unity: History of the Pan-African Congress* (1947: 2nd edn 1963) is a historic text. T. L. Hodgkin, *Nationalism in Colonial Africa* (1956) is a historiographical landmark.

Biographical Studies and Materials

Among the growing number of potentially relevant works in print, the outstanding biography of a European statesman is A. Bullock, *Ernest Bevin: Foreign Secretary* (Oxford, 1983); but other works like K. Harris, *Attlee* (1982) make good use of sources like Dalton's Diary (due for publication as we go to press). Among autobiographers,

Decolonization in Africa

Macmillan quotes widely from his diaries; others, like Lord Chandos, are blander, but occasionally illuminating.

The most interesting biography of a British governor in this period is C. Douglas-Home, *Evelyn Baring: The Last Proconsul* (1978). See also D. Rooney, *Sir Charles Arden-Clarke* (1982). The memoirs of Hugh Foot, *A Start in Freedom* (1964) and Alan Burns, *Colonial Civil Servant* (1949) are interesting, though more inhibited than Hubert Deschamps, *Roi de la Brousse* (Paris, 1975). An interesting memoir from lower down the French colonial hierarchy is M. Méker, *Le temps colonial* (Dakar, 1981).

A large number of African leaders have now published biographies or collected speeches. Kwame Nkrumah's *Autobiography* (Edinburgh, 1957) is still important; it may be compared with C. L. R. James, *Nkrumah and the Ghana Revolution* (1977). Awolowo's *Awo* (Cambridge, 1960) is also good reading. The voluminous editions of Senghor's speeches and essays, used selectively, are interesting. Among formal biographies see B. Weinstein, *Eboué* (NY 1972); D. Goldsworthy, *Tom Mboya* (1982); P. Chabal, *Amilcar Cabral* (Cambridge, 1983); and J. Paden, *Ahmadu Bello, Sardauna of Sokoto* (1986).

244

Maps

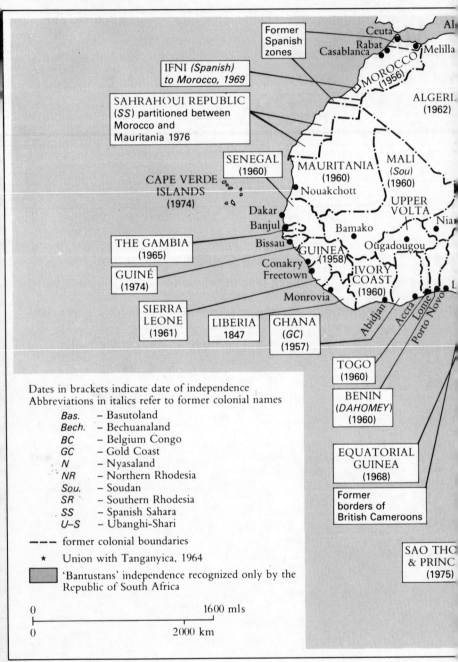

Former
Spanish
zones

Ceuta
Casablanca Rabat
Melilla

MOROCCO
(1956)

Al.

ALGERI.
(1962)

IFNI *(Spanish)*
to Morocco, 1969

SAHRAHOUI REPUBLIC
(SS) partitioned between
Morocco and
Mauritania 1976

SENEGAL
(1960)

MAURITANIA
(1960)
Nouakchott

MALI
(Sou)
(1960)

CAPE VERDE
ISLANDS
(1974)

UPPER
VOLTA

Dakar
Banjul

Bamako

Nia

THE GAMBIA
(1965)

Bissau

GUINEA
(1958)

Ouagadougou

GUINÉ
(1974)

Conakry
Freetown

IVORY
COAST
(1960)

SIERRA
LEONE
(1961)

Monrovia

Abidjan

LIBERIA
1847

GHANA
(GC)
(1957)

Accra
Lome
Porto Novo

L

TOGO
(1960)

BENIN
(DAHOMEY)
(1960)

EQUATORIAL
GUINEA
(1968)

Former
borders of
British Cameroons

SAO THO
& PRINC
(1975)

Dates in brackets indicate date of independence
Abbreviations in italics refer to former colonial names

Bas.	– Basutoland
Bech.	– Bechuanaland
BC	– Belgium Congo
GC	– Gold Coast
N	– Nyasaland
NR	– Northern Rhodesia
Sou.	– Soudan
SR	– Southern Rhodesia
SS	– Spanish Sahara
U–S	– Ubanghi-Shari

- - - former colonial boundaries

★ Union with Tanganyica, 1964

'Bantustans' independence recognized only by the
Republic of South Africa

0 ———————— 1600 mls
0 ———————— 2000 km

Map 1 Political Africa, 1919–87

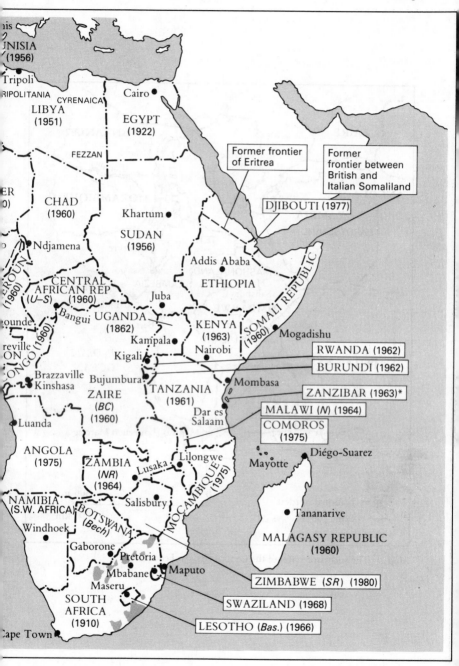

TUNISIA (1956)

Tripoli

TRIPOLITANIA   CYRENAICA

LIBYA (1951)

Cairo

EGYPT (1922)

FEZZAN

Former frontier of Eritrea

Former frontier between British and Italian Somaliland

DJIBOUTI (1977)

CHAD (1960)

Khartum

Ndjamena

SUDAN (1956)

Addis Ababa

CENTRAL AFRICAN REP (U–S) (1960)

ETHIOPIA

Juba

Bangui   UGANDA (1862)

KENYA (1963)

SOMALI REPUBLIC (1960)

Kampala

Nairobi

Mogadishu

Kigali

RWANDA (1962)

Brazzaville   Kinshasa

BURUNDI (1962)

Bujumbura

TANZANIA (1961)

Mombasa

ZANZIBAR (1963)*

ZAIRE (BC) (1960)

Dar es Salaam

MALAWI (N) (1964)

COMOROS (1975)

Luanda

ANGOLA (1975)

ZAMBIA (NR) (1964)

Lilongwe

Mayotte

Diégo-Suarez

Lusaka

MOÇAMBIQUE (1975)

Salisbury

NAMIBIA (S.W. AFRICA)

BOTSWANA (Bech)

Tananarive

Windhoek

MALAGASY REPUBLIC (1960)

Gaborone

Pretoria

Mbabane   Maputo

Maseru

ZIMBABWE (SR) (1980)

SOUTH AFRICA (1910)

SWAZILAND (1968)

Cape Town

LESOTHO (Bas.) (1966)

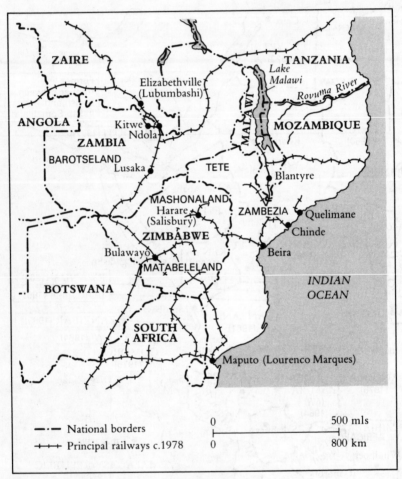

Map 2 The successor states of the Central African Federation

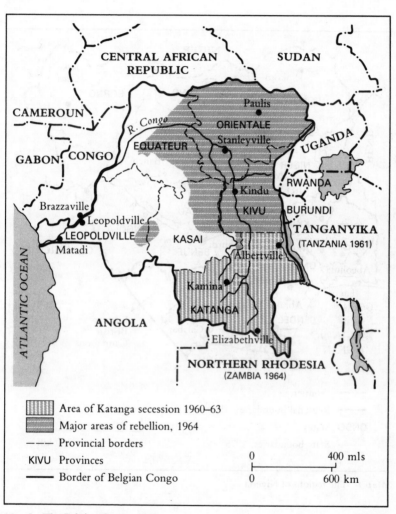

Map 3 The Belgian Congo, 1960

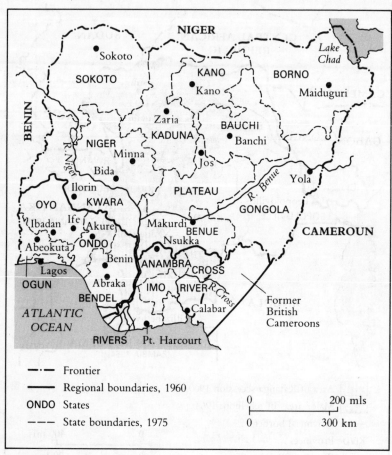

Map 4 The regions of Nigeria

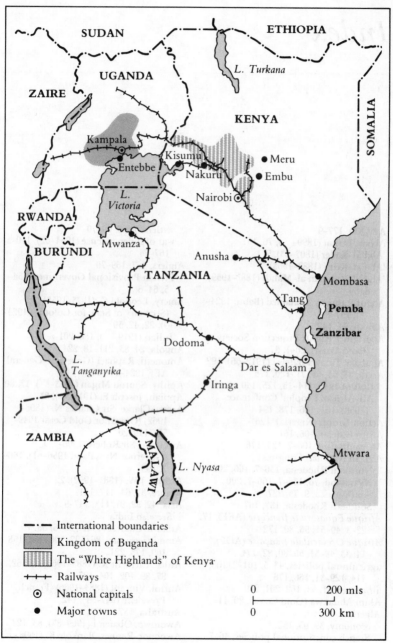

Map 5 Former British East Africa

Index